Camping's Top Secrets

A Lexicon of Camping Tips Only the Experts Know

Third Edition

CLIFF JACOBSON

FALCON GUIDE®

GUILFORD, CONNECTICUT
HELENA, MONTANA
AN IMPRINT OF THE GLOBE PEQUOT PRESS

FALCONGUIDE ®

All photos are by the author unless otherwise indicated.
Text design by Nancy Freeborn
Illustrations by Cliff Moen and Mary Ballachino

Library of Congress Cataloging-in-Publication Data is available.

ISBN-13: 978-0-7627-4017-8
ISBN-10: 0-7627-4017-5

Manufactured in the United States of America
Third Edition/First Printing

Contents

D

E

F

G

H

K

L

M

N

P

R

S

T

U

V

W

Y

Acknowledgments

In my book *Expedition Canoeing: A Guide to Canoeing Wild Rivers in North America,* I said: "Canoeing the wild rivers of the far north makes one understand why primitive man felt so close to God." I am not a religious man, but I have brushed with death often enough in the bush to appreciate the caring spirits who guide my actions. I have spent nearly a lifetime canoeing remote rivers in northern Canada and neither I nor anyone in my charge has ever suffered a serious illness or injury. I believe that I owe much of my good luck to a kindly spirit who watches my back and helps me make wise decisions. I often feel the presence of my "river angel," and I wish to say thanks.

I also wish to credit and say thanks to the following people for their support and encouragement: my friend Dr. Bill Forgey, for his practical tips on wilderness medicine; Dan Cooke; Bob Dannert; Rod Johnson; Gabriel Branby; Bob Reynolds; Darrell Foss; Jim Mandle; Tom Schwinghamer; Paul Swanstrom; Dick Person; Steve Piragis; and my patient wife, Sue Harings.

What! Another Camping Book?

Camping out has changed considerably since the good old days of pine-bough beds, bonfires, and fresh-cut trail shelters. No longer is it ethical to shape the land to suit our whims. There are just too few wild places and too many of us!

As a result, a whole new style of camping has evolved, one geared to the high-tech lightweight equipment of today. Forty-pound canvas tents have been thoughtfully replaced by equally spacious nylon models of one-fourth the weight. Camp stoves have taken over where fires once ruled, and a deluge of new fabrics—polypropylene, polyester pile, Orlon acrylics and Gore-Tex—have challenged traditional fibers. Packsacks, hiking boots, rain gear: Everything has become lighter, more compact, and reliable. Surprisingly good outdoor gear can now be purchased at big-city discount stores—testimony to the growing interest in camping out. Regrettably, even new technology has brought disappointments. Outdoor clothing and footwear have become more stylish and less adapted for use in the wild outdoors. Tents have become exotic, difficult to pitch, and less rainproof than old designs. And today's thick-bladed, serrated knives are better adapted to cutting through metal doors than slicing salami and pine. Have we forsaken old ways that work for fashionable new styles that don't?

Amidst the generally welcome improvements in gear, the one thing that has not changed at all is knowledge of the sport. The wise old scoutmaster who could sniff a coming storm and rig a tight camp in a driving rain has all but been replaced by the well-meaning leader who atones the night in his pickup camper . . . or more likely, doesn't camp at all. Everyone, it seems, has plenty of gear to cope with the elements, but precious few know how to use it. If misery loves company, you'll find plenty of it in the backcountry. Just watch the campers roll home (or to the nearest motel) at the first sign of rain. The notion that bad weather spells bad times afield is so firmly entrenched in the minds of contemporary campers that it is probably pointless for me to argue the truth in the pages of this book. Nonetheless, I shall try.

This book is not intended to take the place of a sport-specific text on back-packing, canoeing, family camping, or the like. Rather, it details hundreds of ideas and procedures that are never found in traditional camping texts—ideas that will make your next campout safer and more enjoyable. Main topics have been alphabetized, everything is indexed for your convenience, and space-consuming anecdotes have been eliminated to make room for the obscure but important things you really need to know.

Some of you may recognize procedures from my books *Expedition Canoe-ing* and *Canoeing and Camping: Beyond the Basics*. These procedures are repeated here for the benefit of those who don't canoe. After all, the rules of backcountry comfort are the same whether you travel by foot, ski, canoe, or truck camper. Foul weather can make you just as miserable in a state park campground as on a remote canoe trail.

I encourage everyone who loves camping to read *Camping and Woodcraft*, by Horace Kephart, which was published in 1917; and *Woodcraft and Camp-ing*, by "Nessmuk" (George Washington Sears), which appeared in 1920. Fortu-nately, reprint editions of these old classics are now available. The theme in both is that the old-timers were not bungling idiots who slashed and trashed the backcountry. They *knew* it took a long time to build a bough bed or a snug shelter, so they devised surprisingly good (and ecological) alternatives. For example, Kephart carried a one-pound mattress tick; Cal Rutstrum—author of *The New Way of the Wilderness* (a *must* read!)—had a down-filled air mattress and a "convertible A-tent." And every woodsman felt that a light tarp was essential for rain—something modern voyageurs are just beginning to admit. If you asked a turn-of-the-twentieth-century woodsman for advice, he'd have been more apt to tell you about the method than the gear. Now, as every mod-ern camper knows, the emphasis is on "things" not "skills."

At one of my seminars, a man wryly suggested that my camping ideas were old hat. "You've just taken the good ideas of Nessmuk, Kephart, and Rutstrum and updated 'em with new technology," he said. "Shhh," I replied. "Promise me you won't tell a soul!"

WHAT'S NEW IN THIS THIRD EDITION?

In a word, plenty! What was intended as a light revision ended with a near rewrite including hundreds of new tips and procedures. Why so many revisions when the basic tenets of camping haven't changed in years? The answer is that if you take camping as seriously as I do, you are always on the prowl for better ways and better stuff.

During the summer I outfit and guide canoe trips on remote rivers in northern Canada, where having one's act together is a tenet of survival and a prerequisite to having a good time. Each new adventure tests old methods and encourages me to think outside the box. When I discover a better plan, I hang onto it forever—or until something better comes along. Some people say this is being opinionated. I prefer to call it wisdom!

Here's wishing you warm winds, fair weather, bug-free days, and enough good camping skills to cope with the worst of times on the best of terms.

ANCHOR

Here's a slick way to make a light, portable anchor for fishing in a canoe. All you need is a basketball net and carabiner (an aluminum link used by mountaineers, available at most camp shops). Tie off the net bottom with cord. Fill the net with rocks, then gather the net perimeter and clip it together with the carabiner. Attach a rope to the "biner" and you're set for action.

You can also make an anchor out of the nylon mesh bags you buy at camping shops. However, few of these bags are as tough as a basketball net.

ANIMALS—BEARS AND OTHER BEASTS

Protecting Foodstuffs

Each year, thousands of campers lose food and equipment to persistent critters. The common advice is to protect foodstuffs by one of these three methods:

1. Store food inside your car.
2. Place food in a critterproof container.
3. Suspend food from a tree limb at least 15 feet off the ground.

Let's look at these three methods.

1. *Store food inside your car.* Not a good plan! Steven Thompson, a Yosemite National Park biologist, says that mother bears teach their young ones how to break into cars. They insert their claws above the rear side door and pull the door frame down to knee level. They climb this "stepladder" into the car. Then they claw through the backseat and into the trunk. Bears have also developed tricks to break into vans. They

look for a van that has a car parked close by, then they lean against the car for leverage to bash in the van's windows. Or they break off the van's bolted windows and get in that way.

Park rangers say that bears often break into cars that contain no food. Perhaps they simply enjoy it. And why not? Animals like to have fun too!

2. *Use a critter-proof container.* A plastic or metal ice chest will deter ravaging raccoons and ground squirrels. Squirrels have sharp teeth and will bore right through a nylon packsack.

   A thick-walled PVC plastic pipe with threaded end caps makes a reliable "food safe" from bears. There are some commercial bearproof containers that are heavy, bulky, and expensive. If you want to know the current technology, check with the managers of national parks like Yellowstone and Glacier, which have a large population of bears.

   An olive- or pickle-barrel pack (see figure W-3), like that preferred by canoeists, will protect foodstuffs from ravaging raccoons and ground squirrels. Barrels are shockproof and waterproof but they *will not* discourage bears!

3. *Hang your food in a tree.* Expert campers usually *do not* store their food in trees to protect it from bears. Instead, they seal their food tightly in plastic to eliminate odors, then they remove the food from the immediate camp area. Setting food packs outside the campsite perimeter is usually enough to foil hungry bruins and other animals. The rationale for this procedure is based on the fact that bears are creatures of habit—they quickly learn that camps, packs, and tin cans contain food. In each campsite there is seldom more than one or two trees with limbs high enough to deter a bruin. Bears aren't stupid; they learn the location of these trees and make daily rounds to secure whatever is suspended from them. When they find something (anything!) hanging from "their" tree, they'll get it down, one way or another. All black bears (even fat old sows) can climb to some degree. And cubs climb like monkeys. If momma can't get your food, the kids will!

   Young grizzlies can "claw climb" like black bears until they are about four years old, when their hooked claws straighten out. Then they will "hug climb" trees, just like you and I. Adult grizzlies have climbed trees and pulled people down! Polar bears are the only bruins that don't climb trees.

Steve Thompson at Yosemite says bears have elaborate schemes for getting food. In an article by Suzanne Charle for the *Milwaukee Journal Sentinal* (November 30, 1997), Thompson described some of these schemes: "One time-honored precaution, hanging bags of food from a rope high in a tree, is now seen as useless. Local residents call the food bags 'bear piñatas.' The bears chew off the rope that has been attached elsewhere, or chew off the branch that is supporting the bag. If the limbs are small, they'll send the cubs out. If that doesn't work, they'll just climb above the bags, launch themselves out of the tree, and grab the bags on the way down."

Recommendation: Double bag (in plastic) all foodstuffs, especially meats. If possible, ask your grocer to vacuum seal smelly foods. Or buy your own vacuum-sealing machine. Set food packs on low ground (to minimize the travel of odors), well away from the confines of campsites and trails. As an added precaution, separate food packs by 50 feet or more. Do not put food packs in trees!

If you're camping in grizzly or polar bear country, locate your kitchen at least 50 yards *downwind* of your tents. Naturally, cooking areas must be scrupulously clean—free of the last Rice Krispie. Nonetheless, human odor is stronger than most food smells: Don't be surprised if the bear smells you before he smells your food!

Bear Encounters

Here's the recommended procedure in the event you meet face-to-face with . . .

Black Bears

Blackies are timid and will ordinarily run away at the first smell of you. Bears don't see very well; what most people interpret as a "charge" is usually nothing more than simple curiosity. Screaming, blowing whistles, and other noise-making will usually send a wild bear running, but an experienced camp bear will remain oblivious to the racket.

The best plan is to hold your ground, spread your arms wide (so you look bigger), talk authoritatively but unthreateningly, and back off slowly. *Do not run!* Take off your pack and put it on top of your head. Place a child on your shoulders. Group your friends together. Bears are intelligent bullies. They assess their odds of success and go for it if they think

Figure A-1. Black bears can be scary when they come into your camp. This big boy was just 25 feet away when the photo was snapped. Note that his ears are up and he's listening—considering his options. We "talked" for more than a minute; then he quietly went away. Along the Fond du Lac River, northwestern Saskatchewan.

they have the upper edge. Do whatever you can to make yourself look bigger and more powerful.

The danger signs are "woofing" and "clacking." If the bear goes "woof, woof, woof" and you hear loud hiccuping sounds with the clacking of teeth, the situation is deteriorating. The bear is mad and unpredictable. If you can beat a path to safer ground or climb a tree, do it. But remember, your safe haven better be close because you can't outrun the bear by far!

The pamphlet *Bears Are Dangerous,* published by the Government of the Northwest Territories, recounts a story of two young people who hiked to Hidden Lake outside of Yellowknife, in Canada's Northwest Territories: "Suddenly, a black bear appeared, forcing the campers to climb trees. The bear ate all the food in camp, then it attempted to climb the trees in which the two campers were hiding. They managed to keep it away by striking it with branches. Finally the bear left, but the campers remained in their trees for five hours before making good their escape."

If you are up a tree and a bear climbs after you, poking it in the face with a branch is a proven plan. Remember, bears climb as well as you!

If you are attacked by a predacious black bear, fight like mad! Do not play dead with a determined black bear! Use all your might—and whatever tools (knife, ax, rock, log) you have—to fend off the attack.

To retreat or fight—how you should react depends largely on whether the attack is *defensive-aggressive* or *predatory.* A bear in a defensive-aggressive mode is trying to protect its interests—its young or food source. Basically, the bear just wants to get you out of the way (eliminate the threat) and as quickly as possible get back to what it was doing before you appeared. In this type of attack, you are best off to play dead and thereby indicate you are no threat. The bear may rough you up some, but if you stay still, it will usually leave quickly.

A predatory attack is another matter. Here, *you* are the food and you will survive only if you fight like mad. The old advice to "play dead with a grizzly and fight back with a black bear" was based on the fact that most black bear attacks are predacious while most grizzly attacks are defensive-aggressive. In any case, you will have just seconds to determine the true motive of a bear attack.

Grizzlies

Grizzlies have been clocked at 45 miles per hour on flat terrain. No way can you outrun one. Grizzlies are shy animals; they will usually run away from you. Nonetheless, grizzlies are king of the hill in their domain; it's doubtful you can bluff them. I was once charged by three grizzlies on the open tundra of Canada and I can vouch for the effectiveness of this procedure:

1. Talk in a moderate, nonthreatening tone to the bear as you slowly back away. *Do not* make eye contact! Let the bear know that you made a mistake and are trying to skedaddle.
2. If the bear runs toward you, interpret this as curiosity, not a charge. Remember, bears don't see very well, and they can't smell you if you're downwind.
3. When the bear is within 50 feet, drop to the ground, *face down, nose in the dirt,* and clasp your hands tightly behind your head. Spread your legs wide so the bear can't turn you over easily. *Note:* Until recently, the recommended method was to assume a tight fetal position, hands behind

the head. I did this, and it worked for me. Discouraging bears is not an exact science!

Research by Stephen Herrero, author of *Bear Attacks: Their Causes and Avoidance* (see appendix A), suggests that the "face down" plan is best. Herrero found that the face is where most serious injury occurs. If the bear bites and claws you, try to remain quiet and passive. If the bear tries to flip you over, do a complete roll and maintain the face-down position. You will probably survive the attack.

In case you're wondering, "my" grizzly bear came within a dozen feet, checked me out, then hightailed it over the next hill. "Your" bear will likely do the same.

What if you see a bear who doesn't see you? Simply leave the area, as quickly and as quietly as possible. It's best if you don't advertise your presence.

Polar Bears

Good luck! These are fast on the flats and they can swim 4 or 5 miles per hour for hours on end in ice water. They will, on rare occasions, eat human flesh. They have been known to stalk humans. Nonetheless, most polar bears will do their best to steer clear of you. It's best you do likewise. You cannot intimidate or outrun these animals. And in their habitat, there is usually no place to hide. You are at their mercy!

I have had several scary polar bear encounters on my canoe trips to Hudson Bay. The most frightening was when a huge male bear slid down a muddy riverbank and followed my canoe across a rapid to the opposite bank. I quickly snubbed the canoe ashore, jumped out, and grabbed my rifle, praying I would not have to shoot. The bear swam to within a dozen feet of me, looked straight at me, then turned and continued downstream. It was quite a rush!

Some General Protective Thoughts

Bears don't like large numbers of people. Two people are more likely to be attacked than six. If a bear comes into your camp, huddle together and spread your arms wide, so as to make a large presence. *Do not* throw rocks at the bear, as advised in the Boundary Waters Canoe Area training film *Leave No Trace—A Wilderness Ethic*. I did this once years ago, and the bear nearly had me for dinner. Regrettably, space does not permit details.

You are safer to sleep inside a tent than on open ground, especially in grizzly country. Evidently, the big bears mistake a human in a sleeping bag for their natural food.

Women who are menstruating may be at greater risk from bear attacks, though there is no clear evidence to support this. Stephen Herrero addresses this topic in detail in his acclaimed book *Bear Attacks*. Bear-wary travelers will want to read it!

Pepper spray (sometimes called "bear mace") contains 2 percent oleoresin capsaicin and derivatives—the flaming ingredients in red pepper. If properly used, it will stop nearly all bears all the time. Herrero observed that even a dangerous mother with cubs will run away from the spray more than 80 percent of the time. Herrero *did not* find a single case where spraying a bear with pepper enraged it and made it more aggressive.

The large, one-pound can sprays up to 30 feet; pocket-size models go half as far and deliver less pepper. Get the *largest* can you can find! A belt holster with a fast release is essential. Bear mace won't do you any good if it's locked away in your pack or dangling from a belt clip you can't quickly unsnap.

Here's some pepper spray advice:

- The effect on the bear may be temporary, so leave immediately after discharging the pepper. Black bears (but not grizzlies) often develop a tolerance for the spray over time. A black bear that has been sprayed before may not be discouraged when sprayed again.
- Everyone in your group should use their spray simultaneously.
- Be sure that the wind *is not* blowing in your face when you spray!
- If possible, stand behind a tree when you spray. The tree will break the bear's impact or at least cause it to slow down. Fire the first blast when the bear is about 10 feet away.
- Try to spray the bear in the face when its mouth is open or it is inhaling.
- Don't practice with your pepper spray (or spray tents, canoes, or other objects with it) in hopes of repelling bears. The bears don't like to be sprayed with pepper, but they do like the taste of it.
- If you must field-test a can of pepper spray, wash it thoroughly with soap and water afterward and clean the nozzle with rubbing alcohol before you take it on a camping trip. The slightest pepper residue will

attract bears. Better yet, buy a "practice can" (it doesn't contain pepper) to perfect your aim.

Pepper spray (the large size can only) is now legal in Canada. Still, your spray may be confiscated if the customs official believes you have no need for it. Say you'll be camping in bear country and you should have no problem. There are many good brands of pepper spray. I prefer Counter Assault (www.counterassault.com; see appendix B) because it is widely available in Canada and is the brand most recognized by Canadian customs officials.

Guns or pepper spray? Dominic Domenici, a U.S. Fish and Wildlife Service officer, believes that pepper spray is far more effective than guns. He says that in one study examining forty cases, 58 percent of humans who shot attacking bears in Wyoming and Montana (outside national parks) received some injury by the bears. But only 8 percent of those who used pepper spray were harmed.

P.S. "Bear mace" works even better on human attackers than on bears! This said, be aware that pepper spray is not 100 percent reliable. Studies suggest that it may not work against enraged animals or seriously starved ones that are determined to eat your food (or you!). And it may not discourage a drug-enraged human attacker who is bent on destruction.

Always Remember
- Never approach a fresh kill or cubs.
- Don't sleep in fishing clothes. Clean fish away from camp. Dispose of fish entrails in the water; wash slime off your boat; establish kitchens downwind of camps.
- Wear a hat or bandanna when cooking to reduce the accumulation (and smell) of grease in your hair. Freeze-dried foods are relatively odorless.
- Never feed a bear.
- If you see a bear in the distance but the bear doesn't see you, retreat quietly. Calling attention to yourself could mark you as a target.

A final note: Desk-bound environmentalists would have you believe that all wild animals are harmless, while Rambo survivalists will suggest otherwise. Facts indicate that you are more at risk when crossing a four-lane highway than in a face-to-face encounter with a bear. Nonetheless, some critters, like some people, are plainly crazy and quite unpredictable. So beware of the small percentage of bears who don't share your live-and-let-live philosophy. Don't overreact to bear encounters; just follow the recommended guidelines. And be aware that you are much safer in seldom, traveled wilderness than in heavily used national parks where bears are used to the sight of people and the taste of their garbage.

For more information about bears, refer to the recommended reading list in appendix A.

AX

The trend today is against the use of axes in the backcountry. The argument is that they are more often used to deface green trees and injure people than to produce firewood. In truth, it is not the tool that is dangerous, it is the person who wields it. Outdoor experts value a good sharp ax. They know it is much simpler to produce fire after a weeklong rain if a splitting tool of some sort is available.

What size ax? Old-time camping books suggest use of the full-length to three-quarter ax under the guise that these are safer than the short hand ax (hatchet). Hogwash! A properly used hand ax is the safest of all edged tools; it is lighter and more compact than a large ax, and when used in conjunction with a folding saw, it will produce all the camp wood you need with surprisingly little effort.

Using an Ax

Here are the rules for safe, efficient use of the hand ax:

1. Saw wood to be split into 12-inch lengths (see the SAW section of this book).
2. Use the hand ax as a *splitting wedge*. Do not chop with it! The folding saw performs all cutting functions.
3. Set the ax head lightly into the end grain of the wood (figure A-2). One person holds the tool while a friend pounds it through with a chunk of log. When splitting very thick logs (more than 6 inches), take multiple splittings off the edges.

     Safety concerns: Hold the ax solidly with both hands. Allow the log hammer to do all the work.

Figure A-2. How to split wood safely with a hand ax.

To produce kindling: Kindling splits easiest from the end grain, a process that's made simpler and safer if you use a stick of wood to hold the upright in place (figure A-3).

Figure A-3. How to split kindling safely with a hand ax.

In case you're wondering, my favorite axes are those built by Gransfors Bruk of Sweden (figure A-4; www.gransfors.us; see appendix B). Every ax is hand- and hammer-forged on century-old machines and hardened to Rockwell 57C, which is harder than U.S. axes and as hard as most good knives. Each completed ax (a work of art!) proudly bears the initials of its maker. If you cut your own firewood, consider the Gransfors splitting ax—it is superior to any U.S.-made maul.

Figure A-4. The author's favorite Gransfors axes, from top to bottom: small forest ax, wildlife hatchet, minihatchet.

Caring for Your Ax

Sharpening: You'll need a flat-mill file and a coarse (soft) natural or synthetic sharpening stone. A fine stone is required if you want a razor edge. I use the coarse stone dry (no lubricant), but I lubricate the fine hone with WD-40 or kerosene. Diamond stones should be lubricated with water. It is important to keep the hone scrupulously clean by frequently flushing its surface with light oil or water, as the case may be (don't mix 'em!), to remove grit. If the lubricant becomes cloudy, it's time to flush it clean. If you don't, the suspended filings will dull the edge.

Large-pore carborundum, aluminum oxide, and diamond hones are best used dry or lubricated with water. Thick cutting oils just gum up fine-grained Arkansas and Wachita stones. I lubricate these with WD-40 or kerosene. For more tips on sharpening stones, see the discussion about sharpening hones in the KNIVES section of this book.

Sharpening procedure: Drive two pegs into the ground about 4 inches apart, or use a peg and log chunk, as illustrated (figure A-5). File perpendicular to the edge. A file guard (tin can lid with hole punched in center) placed over the rat-tail handle is recommended to prevent cut fingers.

File one edge (one side of the blade) uniformly until a burr appears on the opposite edge. The burr is hard to see but easy to feel with a finger. Then file the burred edge until a burr develops on the other side of the blade (the side you first filed).

Then switch to the coarse stone. For greatest safety, hold the ax blade in the palm of one hand and use a circular motion of the stone. Hone each edge uniformly until all the burrs are gone.

Figure A-5. Sharpening an ax.

Check for nicks: Slide a smooth wood or plastic stick *very lightly* along the sharpened edge—you will feel the slightest nick. If the edge feels butter smooth, you're done.

If you want a razor-fine edge—not essential on a working ax—switch to the fine stone and hone the edge perpendicular (no circular motion) to the edge as is recommended for sharpening knives (see page114).

Care of the ax: Axes are forged from carbon steel so they must be kept clean, dry, and rust free. A small amount of gasoline or naphtha (Coleman fuel) will remove pitch and wood stains. Keep ax heads oiled or greased when not in use. The best rust preventative is RIG (Rust Inhibiting Grease) Universal, available from sport and gun shops. Edged tools coated with RIG may be stored for years without rusting.

Blueing the head: Most axes have painted heads to minimize rust. For ease of maintenance and beauty, grind off the paint, buff the head, and apply cold gun blue (available at most hardware and sports shops) to the bright metal. The ax head will develop a mildly rust-resistant blue-black sheen, which is instantly restored by dabbing on more gun blue.

Sheathing the ax: Sheaths that come with edged tools are usually too thin and flimsy for practical field service. Make your own as follows:

1. Obtain two pieces of ⅛-inch-thick sole leather from a leather company or your shoemaker.
2. Soak the leather in warm water until it is soft, then cut two matching pieces, as shown in figure A-6.
3. Contact cement (I suggest Weldwood contact cement) a ¼-inch-wide strip of leather all around the edge. Then rivet on a buckle or Velcro security strap and contact cement the sheath halves together. Rivet the edges of the sheath for greatest security, or have your shoemaker sew it for you. Two-piece hammer drive rivets can be purchased from every leather supply store. Hand axes are never carried on the belt so no belt loop is necessary.

Figure A-6. The heavy sole-leather sheaths shown here require less than one hour of time to make. Leather and rivets can be purchased by mail from several leather companies. PHOTO: MARK LINDBECK

Making a permanently bonded head: Camping books traditionally suggest that you occasionally soak the heads of wood-handled axes in water or oil to expand the handle eye so the head won't come loose. The "water treatment" is dreadfully temporary; oil works only marginally better. Here's a permanent solution:

1. Use a very blunt screwdriver or edge of a flat file as a wedge to drive the factory-installed wooden wedge tightly into the handle eye. You should be able to sink the factory wedge a full ¼ inch to ⅓ inch below the level of the steel ax head.

2. Drive a small steel wedge solidly into the heart of the sunken wooden wedge. The steel wedge will not go in all the way, but its head must be below the level of the steel ax head.

3. Fill the void (trench) with slow-cure or five-minute epoxy. You now have a permanently bonded head that will never come loose.

The Case for the Full-Size Ax

For serious woodshed splitting, you can make a case for a full-size ax with a three-and-a-half-pound head and a 32-inch to 36-inch handle—but only if you don't have a splitting maul! Given the excellent saws and splitting mauls we have today, the big ax has pretty much outlived its usefulness.

If you want something lighter and smaller, but with nearly as much power as a full-size ax, consider the three-quarter ax. And for serious go-light trips in the rain belt, a hatchet-sized splitting maul can't be beat (figure A-7). For example, each year in late October, friends and I make an annual trek to the Boundary Waters Canoe Area in our solo canoes. At this

Figure A-7. A sharp saw and a powerful, short-handled maul are unbeatable for maintaining a cheery fire when rains come to stay. Equally important is the fact that a maul is much safer than an ax.

late date, we're tempting freeze-up and it's usually raining or snowing. But no matter; our five-pound splitting maul quickly gets to the dry heart of rain-drenched logs.

"Chopping" Deadwood with the Big Ax

A large-frame bucksaw is far superior to *any* ax for cutting wood. But if you lose your saw or break the blade, you should know how to use an ax. Here's a safe, efficient way to chop dead, downed wood with a full-size ax.

1. Face the downed log and grasp the ax firmly at the pommel of the handle with one hand. Place the other hand just behind the head. Lift the ax hip-level high, then start your swing. The handle should slide through your "bit" hand (hand closest to the blade) as the blade comes down.

2. Chop three times on one side, then reverse hand positions and chop three times on the other side (figure A-8). This should release the chip, the width of which should roughly equal the diameter of the log. Note that if you don't change hands when you reverse the blade angle, the bit will fly across your body—a dangerous and inefficient situation.

Chop first on one side   and then on the other.

Figure A-8. Change sides and hands every three strokes.

3. When you've cut halfway through the log, rotate it 180 degrees so the ax blade won't break through to the ground where it can nick and dull.

Splitting Logs

Do not set logs upright on the ground to split them—the ax may bury itself into the ground and strike a rock. Instead, chop out a level "splitting" platform and split the upright log from the end grain. Some camping texts suggest that for safety's sake, you should split logs from the side, not the end. I disagree. If you can't hit the center of an upright log with an ax, you need practice or a more accurate friend!

Always chop limbs from the *underside,* as illustrated in figure A-9.

Figure A-9. Always chop limbs from the underside.

Where to Store Your Ax

Keep your ax sheathed and in a pack when it's not being used. Never leave an ax stuck in a log—someone could trip over it! It's better to place the ax on its side, blade tucked under a heavy log or rock, as illustrated in figure A-10.

Figure A-10. Safest way to store an unsheathed ax is with the blade under a log.

BAKING

Reflector ovens and double-pan Dutch ovens are traditional for backcountry baking. However, both require a good hot fire or glowing coals. Modern campers rely almost exclusively on stoves for all their cooking, so the oven should reflect this change in style.

Commercial Ovens

A number of commercial ovens are designed for use with trail stoves. Most popular is the Backpacker's Pantry Outback Oven (www.back packerspantry.com; see appendix B)—a two-piece aluminum bake set that comes complete with a temperature gauge. But the downside of all commercial stove-top ovens is that they add bulk and weight to your kit— they're just one more thing to lug along.

Improvised Ovens

Here are some baking tools and ideas for those who want to go light:

The Gelatin-Mold Oven

You'll need a wide-ring aluminum gelatin mold and a cover of some sort (figure B-1).

1. Grease the mold and put your batter into the outside ring. Decrease the suggested amount of water by up to 25 percent for faster baking.

2. Bring the stove to its normal operating temperature, then reduce the heat to the lowest possible blue-flame setting. Center the gelatin mold over the burner head, top it with a high cover (necessary to allow sufficient room for the baked goods to rise), and relax. Cooking times are nearly identical to those suggested in the baking directions.

3. Cool the mold by setting it in a shallow pan of water for a few moments, then pop out your entree.

Tips for using the gelatin-mold oven:

- Wind reduces the efficiency of the gelatin mold, so use a good wind shield around your stove.
- Large-burner stoves like the Coleman Peak 1 and double-burner models may burn the edges of the bakestuff. An electric stove burner shield—available for a few dollars at most supermarkets—will eliminate this problem. Simply place the shield under the gelatin mold. The air space between the shield and mold bottom will prevent burning. The large-size burner shield will fit large-ring gelatin molds perfectly.

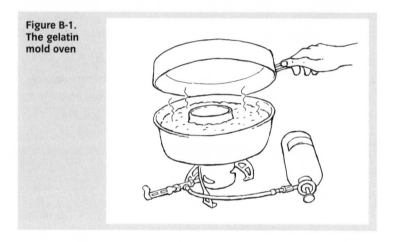

**Figure B-1.
The gelatin
mold oven**

Other uses of the gelatin mold: Your gelatin mold may also be used as a steamer to rehydrate dried fruits and vegetables. Here's how:

1. Place dried fruit or beans in the gelatin mold ring with about two tablespoons of water.
2. Fill a stainless-steel Sierra cup with water and set it on the chimney of the mold.
3. Cover the mold and cup and turn the stove to medium high. Boiling water from the Sierra cup will vaporize and steam your fruit or vegetables to tenderness in a fraction of the time of simple soaking. It's the steam that does the trick!

You can also fire the gelatin mold with a small (2⅝-ounce) can of Sterno or a small tin can filled with rubbing alcohol. Don't use the large-size cans of Sterno; they put out too much heat. To ensure ample draft, use a pair of sticks to prop the ring about ½ inch above the Sterno. You must ventilate the high cover with a matchstick or the Sterno (or alcohol) will go out.

You may also use the gelatin mold as a pot support on your stove. To heat a single cup of water on your trail stove, set a water-filled Sierra cup into the gelatin mold chimney. A cover will speed heating and save stove fuel.

Double-Pan Method of Baking

Use this method if you don't have a gelatin mold. You'll need two nesting skillets, a high cover, and a half-dozen small nails or stones.

1. Evenly scatter some nails or stones onto the surface of the large (bottom) frying pan. *Don't* use stones from a lakeshore or riverbank; the trapped moisture could cause those stones to explode when heated. Small sticks, or tiny balls rolled from aluminum foil, may be used in place of nails or stones.

2. Place your bakestuff into the small frying pan and set it on top of the nails (the two pans must be separated by nails or stones to prevent the food's burning).

3. Cover the unit and place it on your stove. Use the lowest possible blue-flame setting.

Warning: Don't use this method with a thin aluminum skillet on the bottom; you'll burn a hole right through it!

Figure B-2. The double-pan oven.

BANNOCK (CAMP BREAD)

Bannock is bread that is traditionally baked before an open fire in a large straight-sided skillet. Bannock is fast and easy to make—no need for special ovens, aluminum foil, pot covers, or baking thermometers. Just grease the skillet, press in the dough, fry lightly for a minute or three, then prop the pan before a cheery blaze as illustrated in figure B-3. No wondering "when it's done"— the beauty of bannock is that you watch it bake!

Ingredients: In the old days, sourdough was the preferred ingredient; now most campers use commercial mixes that are handier but less tasty. Here's my favorite made-from-scratch recipe, along with a scrumptious sourdough version:

Easy Scratch Bannock

In an plastic bag or a bowl, mix 2 cups of flour, 3 rounded teaspoons of baking powder, 1 heaping tablespoon of nonfat dry milk, and 1 teaspoon of salt.

To this, add 5 tablespoons of liquid margarine or canola oil and enough cold water to make a stiff dough. Work the dough just enough to mix the ingredients. If you knead too long, the bannock will be tough.

Now mix in 2 tablespoons of honey and/or a few spoonfuls of blueberry jam. Sprinkle cinnamon and sugar and/or brown sugar on top. Creatively lace the surface of the bannock with liquid margarine (optional). Bake as directed below.

Baking the bannock: Gently fry the bannock on very low heat (on a mix of hot ashes and coals) until it is firm—about three to five minutes. If you prop the bannock before the bottom is solid, the dough may slide out of the pan!

Prop the pan at a 45-degree angle to the flames and relax. In about twenty minutes the bread will start turning golden brown. The bannock is done when a wood sliver comes out clean. Mmmm, good—and enough calories for a half-day hike!

Tips: Don't make the batter too thick—½-inch thick is about right. Use a frying pan with relatively straight sides so the dough won't slide out when propped before the fire; avoid thin aluminum skillets, which may warp, and Teflon-coated ones, which may flake from the heat.

Figure B-3. When the bannock is solid, prop the frying pan before the fire at a 60-degree angle.

Serious Sourdough Bannock

Put about 2 cups of flour, 1 tablespoon sugar, and one-half cake of yeast into a plastic bucket with a loose-fitting lid. Add enough warm water to make a pancakelike batter. Let the mixture sit at room temperature about three days until it "sours."

Making the bannock: Remove about 1 cup of well-stirred liquid and place it in a mixing bowl. To keep the unused mix from oversouring, replace the amount of batter you take with an equal amount of fresh flour and water.

Add about ¼ teaspoon baking soda (the secret is in the soda—don't add too much!). Mix thoroughly. A chemical change will occur and the mixture will bubble up into a meringuelike fluff. Add a dash of salt, about a tablespoon of sugar to taste (don't add too much!), a little melted shortening, and enough flour to make a stiff dough. Make a stiff "working" dough for bread or rolls; thin it out for pancakes. Options are endless.

You can keep sourdough almost forever if you keep diluting it with fresh flour and water. The mix will oversour (possibly explode—or at best, ooze out of your bucket) if you don't "use it and dilute it" on a regular basis. Refrigerating the working mix stops the chemical reaction. Sourdough can be dried and stored and used to start a new mix.

Tips:

- Don't store sourdough in an aluminum pot: A chemical reaction will occur that will adversely affect the flavor. Stainless steel and stoneware are okay.

- Butter or margarine has better flavor than cooking oil.
- The most convenient way to carry sourdough on the trail is to mix half a cup of starter with flour until you get a soft ball. Roll the ball in more flour and store it in a plastic bag half filled with flour. This should keep a week or more. (Thanks to Scott Power for this useful tip, which I discovered in his delightful book, *Cooking the Sourdough Way: Tips, Stoves, and Recipes* [ICS Books, 1994]. When Scott graduated from high school, he and a friend overwintered in Dr. Bill Forgey's log cabin near Hudson Bay. Scott—a superb wilderness chef—developed a wealth of scrumptious recipes that you'll want to try.)

BINOCULARS

Binoculars are worth bringing along on wilderness canoe trips. They enable you to quickly locate portage trails and campsites on complex lakes, and they are a wonderful tool for checking rapids. A monocular is not good enough; you need two-eye depth perception for interpreting river dangers.

BOOTS

Today's hiker chooses the lightest, most flexible footwear he or she can find. The trend began when we quit thumbing our noses at Native peoples—American Indians and Eskimos—who routinely traveled the most difficult terrain while wearing moccasins, sandals, or no shoes at all. The coup de grace was quietly administered when American and British mountaineers were outfooted by sandal-wearing Sherpas who casually carried loads far in excess of those toted by well-heeled climbers. Specialized lightweight running shoes set the trend; featherweight hiking boots logically followed suit.

Which Boots Are for You?

There are boots of all leather, leather and nylon, pure (synthetic) rubber, or leather and rubber combinations. There's also a diversity of unique winter wear. Here are the differences:

Combination leather and nylon boots are light, supple, comfortable, and most popular. They require almost no break-in. The best models are suitable for the most strenuous off-trail applications, with the exception of rock climbing or boulder hiking. Unfortunately, most of these combo boots cannot be resoled when they wear out—a factor to consider if you'll subject them to heavy use.

Supple, all-leather boots that can be resoled (check 'em out, most can't!) are the sturdiest, most reliable, and probably the best buy. All-leather boots will outlast leather/fabric combos by decades.

Gore-Tex liners: Some of the best boots (especially leather/fabric ones) come with liners of waterproof Gore-Tex. Though Gore-Tex liners perform admirably over the short haul, they may not be reliable in the long run. If the Gore-Tex liner in a fabric foot fails, you're doomed to wet feet—an instant displeasure the moment you walk through dew-moistened grass. And these boots are hot! Yes, Gore-Tex does "breathe," but not very well. If you flat move out when you hike, you won't like Gore-Tex boots at all. Traditional all-leather boots can be made acceptably water resistant by a judicious application of wax or grease, but fabric ones cannot.

Despite convincing advertising, Gore-Tex boots have not proven reliable enough for day-in, day-out use in wet country. And neither has any brand of all-leather boots. If you want truly waterproof footwear, follow the lead of lobster fishermen and Alaskan guides and select knee-high rubber barn boots or green "Wellies," as the British call them. Or check out the Chota line of lightweight neoprene boots and shoes (www.chotaoutdoor gear.com; see appendix B). The QuickLace Mukluk is my favorite for canoeing. Neoprene is a good insulator, so these boots also work well for active winter sports like snowshoeing. For occasional wet weather—stepping in and out of water—the vote goes to the leather/rubber Maine Hunting Shoe offered by L.L. Bean (www.llbean.com), which incidentally comes in women's and children's sizes.

Knee-high Tingley rubber overshoes (figure B-4; www.tingleyrubber .com; see appendix B) are the choice of many wilderness canoeists who must alternately paddle, portage, and wade in cold water. Tingleys are very flexible; they roll to fist size and their soft, nonaggressive rubber soles won't slip on wet rocks. These boots are actually better for rock-hopping than most wet shoes that are built for the purpose. Lightweight Tingley boots are sold in stores that service construction workers and other outdoor professionals. They are inexpensive.

Wear wool socks inside canvas sneakers, and Tingleys over the sneakers, and you're set for an arctic canoe expedition or a sloppy walk through a swamp. For transitional cold in near-freezing, sloppy conditions, substitute wool-felt snowmobile boot liners for the running shoes. Be sure to wear warm insoles inside (or under) the felt boot liners!

Tips:

sneakers worn inside

Figure B-4. Tingley rubber overshoes.

- Wear two pairs of wool socks—lightweight liner and medium weight—inside your boots. Wear the lightweight liner *inside out,* so the abrasive seams (which can produce hot spots and subsequently blisters) will not touch your skin.

- Old-fashioned sneakers were made from cotton canvas that provided good ventilation. Modern tennies are mostly plastic, which gets dreadfully hot. Here's a cool tip from Rod Johnson, a world-class hiker/mountaineer and the owner of Midwest Mountaineering (www.midwestmtn.com) in Minneapolis: Rod says your feet will stay a lot cooler if you cut the hot foam tongue out of your trail shoes. It really works! And surprisingly, you don't feel the pressure of laces at all. This trick cools down everyday running shoes too!

How to Break in New Boots

The traditional method: Wear boots an hour or two each day until they fit properly. This painful procedure takes about a week.

The preferred method: Fill each new boot full of lukewarm tap water. Allow the water to soak in for about fifteen seconds, then pour it out. Now put on the boots (with the correct socks, of course) and walk them dry—takes about three hours and results in about 50 percent break-in. Wear the boots around the house for about an hour each day for a week following the water treatment, and they'll be sufficiently broken in for hiking.

Care of Boots

Sponge dirt and grime off leather boots with saddle soap and water. Work up a good lather, then remove the suds with a damp sponge. Gentle sponging with plain soap and water is the best way to clean the fabric panels on leather/fabric boots.

Allow boots to dry thoroughly, away from heat, then apply an oil-based preservative like mink oil (with or without silicone) to oil-tanned leather. Apply a wax-based compound like Sno-Seal to chrome-tanned leather. Waxes do a much better job of waterproofing than oils and greases. Fortunately, waxes are compatible with oils and greases, if used sparingly. You can improve the weather resistance of oil-tanned boots considerably by topping the base oil (which should be well absorbed into the leather pores) with waxed-based compounds.

To apply boot grease or wax: Melt the preservative (leave the tin in hot sunlight for a few minutes) and apply it to lightly warmed leather with your bare hands. Rub in thoroughly and allow boots to "sunbathe" until the excess preservative is absorbed. Repeat application of the product until it is no longer absorbed by the leather. A dry rag may be used to remove excess grease that remains after the second application.

To dry wet boots: Never put boots too near a fire (if you can't hold your hand near the flame for thirty seconds, it's too hot for your boots!) or in an oven to dry them. You can speed the drying of wet boots by stuffing them with fire-warmed pebbles placed inside socks.

Always carry some boot wax in a 35-millimeter film canister on all your outings. Apply it frequently in wet weather.

Removing mold from boots and leather gear: Boots and leather goods stored in damp areas (basements) are sure to mold. The best way to remove mold is with a 25 percent solution of vinegar, household ammonia, or oxygen bleach, which will go deep into the pores of the leather and kill fungal hyphae. Thoroughly rinse the treated leather with clear water and allow it to dry before you apply preservatives. Sunlight kills fungus too, so give your leather goods a frequent airing outdoors.

To improve the warmth of boots: Install warm insoles! Three-eighths- to ½-inch-thick wool-felt snowmobile-boot insoles (80 percent wool, 20 percent polyester) are probably the best all-around choice, but closed-cell neoprene or EVA (ethyl vinyl acetate) insoles are less compressible and warmer. However, closed-cell foam insoles may be too hot under some conditions. You should have at least two pairs of insoles for your winter boots. Change insoles every day.

Oversocks: If your boots are too small to accept warm insoles, try wearing thick wool socks over them. Of course, the sock bottoms will quickly wear through, but what is left will add considerable warmth.

Winter Boots

Military surplus rubber "Mickey Mouse" boots are among the warmest mass-produced boots you can buy. However, they are very uncomfortable for walking. Pure white "bunny" boots—another surplus item—which are made from wool felt, are wonderfully warm and are great for hiking. Wear rubbers or Tingley boots over them in wet snow.

Canadian Sorel boots, or fabric-top snowmobile boots, are the preferred choice for one-day use but become damp after a good workout. The felt liners in these boots *must* be changed daily or frostbite may result.

Mukluks are roomy knee-high moccasins that are designed for snow. They have a canvas or soft leather outer shell and a wool or synthetic liner that is usually removable. Traditional Native American–style mukluks, like those made in Ely, Minnesota, by Patti Steger Holmberg, are *by far* the warmest, most comfortable, and breathtakingly beautiful winter footwear you can buy (www.muk-luks.com; see appendix B). World-famous arctic explorer Will Steger swears by Steger muk luks, as do most sled dog racers and snowshoers. There are more than a dozen styles of Steger mukluks and moccasins.

Professional mushers also like Dan Cooke's Cordura nylon Polar Mukluks, which have been used by top finishers in the Iditarod sled dog race

canvas or leather uppers →

waterproof soles

← leather bottoms

Figure B-5. Traditional mukluks.

(www.cookecustomsewing.com; see appendix B). They're insulated with 400-gram Thinsulate and have a ½-inch-thick closed-cell foam insole sewn into the bottom for extra warmth.

Foot wraps: The late Gil Phillips, known by the Boy Scouts as the "foam man," perfected the use of low-cost open-cell polyurethane foam for clothing, sleeping bags, and footwear. Gil and his Scouts relied on foam "everything" for their subzero encampments. Gil's proven system is recommended by the Boy Scouts of America and is described in detail in the Boy Scout's *Fieldbook* and in *Okpik: Cold Weather Camping,* which are available from Boy Scout suppliers. Here's the basic plan:

You'll need a loose-fitting canvas or nylon mukluk (military-surplus models are sometimes available) and two circular pieces of soft, 1-inch-thick open-cell polyurethane foam, like that used for pillow padding.

Fold the foam in half, then quarter it, as illustrated in figure B-6. Pull aside an outside foam layer and put your foot inside with the single foam layer at your heel. Wrap the double layers of foam right and left around your foot and insert both your "foot and foam" into the mukluk. On long trips, dry and refold the foam liner every few days. Foam foot wraps are incredibly warm, even without socks!

Boot liner tip 1: Two thin felt liners are warmer than one thick one. In 2003 I attended an arctic survival school in Spitsbergen, Norway (latitude 74° north). Temperatures plunged to 30 degrees below zero. Our winter survival instructor wore three ⅛-inch-thick wool felt liners (nested one inside the other) and double felt insoles inside his knee-high mukluks. His feet were never cold, even after hours of standing around on glacial ice.

Boot liner tip 2: To dry damp wool-felt liners in below-freezing weather, allow them to freeze, then knock off the ice crystals. Place them inside (at the foot of) your sleeping bag when you retire. They should be dry enough to wear by morning.

Boots in Summary

- For relatively dry three-season use, traditional lightweight all-leather boots are best. Combination leather and fabric boots tend to be less waterproof but lighter, more comfortable, and cooler.
- For mixed (wet and dry) conditions, leather top/rubber bottom shoepacs like the traditional L.L. Bean Maine Hunting Shoes work best. "Bean boots" are the most popular boots in the world. Millions

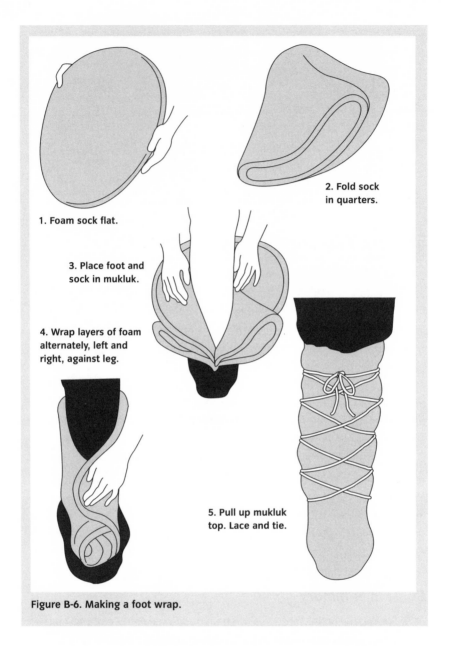

1. Foam sock flat.

2. Fold sock in quarters.

3. Place foot and sock in mukluk.

4. Wrap layers of foam alternately, left and right, against leg.

5. Pull up mukluk top. Lace and tie.

Figure B-6. Making a foot wrap.

of pairs have been sold . . . and resoled. These are by far the best boots for typical fall hiking and hunting in the wetland states.

• Chota neoprene mukluks and Tingley rubber boots, worn over sneakers, are good for boating; they provide good traction for rock hopping. Tingleys fit more loosely than pull-on rubber barn boots—they may come off your feet if you wear them in sticky mud. The neoprene Chotas are warm enough for mild winter use.

- Mickey Mouse boots are best for standing around. Sorels or fabric-top snowmobile boots work well if the felt liners are changed every day.
- White bunny boots or felt-lined canvas mukluks (with warm insoles) are the best cold-weather combination for dry snow.
- Foam foot wraps really work, even in severe weather.

BOTTLES AND FOOD TUBES

Various sizes and shapes of polyethylene bottles are commonly used by campers to store liquid and semiliquid foods like jam, peanut butter, pancake syrup, and cooking oil. Most of the plastic containers on supermarket shelves are too flimsy for strenuous camping trips; you need thick-walled, tough containers for serious backwoods use.

By far the most reliable containers for foodstuffs are Nalgenes (www .usplastic.com; see appendix B). Nalgene bottles were originally designed for packaging chemicals, so you know they're bombproof. Nalgene containers are positively leakproof and deservedly expensive. All the best camping stores carry them.

Free bottles (figure B-7): A decade ago, hospitals and clinics threw out plastic "sterile water for irrigation" (SWIG) bottles after a single use. You could get a box full for the asking. SWIG bottles were tough as nails, didn't absorb odors, and had graduated markings and a ring for hanging. Now the medical community has switched to sterile plastic bladders, which are useless for camping. But your local clinic may have some of the old bottles around. It's worth a check.

Most every liquid—from pop to pancake syrup—now comes in plastic bottles. The bottles, but not the flip-up tops, are generally reliable. Either replace the tops with screw caps (available at wine stores) or melt the pop-up openings shut in the flame of your trail stove.

Plastic food containers will retain odors after use. A thorough washing won't help much, but a mixture of baking soda and water will. Allow the soda-water solution to remain in the bottles for two weeks and odors will all but disappear.

Figure B-7. Sterile water for irrigation bottles.

Plastic food tubes, which are available at camping stores, resemble large toothpaste tubes. They are commonly used to hold jam, peanut butter, and other semiliquids. The tubes are filled from the open back end and are sealed with a marginally effective plastic clip. To use a food tube, unscrew the cap and squeeze the container (like a toothpaste tube). The idea sounds great but the product is unreliable, especially when the tubes are filled more than two-thirds full. Expert campers don't trust food tubes. I suggest you don't either!

BUGS—MOSQUITOES, FLIES, NO-SEE-UMS, AND TICKS
Colors and Biting Insects

Dark colors, especially navy blue and black, attract insects. Powder blue, yellow, mist green, white, and other light colors have a neutral or mild repelling effect. Avoid dark blue rain suits (the most popular color)! Contrary to popular belief, *red* does not repel blackflies (almost nothing really repels them!). Red is a fairly neutral color that neither repels nor attracts insects.

Know Your Enemies

Mosquitoes

They like to bite at dawn and dusk and just before or after a rain. They seem to like navy blue colors more than other insects. Air Force blue wool pants and shirts are an abomination in the woods and are nearly impossible to wear on buggy days. Mosquitoes are mild-mannered compared to flies. Most repellents will keep them away.

Horseflies and Deerflies

Horseflies and deerflies are much larger than houseflies. They're most active at midday when the sun is up. They zoom in fast and take a quick bite, which may become infected if you don't clean it fast. Flies can bite through thin liner socks but not through thick wool ones.

Blackflies

In the northern states and Canada, blackflies, which are about the size of rice grains, are the most dreaded pests. They're most active in the calm of dawn and dusk, and they breed in fast water—a reason why canoeists don't like to camp by rapids and falls. Big winds and temperatures below 40 degrees Fahrenheit usually keep them away. Blackflies have tiny mouths so you may not feel their bite—but they leave a bloody wound that is easily infected and may swell to golf-ball size. The good news is that the worst-biting species hatch in spring and only have one generation. Adults live six to eight weeks. Most blackflies are gone by late June in the north-

Figure B-8. A head net is essential if you camp in blackfly country. Along the Hood River in Nunavut, Canada.

ern states and southern Canada. In the high arctic they hang around till the first fall frost.

Blackflies prefer the constricted areas around wrists, ankles, behind the ear, etc., and they hone in on eyes, ears, and nostrils. Only the most powerful—nearly pure DEET—repellents will discourage them, and then not much. Closely woven clothing, neck-to-toe long johns, head nets, bug jackets, and full "body armor"—like the Susie bug net, described on page 36—are the best way to keep them at bay. Tuck your trousers into your boots or blouse them over the top with military blousing bands or elastic cords. Velcro tabs on shirt cuffs will seal your armor completely. If you don't want to get bitten in blackfly country, stay home! Nothing else really works.

Biting Midges (No-see-ums)

They're called no-see-ums because they're so tiny they can fly through the holes in conventional mosquito netting. Their bite feels like the jab of a sharp needle. The pain goes away fast but the wound itches for some time. The tiny holes in no-see-um netting are hard to see through and they restrict ventilation. Tents that have no-see-um nets become intolerably hot on bright sunny days—when no-see-ums are about. Standard wide-mesh mosquito netting will keep no-see-ums at bay if you spray the net with repellent.

Ticks

Watch out for deer ticks, which carry Lyme disease (see page 125), and the lone star tick, which is the host for Rocky Mountain spotted fever.

Removing an embedded tick:

Ticks must be on your body for a long time in order to bite. If you remove them within six hours, you're probably safe. A vigorous shower will remove most ticks before they dig in.

Don't pour gasoline, alcohol, or other chemicals over an embedded tick, and don't cover one with Vaseline or heat one with a match or ciga-rette: This could cause the tick to disgorge the contents of its stomach into you!

Do carefully scoop under the tick's body and slowly pull it from your skin. A blunt tweezer works okay if you're careful, but the Sawyer Tick Plier (figure B-9) is foolproof. William Forgey, M.D., author of *Wilderness Medi-cine: Beyond First Aid* (see appendix A), recommends the Sawyer Extractor

Sawyer Tick Plier

THE EXTRACTOR

Figure B-9. The Tick Plier and Extractor.

(it looks like a syringe, but produces a strong vacuum) to draw out tick saliva and other venoms. (Visit Sawyer at www.sawyerproducts.com, or see appendix B.)

Finally, wash the affected area with soap and water and apply an antiseptic and adhesive bandage.

Repellents and Insecticides: Your Best Hope Is Bug Dope!
DEET

The most effective repellents contain DEET—a chemical that contains N,N-diethyl-meta-toluamide. Generally, the more DEET a repellent has, the longer it works. However, too much DEET may burn sensitive skin and dissolve plastics—eyeglasses, Swiss Army knife handles, and plastic-coated fabrics. A bottle of DEET once leaked through a friend's trouser pocket. The repellent dissolved a huge swatch of his polypropylene underwear in a most embarrassing place!

No one knows for sure how much DEET is needed to keep bugs away. Everyone's body chemistry is different. However, my own experience in the Canadian bush suggests that 25 percent DEET, *in a mixture with other ingredients,* will keep away most insects. The remainder of the repellent should be a soothing lotion or alcohol. Lotion is kinder to your skin and it evaporates more slowly than alcohol, so the repellent lasts much longer. Save pure DEET as a last resort for arctic rivers where blackflies number in the billions and the lesser repellents you've tried don't work.

Caution: Children should *never* use pure DEET—it will burn their sensitive skin!

Permethrin

Permethrin is an insecticide. You put it on your clothes, not your skin. (Human skin metabolizes the chemical and renders it useless in a short time.) It's the best tick protection you can buy.

The agricultural grade permethrin you get at garden shops will work, but it smells awful and it doesn't bond to fabrics. I like Sawyer's Premium Insect Repellent (it contains 0.5 percent permethrin), which is odorless, bonds well to fabrics, and lasts six weeks. Some clothing makers, notably Ex Officio (Buzz Off clothing) and L.L. Bean, offer clothes that are treated with permethrin—naturally, with EPA approval. The commercially treated garments contain a higher concentration of permethrin than you would normally apply yourself, so the treatment lasts longer and survives more washing cycles. The EPA recently granted Sawyer Products registration for a clothing treatment kit that's similar to the one used by the military—you soak your clothes in the permethrin solution for two hours then hang dry the clothes. The treatment lasts through six washings.

The beauty of permethrin is that you apply it to your clothes, not your skin. And the treatment lasts a very long time. Spray your tent netting with permethrin and watch bugs die! Blackflies that are enclosed within a tent or netted tarp go nuts and crawl to the highest point, so dope these places too.

Natural Repellents

Big claims are made for "natural" insect repellents that don't contain DEET. Ingredients may include cedar oil, eucalyptus oil, tea tree oil, geranium oil, pure vanilla extract, rubbing alcohol, and spices like cinnamon, basil, thyme, garlic, catnip, spearmint, and more.

How well do these "natural" repellents work? For casual backyard use on mostly mild-mannered mosquitoes, they are adequate. But add blackflies—or hours of exposure—and you'll want DEET. Do Bengay, Vick's VapoRub, and Skin-So-Soft lotion repel mosquitoes? Yes, but not very well and not for long.

Tip: If you're in the north woods and don't have bug dope, peel strips of bark from spruce trees and rub the inner bark on your skin. Or cover exposed areas with mud.

Build a Skin Barrier with Sunblock

Kurt Avery, president of Sawyer Products, suggests you rub sunblock deep into your skin, wait ten minutes, then apply the insect repellent. The sunblock keeps your body from absorbing too much of the repellent. If possible, select one of the new "bonding base" sunblocks that penetrate deep into your skin. Film-base sunblocks—like the kind available everywhere—cover just the surface of your skin.

Head Nets and Bug Jackets

Head nets are essential for early-season trips in the northern states and Canada. Nonmilitary styles that don't have a hoop around the face are best because they roll to fist size and fit in your pocket. You can make a head net in a few minutes. Just sew up a wide rectangle of mosquito net large enough to fit over your head and wide-brimmed hat. Make the net long enough to drape lazily on your shoulders. *Don't* sew an elastic band into the hem. Spray the hem with repellent and even blackflies will be confused. Spray the entire net if no-see-ums are about.

Figure B-10. A bug jacket, like this DEET-impregnated model, is cool and comfortable and it repels the meanest blackflies.

Head nets are best constructed of dark-colored standard-mesh mosquito net, both for good visibility and ventilation. It's difficult to see through milk-colored no-see-um net. If you can't find a dark-colored head net, buy a light-colored one and darken the eye panel with black marker or spray paint.

Bug jackets armor your body against biting insects. Some styles rely on chemicals (DEET or permethrin) to keep bugs away; others block them with close-knit mesh. Chemically treated jackets are cooler to wear and they prevent bugs from landing—a plus when you're eating or drinking. I've spent a lot of time fighting bugs in the Canadian north, so I'm very picky about bug jackets. Here are three of my favorites:

- *Chemically treated (DEET) style:* Uncle Keith's Northern Canadian Bug-Free Insect Repellent Jacket. This wide-mesh cotton-polyester jacket has a large hood (you'll need a head net) and zipper closure. To activate the jacket you soak it in pure (100 percent) DEET overnight, then hang it out to dry. With frequent everyday use, the treatment lasts about two weeks. It is easily recharged with DEET in the field. This jacket is cool, compact, and comfortable. It's available (at this writing) only in Canada. The Arctic Trading Company, in Churchill, Manitoba (www.arctictradingco.com; see appendix B) will ship these jackets (without the DEET) to U.S. customers. You can buy full-strength DEET at most sport shops and treat the jacket yourself. Or spray it with permethrin.

- *Chemical-free:* The Original Bug Shirt (made in Canada) combines fine-mesh netting with ultralight, densely woven cotton or polyester microfiber (www.bugshirt.com; see appendix B). The zippered hood has an integral face mask so you don't need a head net (you have to unzip to eat). Cord-lock closures at the wrist and waist provide an impenetrable seal.

- *Make your own bug jacket:* Impregnate (using a spray can or soaker kit) any light-colored cotton or polyester long-sleeve shirt with permethrin. Add a head net and you're set for battle.

Susie Bug Net

First, you apply DEET to all exposed skin. As more insects gather, you add a head net, then a DEET-impregnated bug jacket. Ultimately, you rant and

swear, then in disgust retire to your insectproof tent. Meanwhile, friends nearby enjoy a bug-free after-dinner brandy and a glorious sunset inside their "Susie bug net"—a personal-size bug armor designed by my wife, Sue Harings:

Materials needed: A piece of mosquito netting 12 feet long and 7 feet wide, plus enough ⅛-inch-diameter shock cord to span the hem. Don't use no-see-um net: It's not strong enough and you can't see through it.

Procedure: Fold the netting in half to produce a rectangular sheet that measures 6 feet by 7 feet. Sew up the two long sides, hem the bottom and install the bungee cord in the hem. The finished net will weigh less than a pound and compress to football size.

Here are some uses for your Susie bug net:

Figure B-11. Susie bug net.

1. Eat inside it; there's room for two.
2. Sleep out under the stars. The net covers you from head to toe. Cinch the bungee cord tightly around the foot of your sleeping bag.
3. Use it as a portable outhouse when bugs are bad.
4. Bathe in it! Amble to the beach as a ghostly apparition in your Susie bug net. Wear your life vest and you'll float confidently inside your bug armor.
5. Lay the net over breads, cheese, and lunch meats to keep flies away.
6. Rig a tripod inside and you have a tiny bugproof tepee in which to wash dishes, cook, and make repairs.

Roll and stuff your Susie bug net under a pack flap so it will be available at meals and river rest stops.

If you don't want to make your own, the Susie bug net is available from Cooke Custom Sewing (see appendix B).

Some Final "Repelling" Tips

- Bugs will avoid your face if you saturate a cowboy neckerchief with repellent and tie it loosely around your neck. Spray the underside of your hat brim too!

- Some of the most effective first-aid products for bug bites contain aloe, a plant-derived ingredient that has been around for thousands of years. Aloe soothes inflammation, inhibits swelling, and keeps skin moist. It also soothes burns and kills bacteria and fungi. To be effective, aloe should make up at least 80 percent of the product's formula.

- Liquid or cream repellents are much more potent (a better buy) than sprays.

- Household ammonia and water will cut the sting of mosquito bites. For bee, wasp, and hornet stings, apply a wet salt pack and allow it to dry. The salt will draw the pain away quickly.

- Sew Velcro tabs to your shirt cuffs (figure B-12) so you can seal off this area from black-flies and mosquitoes.

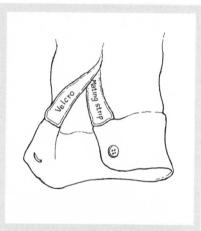

Figure B-12. Sew Velcro tabs to your shirt cuffs to keep bugs out.

BUSH LIVING

Sharron Chatterton is a retired wilderness canoe guide, college instructor, and writer who lives a contemplative life in a lakeside cabin near Teslin, Yukon, Canada. Here she explains how the solitude and demands of bush living shape the personality of those who live and work in wild places.

—CJ

The wilderness promotes traits that encourage survival. Surrounded by the unpredictable and beyond rescue, wilderness travelers safeguard unknown outcomes against disaster. Their goal is safe arrival to their desti-

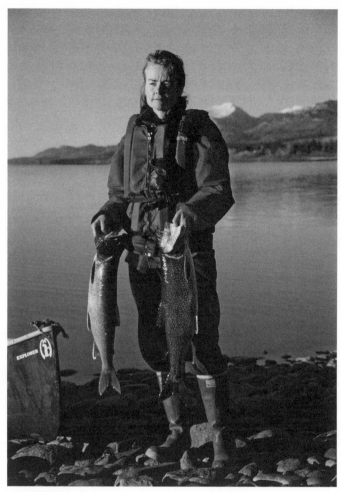
Sharron Chatterton.

nation, not arrival by some time or date. Some "great feats" are simply their cautious journeys.

Wilderness makes an individual self-reliant—able to function alone, to perform all tasks independently, and to know the adaptive capability of every tool. To the bush traveler, rescue is an urban myth—there are no buffers against irresponsibility! Wilderness dwellers accept what *is*, not what was or ought to be. They plan carefully and they don't take chances. Actions are purposeful; tasks are always completed. To use energy on valueless projects or to leave important work undone is unthinkable. There is too much to do to get bored.

Long periods spent in silence creates an ease without talk, value for the understandings that flow without language, and a need for silence. Silence conserves energy, frees ones attention for more important work and, lacking confrontation, creates gentleness. Simple wisdom breeds in silence.

Wilderness travelers become hyperalert and observant. The land exhibits what happened, is happening, and might happen next to the ears, eyes, nose, and skin. These sensors function in overdrive, constantly receiving information.

Some believe that wilderness living breeds antisocial behavior. In truth, the wilderness man or woman becomes *asocial*—he or she has a lingering love of society but little need for it. The wilderness, not the nation that manages it, evokes their allegiance. This alienation from political boundaries and reassociation with the natural world defines the "wilderness heart."

Survival is the hidden foundation of bush morality. It is what allows one to kill animals to eat, blaze trees to mark a return trail, or sidestep a slipper orchid. An experienced bush dweller learns never to interfere with another. To pass without offering help is a cardinal sin. To solicit help unnecessarily is another. Survival encourages cordiality among neighbors—you might have to depend upon one for help.

There are deeper effects of wilderness than those on human personality: There is a growing need to reduce belongings, to hunt and gather, and to be nomadic. Nature—not other humans—controls the routine. There is a growing intimacy with animals and with death. Consciousness passes old barriers and metaphysical experiences occur. Wilderness rearranges behavior, reconfigures mental constructs, and transforms the inner self forever.

Yet personality change is what we first perceive in committed wilderness travelers. We see it in epic soloists, long-distance trekkers, and in those who work in wild places—guides, researchers, and itinerant wanderers. In fact, all of us, even we who paddle a simple slough alone or walk a dog along the bluffs—even farmers, loggers, and deep sea fishermen whose wilderness experiences we consistently deny—have personalities deeply marked by wilderness.

CAMERA

Waterproof protection: Most photographers rely on waterproof Pelican or Otter boxes to protect their cameras from rain or a boat capsize. These boxes are reliable if you take certain precautions (see WATERPROOF BAGS AND BOXES, page 227).

Regrettably, the wonderful military assault gas-mask bags are no longer available. They were constructed from rubberized canvas and were ideal camera containers. Vinyl copies aren't as rugged or waterproof. Waterproof "dry bags" that have roll-down closures or watertight zippers are the current "soft bag" options.

Tip: Make a cylinder of closed-cell foam that will fit snugly inside your waterproof dry bag. Cut a circular bottom. Glue or duct tape the pieces together. The foam will protect your camera from knocks and shield it from the sun.

Some boaters still use metal GI ammo boxes. But beware of damaged and rotten seals. The seals are easy to replace—if you can find them!

You can rig a quick waterproof "shoot-through" bag by placing your camera inside an Aloksak waterproof plastic bag (see page 227).

CANOE- AND BOAT-RIGGING TIPS

(See my books *Expedition Canoeing* and *Canoeing and Camping* for a wealth of detailed canoeing and canoe-rigging tips.)

Compass: For ease in navigating complex lakes, secure a wrist compass around the aft canoe thwart. This will enable you to simultaneously paddle and follow a plotted course.

Custom improvements: Thread loops of fabric shock cord through holes drilled in the canoe's thwarts and deck plates. End lines (painters) stored under the shock-cord loops will stay put in a capsize and on portages. Oddities can be secured under the thwart cords.

Fiberglass and Royalex canoes should have lining holes or rings installed at cutwater, not high on the deck as is the common practice. See figure C-1.

Figure C-1. End lines, shock cords, and lining holes.

Multiuse bailer: A two-quart plastic water pitcher tied to a canoe thwart makes a handy bailer and is useful for mixing powdered drinks in camp.

Canoe pockets you can portage: Where to store small items like eyeglasses, suntan lotion, and repellent is always a problem on canoe trips. Of course, you can store these small items in packsacks, but getting to them is a hassle. So why not install pockets in your canoe?

An early pioneer of canoe pockets was Verlen Kruger, whose 7,000-mile canoe trip from Montreal to the Bering Sea made canoeing history in 1971. Verlen simply attached plastic bicycle baskets to his canoe thwarts. The baskets provided a convenient—though not capsize proof—place to store small items.

Thwart bags are the modern alternative to bicycle baskets. Most clip or Velcro to a canoe thwart. Unfortunately, few thwart bag makers have given much thought as to what to do with these bags when it's time to portage.

You can turn any small fanny pack or nylon briefcase into a "portage-able" thwart bag by simply sewing on buckles or Velcro tabs that will secure around a thwart. Add a detachable shoulder strap and you'll be set for the portage.

You can buy commercial thwart bags from Cooke Custom Sewing, Granite Gear, Frost River, and Duluth Pack (see appendix B).

Seat improvements: Drill holes in canoe and boat seats so they won't pool water when it rains. Glue (contact cement) closed-cell foam to the surface of canoe and boat seats to increase comfort and warmth. The foam will also add flotation to the craft.

Emergency repair kit: The only emergency repair kit you really need for a canoe or boat is a roll of 2-inch-wide silver duct tape. Duct tape sticks to anything. Use it for emergency repairs on all your camping gear.

Paint decks on aluminum canoes flat black to reduce glare.

For kneeling comfort when paddling, glue foam knee pads into your canoe. You can buy precut knee pads at canoe and kayak shops or just cut up a closed-cell foam sleeping pad. Weldwood contact cement is the most reliable adhesive and will work on any surface.

Tying canoes on cars: Best hitch for this is the power cinch. See the section KNOTS, HITCHES, AND LASHINGS on page 117.

Yoke: A yoke is essential if you plan to carry your canoe alone for even short distances. A curved hardwood yoke, with overstuffed foam-filled shoulder pads, is the most comfortable combination. Commercial yokes cost upward of $40 and are seldom very good. You can make a much better yoke than you can buy.

Make your yoke from white ash (preferred) and finish to the dimensions illustrated in figure C-2. The completed yoke should have some flex, which will take the sting out of a rigorous carry. Use open-cell polyurethane foam

Figure C-2. A homemade yoke with drainage holes will take the sting out of a long carry.

Figure C-3. A curved hardwood yoke with overstuffed foam shoulder pads is the most comfortable device for carrying a canoe or kayak. At top is a home-made yoke with Old Town Canoe Company brackets. At bottom is the Bell Canoeworks universal portage yoke. Note the nice star-wheel bracket.

(pillow padding) for the shoulder pads. Naugahyde or other heavy plastic upholstery material is the best covering fabric. Attach the yoke to the balance point of the canoe (some prefer a slightly tail-heavy arrangement) with bolts or wood clamps. The clamp and wing nut setup is best if you plan to carry a third person in the canoe. You can easily remove the yoke to provide more room for your passenger.

Make a Belly Cover for Your Canoe

If you've ever paddled a canoe in icy wind-whipped rain, fought the waves of a big lake, or edged down huge rapids, you know the value of a canoe cover. My book *Expedition Canoeing* has detailed plans for making the Jacobson three-piece tandem cover, the Jacobson two-piece solo cover, and the split-center dogsled model designed by arctic canoeist Bob O'Hara. Commercial versions of this cover are available from Cooke Custom Sewing (see appendix B). Dan Cooke supplies a no-shrink Mylar template, which ensures a perfect fit on any canoe.

You don't need a full splash cover unless you're a white-water fanatic or are canoeing the Canadian north. The one-piece "expandable belly" described next provides enough protection for all but the most severe conditions. If you can sew a straight stitch, you can make a belly cover in about three hours.

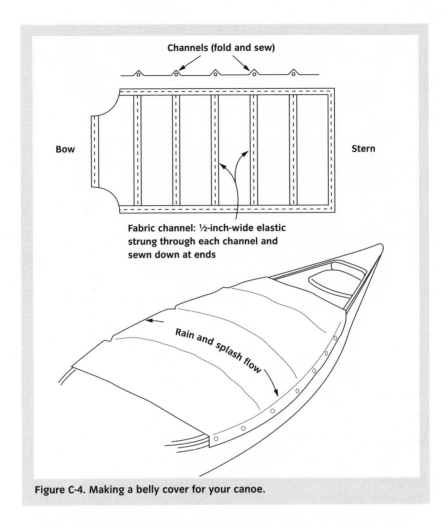

Figure C-4. Making a belly cover for your canoe.

The belly section described below weighs about a pound and stuffs to football size. You can use it as a small sail or tablecloth or as a rain cover for packs and firewood.

Materials:

1. Pattern: None! The canoe is your pattern.
2. Snaps: Twenty-four brass snaps. Check 'em with a magnet to be sure they're not plated steel.
3. Waterproof nylon: A weight of 2.5 ounces per square yard is strong enough for friendly waterways; 4-ounce to 6-ounce stuff is best for the arctic barrens.

4. One-inch-wide seam tape or nylon webbing—about 20 feet.
5. Extras: 2-inch-wide Velcro, 1-inch-wide pajama elastic.

Procedure:

1. Pop rivet snaps through the hull, 2 inches below the rails, 8 inches apart. Begin the snap line at the rear edge of the front seat and end it at the back thwart. Use an aluminum backup washer behind each rivet. You'll need about twelve snaps for each side of the canoe.
2. Cut a 60-inch-wide piece of fabric that reaches from the front edge of the bow seat to the rear thwart. Hem all sides then sew seam tape to the inside hem. Next, fold over and sew the "water deflector channels," illustrated in figure C-4. Thread pajama elastic through the channels and rear hem. Tighten the elastic slightly, then sew down the ends.
3. Set snaps through the hem to match those on the canoe. Nylon stretches when wet and shrinks when dry, so don't pull the material too tightly!

You can modify the belly to accept a passenger by installing a quick-release skirt in the center.

Gel-Coat Repair and Maintenance Tricks

It's doubtful that you'll ever have to repair major damage to a well-built fiberglass or Kevlar canoe or boat. However, you may need to mend chipped gel coat on the bottom—easy, if you *don't* follow the manufacturer's directions. The recommended procedure calls for filling the break with color-matched liquid gel coat, then sanding and polishing to blend the repair.

Nothing could be more difficult or frustrating. Catalyzed liquid gel coat is runny; you must prop the boat at an awkward angle to level the flow, then build a well of masking tape to contain the resin. Then you have to nurse the slowly hardening liquid with a flat stick to keep it from overflowing the well.

Here's an easier way:

1. Remove the shards of damaged gel coat.
2. Mask the work area, then catalyze polyester or gray auto-body putty (use extra MEKP hardening agent to produce a "hot" mix) and work it into the

break to overflowing. The putty is thick and won't run, so there's no need to prop the canoe or build a tape well. *Caution:* MEKP (methyl ethyl ketone peroxide) is toxic and can cause blindness. Wear safety goggles and rubber gloves! And mix everything in a well-ventilated area.

3. When the putty is firm (about five minutes), slice off the excess with your jackknife. Allow the remainder to cure for another half hour, then sand it level with progressive grits of sandpaper. Finish to silky smooth-ness with wet 400-grit sandpaper.

4. Spray paint the patch with matching auto acrylic. When the paint has dried, buff it out with a mixture of paste wax and pumice. Or use a commercial fiberglass boat wax (it contains pumice), which you can get at any marina.

Your patch is now complete. The whole process takes about an hour.

To keep gel coat looking like new: Occasionally use a commercial hull cleaner (I've had good results with Star brite) to remove scum lines and stains from fiberglass and Kevlar gel coat. Paste wax will brighten and pro-tect the hull. Canoe retailers often wipe on a coat of Lemon Pledge before they display their fiberglass canoes and boats in the store.

CANTEEN

Only cheechakos and bona fide cowboys use traditional canteens these days. Expert campers rely on poly bottles to carry thirst quenchers. Plastic bottles are cheaper, lighter, and easier to pack than metal canteens.

Some backpackers and paddlers prefer the convenience of a self-contained hydration system, like the popular CamelBak, which you wear on your back (it has pack straps). Water is held inside a plastic bladder that is protected by a tough nylon cover. Water is delivered via a plastic tube that has a sophisticated no-leak mouthpiece. Hydration systems are great for people on the go, especially those who must have their hands free.

Plastic soda bottles make fine canteens, and they fit nicely into the side pockets of small hiking packs. Several companies make insulated (neo-prene) covers for these bottles.

Tip: Fill your water bottle four-fifths full of water and freeze it to assure a supply of cold water during the next day's hike. In below-freezing weather, carry your bottle *upside down* in your pack. This will prevent ice from forming in the mouthpiece.

Web handle for hanging ←

↖ Sew nylon webbing all around wine bladder.

Figure C-5. Wine bladder water bag.

A glass vacuum bottle, sans cup, makes a surprisingly good canteen. Modern vacuum bottles are quite strong and lightweight; they assure a cold (or hot) drink throughout the day.

The traditional bota, or wine bladder, remains popular with skiers. It also makes a fine, easy-to-carry canteen for summer hiking.

Here's a good way to warm up your sleeping bag on a cold night: Pour boiling water into your canteen, roll the canteen in a towel or shirt, and take this homemade hot-water bottle to bed.

Do not put carbonated beverages or alcohol into an aluminum canteen. These products will react with the aluminum!

The tough Mylar bag (bladder), which lines wine boxes, makes a great "giant" canteen (figure C-5). Sew tough nylon around the bladder so you can hang the unit from a tree and dispense liquid through the efficient rubber faucetlike spout. *Note:* The rubber spouts are easy to remove if you grasp the lip with a thumbnail and pull. No amount of twisting and forcing will break it loose.

Here's how to make a collapsible nylon water bucket:

1. Cut a 3-foot-diameter circle of waterproof nylon (taffeta or ripstop).
2. Gather the circular edge of the material to form a bag, then sew the pleated mouth, leaving an approximate 3-inch opening.
3. Sew seam binding all around the mouth of the bag. Sew a handle of nylon webbing across the mouth.

This water bag (which I call a "spider") is very compact. It will stand freely if you don't overfill it. *Tip:* Attach a stout 10-foot rope to the handle of the spider so you can toss it into the water from a riverbank. Water will stay inside when you drag the spider up the bank (figure C-6).

Figure C-6. Spider water bag.

CARTOP CARRIERS (CANOE RACKS)

Canoeists still mourn the passing of car rain gutters, which accepted all manners of clamp-on devices. No current system is as secure as racks that bolt directly to the drip eaves of the car. My 1986 Chevy van has rain gutters, and I plan to keep it forever. I'm convinced that the world's first closed cars had rain gutters because they were designed by canoeists for canoeists!

Regrettably, the days of the wonderful generic racks that attach to a car's drip eaves are over. With the exception of full-size vans and a few SUVs, all of today's vehicles have airplane-style doors that require specially fitted brackets. Thule and Yakima lead the way in gutterless designs and offer racks to fit nearly every car model.

Caution: The load brackets that come with gutterless carriers are built to fit the rooflines of specific vehicles. Do not jury-rig them to fit cars for which they are not designed!

Even if you don't plan to buy a second canoe, you may need to shuttle a friend's, so be sure to order double-length (80 inches) crossbars—the factory standard 48-inch carrier is too short to carry paired canoes. Be sure your cartop carrier has locking bars to prevent theft. Even then, many paddlers prefer to remove their expensive racks and store them inside their cars when they're on the river.

Never set canoes on hard, unpadded carriers—the gunnels are sure to be damaged. Here's how to protect your canoe, your car, and your peace of mind:

1. Sew or duct tape scrap carpeting around the crossbars. This ancient low-tech method is still the best way to protect fine woodwork. Most "show" canoes ride on old-fashioned carpeted racks. Carpeting tells the canoe world you care about your canoe!

2. Yakima, Quick-N-Easy, and a few other companies use tubular aluminum conduit crossbars (Yakima covers theirs with plastic). Some canoeists armor the conduit with rubber heater hose—it slides on easily if you lubricate the rubber with brake fluid.

3. You can bolt L-shaped plastic gunnel brackets (an optional accessory) to the crossbars. The brackets provide a wide, protective bearing surface for the canoe's gunnels and prevent the craft from shifting in wind—a safety advantage. If your canoe has wooden rails, you may want to glue closed-cell foam or scrap carpeting to the hard plastic faces of the brackets.

Watch out that you don't hit your head on the ends of oversize canoe racks when you get in and out of your car. To cushion the occasional blow, some canoeists replace the plastic caps on the ends of the crossbars with thick rubber furniture tips. Others tie short pieces of brightly colored surveying ribbon to the bar ends so they'll be more visible in dim light. One friend has impaled tennis balls on the ends of his canoe rack; another has tied small bells to the crossbars. The bells jingle in the slightest breeze—a reminder to be careful.

Tie-down Procedures

Separately tie down each canoe you carry! Do it right and the canoe will remain rock solid even at illegal speeds. Here are the rules for safe travel:

1. Run *two* strong ropes or straps over the belly of the canoe and secure each to its respective crossbar. Do not string one long rope from crossbar to crossbar—it could loosen at highway speeds and the canoe could come off the car!

2. Attach *two* lines to the bow and *two* lines to the stern of each craft. Secure each line to eye bolts in the bumpers, to padded S hooks that ride in secure notches under the bumper, or to loops of webbing or Kevlar cord secured to bolts or fittings under the hood (figure C-7)—the latter is the best plan for cars that have plastic bumpers. Pull the webbing up through the crack between the hood and fender when you need it. Don't wind ropes around bumpers; sharp bumper edges (even plastic ones) can cut or abrade them.

3. Don't use rubber tie-downs or elastic shock cords to secure canoes to cars! There should be a law against using these stretchy devices.

Straps or ropes? Many paddlers prefer heavy-duty straps to ropes for cartopping canoes. Straps are fast and easy to adjust and they stay tight in

Figure C-7. For cars that don't have metal bumpers, attach tie-down lines to loops of nylon webbing or cord that are secured to a bracket or bolt under the hood.

any weather. But straps may be stolen if you leave them on the cartop carrier while you're off paddling. Ropes are a low theft item and can be left tied to the roof rack for a quick tie down and getaway after the trip. *Caution:* Don't toss straps over the roof of your vehicle when you load your canoe—the metal buckles may take a chunk out of the canoe or car! Straps are best passed to a friend or—if they're long enough—walked around the car. Ropes are safe to throw. Straps are more reliable than ropes only if you don't know how to tie the right knots! Most serious canoeists I know prefer ropes to straps. Exceptions: when carrying a single canoe on a small, narrow car or a bunch of canoes on a trailer.

Concerns for Carrying Fragile and Paired Canoes

You can break the back of a fragile canoe if you secure its ends too tightly. For this reason, many canoeists prefer to tie only the bow. Racers *never* tie down the tail of their ultralight canoes!

Whenever you carry two canoes side by side on an overhead rack, always pad the inside of one of the canoes so the finish won't be galled if the two crafts shift sideways and touch.

Finally, if you carry two canoes on a double rack, place the lightest and most fragile canoe on the passenger side of the carrier. This will allow the sturdier and more rigidly tied craft on the driver's side to take the abuse of high winds generated by passing trucks.

CHILDREN (TIPS FOR CAMPING WITH KIDS)

Rain Gear

The best rain gear for young children is an inexpensive plastic poncho, a coated nylon windbreaker, and a sou'wester-style hat. Trim the poncho to fit with scissors. Waterproof the stitching of the coated jacket with seam sealant (every camp shop has it). Be sure to glue the seams on the sou'wester hat too.

Rationale: The youngster wears the coated wind shell under the poncho—it keeps arms dry and provides a secondary "drip" layer in prolonged rain. The sou'wester hat is worn over the poncho hood and is tied beneath the chin. Together, these garments provide serviceable and inexpensive protection from rain.

Emergency rain gear for kids (or adults) may be fashioned from a large leaf-and-lawn-size garbage bag. Cut head and arm holes, provide a sou'wester hat, and you'll stay reasonably dry.

Wet-weather footgear: Running shoes and galoshes, or any rubber boots sized large enough to fit over the sneakers, are all you need. When rains quit, the boots are removed and freedom of foot is instantly restored.

Camp Clothing and Sleeping Gear

Cotton clothing (except underwear) should be *avoided* except in the predictable heat of mid-July. Woolens may be too scratchy for some youngsters, so the logical solution is Orlon acrylic. Acrylic sweaters, gloves, and hats dry quickly after a wetting and retain their insulating properties when damp or soiled. Acrylic garments are also quite inexpensive; they are ideal for spring canoe and boat trips, for adults as well as kids.

Hats: Kids need three hats on a camping trip—a brimmed cap for sun, a warm stocking cap (wool or acrylic) for chilly days, and the traditional sou'wester for rain.

Sleeping gear: Kids do not need air mattresses or foam pads for comfort. Their young bones will happily conform to the most uneven ground!

You must provide a foam pad (not an air mattress—these conduct cold!) if down sleeping bags are used. Body weight compresses the underside of a down bag to near-zero thickness, and chilling will result unless insulation is provided. The typical polyester (Polarguard, Quallofil, or Hollofil) sleeping bag provides sufficient insulation below so that, except in very cold weather, mattresses may be omitted.

Sleeping bags are unnecessary for typical summer camping. One or two light wool or fluffy acrylic blankets, folded as illustrated (figure C-8), will provide plenty of warmth in temperatures to 45 degrees.

Increasing the warmth of a sleeping bag: The warmth of a sleeping bag is partly related to the amount of space the body has to heat. By reducing dead-air space, you'll increase warmth. Figure C-9 shows an easy way to reduce the dimensions, and add warmth, to the typical station-wagon-sized sleeping bag. A flannel "draft collar" sewn to the top of a sleeping bag will increase warmth considerably.

Insects (see BUGS, page 30): A head net *and* a Susie bug net are wise investments if you'll be camping in buggy country. Choose mild, cream-

One blanket

a. Two blankets

b.

Figure C-8. For summer use, blankets work as well as a sleeping bag. Here's how to fold them for maximum warmth.

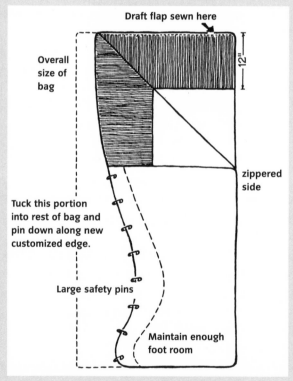

Draft flap sewn here

Overall size of bag

12"

zippered side

Tuck this portion into rest of bag and pin down along new customized edge.

Large safety pins

Maintain enough foot room

Figure C-9. Customizing a sleeping bag for children.

based repellents rather than more powerful chemicals, which may burn sensitive young skin.

Toys: Kids will want to bring a favorite doll or teddy bear. Be sure to provide a "raincoat" (plastic bag) for the toy, so it won't be ruined in foul weather.

CLOTHING

How to Tell the Real Thing from Designer Wear!

With today's "outdoor look," you'd think it would be easy to locate suitable clothing for backcountry camping. Hardly! Only a handful of manufacturers currently offer attire that is truly functional. The vast majority of clothing makers are simply producing stylish garments that parrot the outdoor look. Here's how to tell designer campwear from the real thing.

Fit: Outdoor clothing should be cut large enough to permit unrestricted movement of arms and legs, even when extra clothing is worn beneath. Shirt and jacket sleeves should be generously sized, even to the point of billowing.

Designer outdoor wear is almost always restrictive in the arms and chest and is usually cut on the short side. This style looks flattering but is an abomination in the wilds. *A rule of thumb:* Properly sized wind and rain gear should have sleeves that are three times the diameter of your arms!

Hoods: Designer hoods are slim, trim, and stow away into collars. Wilderness hoods are large enough to fit over a brimmed hat. Hood zippers continue to the nose. This continuous-zipper design naturally precludes a stowaway feature essential to the designer look.

Designer wear also features more pockets than you can possibly use, suggesting utility and driving up tailoring costs. Really now, when was the last time you used more than two pockets in your parka or rain jacket?

The least expensive and most versatile trousers for camping are military surplus chinos and fatigues. For cold-weather use, surplus wool trousers are the norm. Trouser legs should hang straight (no cuffs) so they won't trap the environment as you walk through it.

Wool or synthetic? Despite the ballyhoo over synthetic fabrics like polypropylene, fleece, and chemically treated polyesters, good wool still performs as well or better in cold, damp weather. In practice, the human body is less sensitive than the machines used to prove manufacturers' claims of superiority.

I tried a variety of natural and synthetic fabrics when I attended the winter work and survival school in Spitsbergen, Norway. Wool was rated the warmest fabric of them all! And there was no guesswork to the ratings because students were wired with sensors whose data were later fed into a computer. Skin temperatures don't lie! When it comes to longevity, good wool outlasts them all.

Still, synthetics have their place—as wind stoppers, dry liners, comfy fleece outergarments, and underwear for those who can't stand wool (even soft merino wool) next to their skin.

Buy what you can afford, but don't be swept off your feet by exotic claims for space-age fabrics. Except in the heat of summer, only cotton in pure form is unsuitable for camping.

Summer wind parka: Your most useful garment on a camping trip is a simple, porous, nylon wind shell. Emphasize "simple" and "porous." You don't need a fancy hood that turns with your head, armpit zippers, or a microfiber liner. You *do need* a hood that will fit over your wide-brim hat, a zipper that runs almost to your nose (and seals your throat), excellent ventilation, and a large enough size to fit over your fleece jacket or Norwegian wool sweater. Your wind shell should roll to fist size and weigh almost nothing. You can buy nylon shells like this at any discount store; they are inexpensive.

Why no bells and whistles on a wind parka? Because they add weight and bulk and provide little real utility. Forget coated fabrics and Gore-Tex —they are not breathable (porous) enough for active wear. You may put on and take off your wind shell dozens of times a day as you adjust your comfort system. If your jacket is too bulky to stuff into a pack pocket or to loop around your waist, you'll wish you'd left it at home!

Winter wind parka: Same rules as for the summer parka, with these exceptions:

- Tightly woven cotton or cotton-polyester is softer and more flexible than nylon in extremely cold temperatures.
- Size should be knee length and one size larger than your usual summer parka.
- An anorak style provides more freedom of movement than a full-zip model—and the constantly connected anorak zipper is less likely to

jam. For extreme subzero temperatures, choose buttons, snaps, or Velcro over zippers. A winter parka must have a protective beard flap behind the zipper.

- A fur-trimmed hood (coyote fur doesn't frost up and it's not too pricey) is essential in bitter cold and blowing wind.

- Gore-Tex can be dangerous in bitter cold temperatures (especially if you are very active) because its tiny pores can't eliminate perspiration as fast as it's produced. Condensation builds and produces a sauna inside. When you remove the Gore-Tex jacket, the trapped moisture freezes and the fabric becomes stiff as a board. Under some conditions, the garment may even freeze on you! High porosity is essential in active cold-weather clothing! Note: Treating a porous cotton or nylon windbreaker with a water-repellent like Scotchguard will reduce its porosity and its ability to move moisture.

Blue jeans are a particularly bad choice and have accounted for several deaths due to hypothermia. Even in the heat of summer, there are better choices than pure cotton.

Long underwear: I've tried many brands; these are my current favorites:

- Icebreaker (www.icebreaker.com; see appendix B): Stylish underwear and outerwear woven from silky soft pure merino wool. Beautiful, functional, and wonderfully warm. The flat-finished weave is less likely to catch on brush and unravel. I just love the merino T-shirt!

- Klar Ullfrotté: Underlayer, mid-layer and outer-layer garments woven from two-thirds pure merino wool and one-third polyamide (for strength and elasticity). First choice of the Scandinavian military and widely used by police departments and rescue personnel the world over, Klar Ullfrotté may be the warmest long underwear on the planet.

- Smartwool (www.smartwool.com; see appendix B): Everyone knows about Smartwool socks. But their merino T-shirts and long johns are terrific too.

- Thermax: This nonallergenic DuPont fabric insulates well, even when wet. It breathes in hot weather, feels nice against the skin, and it doesn't smell—even when it goes unwashed for days. My wife, Sue Harings, who is very conscious of odors, insisted that I recommend

Thermax and its relative Thermistat by name. Available from Cabela's (www.cabelas.com; see appendix B).

Tip: Pack a small nylon sack inside your clothes bag or pack to serve as a dirty laundry bag to keep dirty clothing separate from clean items.

Care and Cleaning of Clothing

Woolens may be dry-cleaned or washed by hand or machine (gentle cycle only). The best method is to hand wash—a three-minute soak in a mild detergent (Woolite, Ivory Snow, or any mild dishwashing detergent), then hand rinse and spin dry in a machine.

Spun-dry woolens are best dried flat or hung on wooden hangers, out of direct sunlight.

Woolen outergarments should be washed in cold or lukewarm water to prevent shrinkage and prolong the life of the fibers. But cold water may not destroy the bacteria and body odor that accumulates in garments worn next to the skin. Klar Ullfrotté—a Swedish company that supplies merino wool long underwear to the Swedish and Norwegian military—recommends that you wash their woolens in 60 degree Celsius (140 degree Fahrenheit) water, which will kill many microorganisms. Most good woolens are conditioned and preshrunk in very hot water during the manufacturing process. The manufacturer's label will tell you what you need to know. An advantage of wool is that it will withstand higher washing temperatures than most synthetics. And when it comes to longevity, wool outlasts them all.

To alter the fit of wool garments: Everyone knows that woolens shrink when exposed to hot water and rough handling. However, shrunken garments can also be restored to a semblance of their original shape by rewashing, stretching, and slow drying. These unique characteristics of wool will enable you to get a custom fit from military surplus and garage-sale items.

For example, the sleeves on most shirts are too long for me so I shrink them by washing them (just the sleeves) in very hot water. The shirt is then spun dry in a hot clothes dryer. Careful monitoring of the drying process produces the exact sleeve length I want. When sleeves have shrunk, they'll hold their size for the lifetime of the garment. This procedure is not unique. For years, lobster fishermen have boiled their wool mittens to make them warmer and more resistant to wind. This is the same principle used in the manufacture of world-famous Dachstein mittens and sweaters. Wool hats, gloves—anything—can be made more wind- and waterproof by "boiling."

Polypropylene garments cannot be dry-cleaned. The solvent will dissolve the plastic fibers. Hand or machine wash in cold water and air-dry. Polypropylene melts at very low temperatures, so don't ever place these garments in a hot clothes dryer or too near a fire.

Polypropylene accumulates body oils and smells quite ripe after a few days afield. Embedded grime also reduces the thermal efficiency of the fibers, so wash these garments frequently. Because of their tendency to retain odors, hunters are switching from polypropylene underwear back to conventional fabrics. Deer can probably smell a sweaty polypro undershirt a mile away when the wind is right!

Gore-Tex must be washed frequently to maintain waterproofness. Ivory Snow was the recommended soap for early Gore-Tex garments; now any good powdered or liquid laundry detergent can be used. Wash in cold water and rinse thoroughly—you must get *all* the detergent out! Better yet, use one of the efficient, complete-rinsing Gore-Tex cleansers sold at camping shops. Air- or tumble dry Gore-Tex products at low heat. Do not dry-clean Gore-Tex items; you'll destroy them beyond repair!

Coated fabrics (rain gear) must never be dry-cleaned or machine washed. Hand wash them in warm water with any good detergent. Rinse and air-dry.

Be sure coated fabrics are bone dry before you store them. The stitching and nylon won't rot but the polyurethane coatings will. Certain microorganisms attack polyurethane coatings, which will cause separation (peeling) of the chemical from the fabric.

To Dry Clothing When There's No Wind and the Sun's Not Shining

Method 1. Wring as much water from the fabric as you can. Then tightly roll the clothes in a cotton towel, or better yet, an absorbent synthetic chamois or Packtowl. Set the rolled towel aside for a few minutes. Next, heat some rocks in the fire or in a covered pan on your stove. Remove the damp clothes from their towel wrapping and roll the heated rocks inside the clothes. Small articles of clothing—like socks and underwear—will usually be dry enough to wear in about an hour. Old-time woodsmen commonly placed hot rocks in their wet socks to dry them.

Method 2. Wring out the water and roll in a towel, as above. When you prepare supper on your trail stove, place a pair of socks or a thin article of folded clothing on top of the cover of your cooking pot. Heat from your cooking pot will help dry your clothes. Sounds weird but it works real well!

Method 3. String a parachute-cord ridge line inside your tent and pin (use diaper pins) your damp (towel-wrung) clothes to the line. Clothes should hang straight, not be folded over the cord. Secure a candle lantern to the ridge line (it *must not* touch your clothes or tent!). Close the tent. Your things will be much drier in an hour. Even without a candle lantern, your clothes will dry some if you simply allow them to hang all night.

Note: Normal tent temperatures average about 10 degrees warmer than the outside temperature. A candle lantern may add another 10 to 15 degrees. *Warning:* Do not leave a burning candle in a tent unattended!

None of these methods produce perfect results. The best plan is to use all three.

COMPASS

The most practical and reliable field compass is the Silva system orienteering type. This compass features a built-in protractor, which allows you to compute bearings without orienting the map to north, and a liquid-dampened needle that stops in three seconds. Detailed instructions come with all orienteering compasses. However, you should know how to determine declination.

Declination is the angular difference between geographic or true north and the direction the compass needle points. As you can see from the standard declination diagram in figure C-10, the difference can be quite large, especially if you live in the far East or West.

Declination values are constantly changing. Values (to the nearest fraction of a degree) are given in the legend of all topographic maps. Or you can access them—for any place in the world—from these Web sites:

United States: www.ngdc.noaa.gov/seg/geomag/jsp/struts /calcDeclination

Canada: http://gsc.nrcan.gc.ca/geomag/field/mdcalc_e.php

To adjust your compass for declination, apply the rhyme: *Declination east, compass least, or declination west, compass best.*

Example: You are traveling in California where the declination, as given

Figure C-10. Standard declination diagram.

in the diagram (and your topo map sheet), is 16 degrees east. You have computed a *true* map heading to an objective, using the protractor function of your orienteering compass. Your true map heading is due east, or 90 degrees. Adjust this figure for declination by applying the "east is least" (subtract) rhyme: Simply subtract 16 degrees from 90 degrees and travel on a magnetic heading of 74 degrees.

Conversely, the declination would be added (west is best) to your map bearing if you lived in New York, east of the zero (agonic) declination line.

Note: It makes no difference in which cardinal direction you are traveling on your map sheet. The declination in your area holds constant for the entire map sheet (usually), and there is seldom more than a few degrees of difference from one area of a state to another. Once you have determined your area declination, you need only remember the rhyme to apply it to any true direction computed from your map.

One degree of compass error equals approximately 92 feet per mile of ground error, so you must consider declination when traveling in regions substantially distant from the agonic line.

A detailed discussion of the compass and navigational techniques is found in my book *Basic Essentials: Map and Compass.*

Your watch as a compass: You'll need a conventional dial watch for this procedure. Hold the watch level and rotate it until the hour hand points to the sun. Halfway between the hour hand and the 12 on the watch dial is due south. This procedure is reasonably accurate providing your watch is correctly set for the right time zone . . . and you are north of the equator.

Your compass as a watch: The sun will be at these approximate bearings at these approximate times:

East	6:00 A.M.
Southeast	9:00 A.M.
South	noon
Southwest	3:00 P.M.
West	6:00 P.M..

Compass or GPS? Now that just about everyone owns a global positioning system (GPS) unit, you can toss away your magnetic compass. Right? Hardly! You *must* understand how to use a compass in order to effectively use a GPS unit. See the GPS section on page 105. A GPS complements a compass; it doesn't replace it!

CONTACT CEMENT

This is the best adhesive to use for gluing fabrics and/or porous items. Useful applications include patching holes in canvas tents and bags, gluing foam knee pads into canoes, repairing holes and tears in nylon fabrics, etc. Weldwood contact cement, in my experience, is the most reliable.

COOKING AND FOOD IDEAS (SEE ALSO BAKING)

Cookware

Prepackaged Trail King cooksets are a waste of money. Pot sizes are usually awkward and the frying pans are awful. Experienced campers usually assemble their own cookware, buying only those items they need.

Pots may be aluminum, stainless steel, or porcelain-lined steel. The concern that cooking in aluminum may cause Alzheimer's disease has been dismissed, and in any case is hardly a concern considering the minimal use received by camp cookwear. Choose low-sided broad pots rather than high narrow ones. A low center of gravity is important if you're cooking on a less-than-rock-stable trail stove. For a crew of eight, you'll need three nesting pots, the largest of which is twenty-four cups.

You'll find better cookware at kitchen supply and discount stores than at camping shops. What works at home works afield, providing it has a tight-fitting cover and is sized to nest with the rest of your pots and pans. Wire bail handles are necessary only if you do all your cooking on an open fire. One long pot handle or two protruding metal "ears" per pot are adequate if you have insulated pot holders, gloves, bandannas, or pliers.

Engrave lines on the *inside* of the pot sides at two-cup intervals and scratch the total capacity (e.g., sixteen cups) just below the rim. This will eliminate guesswork and the need for measuring cups at mealtime.

Skillets: The "camping" skillets I've seen are either too thin, too small, or the handles are weak or awkward to use. I prefer to purchase a high-grade Teflon-lined skillet (10- or 12-inch diameter) at my local discount store and cut off the Bakelite handle with a hacksaw. Then I make a universal-style, quickly removable handle from 0.187-inch-diameter spring wire (see figure C-11). The mounting bracket on the skillet is made from hardware store aluminum flat stock. Two brass bolts secure the bracket to the pan. You can order a spring wire handle kit like the one described from Chosen Valley Canoe Accessories (www.gear4portaging.com; see appendix B). You get two handles, mounting brackets, and hardware.

I also outfit my large "spaghetti" pot with a rigid wire handle (figure C-11), so I'll have better control when I drain liquid. When a pan wears out, I unbolt the bracket and transfer it to a new pan—no need to make a new one.

Store your cookset in a nylon bag.

Teakettle: A teakettle heats faster and is less tippy than a coffee pot and you can pour with one hand. An eight-cup kettle is about right for four; a twenty-cup model is better for groups of eight or more. Teapots are ordinarily left on the fire as a major supply of boiling water, so consider an oversize (twenty-cup) kettle, even for small groups. A large teapot will speed heating of dishwater and save stove fuel.

On a long hike, you may want to stop for tea—so always pack your teakettle (in a fabric bag) at the top of your pack where you can get it quickly.

Utensils: Experienced campers carry only an insulated plastic cup (it keeps things hotter and colder than metal cups), a metal spoon, and a sturdy plastic bowl. The individual belt knife or pocketknife performs all

Figure C-11. A quickly removable spring-wire handle works on all pans and pots.

cutting chores. Forks—useful for vehicle camping—are a luxury. It's best to have identical, colored nesting bowls. Keep bowls in a fabric bag, stored inside your smallest cook pot. To prevent the spread of illness, each person should always use the same bowl.

You'll need these cooking utensils:

1. Pancake turner (wood is best; plastic burns!)
2. Rubber spatula for scraping uneaten food from pots and bowls
3. Aluminum pliers or "pot grabber" (I prefer the official Boy Scout model.)
4. Wooden stirring spoon
5. Small wire whip for reconstituting instant mixes
6. Salt, pepper, and other spices (best stored in 35-millimeter plastic film canisters)

7. Small sheath knife or French folding picnic knife (An extra knife is always welcome in the kitchen.)

Tip: Be sure your cup has a plastic snap-on lid that will keep coffee hot and heat-seeking insects out. *Make a leash for your lid:* Drill a small hole through an edge of the mug lid and tie a piece of heavy fishing line through the hole. Tie the other end of the line to the mug handle (see figure C-12).

A fabric utensil roll (figure C-13) is used to store tools and spices. Set snaps or Velcro tabs at the top as illustrated so you can hang the roll from a tight line, out of contact with wet ground. If you string a tight rope under your rain tarp (see TARPS, page 181) and hang your utensil roll from it, everything will remain dry in the rain.

Commercial utensil rolls, patterned after my design, may be purchased from Duluth Pack or Frost River (see appendix B).

Blacken your pot bottoms: Pots that are used on open fires get quite black outside. Some experts suggest that you coat the exposed surfaces with liquid soap or shaving cream so the carbon black will clean easily. The result is an awful mess for the dish-washing crew. I leave pots black (they cook faster and more evenly) and keep them inside a plastic-lined nylon sack between uses.

Aluma Black, a chemical used to blacken aluminum gun sights and mounts, works wonders on pot bottoms. Just daub the chemical on the pot, allow it to dry, and a rich blue black color will result. Aluma Black is

Figure C-12. Your cup should have a snap-on lid to keep bugs out—and a leash so you won't lose the lid. Note the snap on the handle for attachment to a pack.

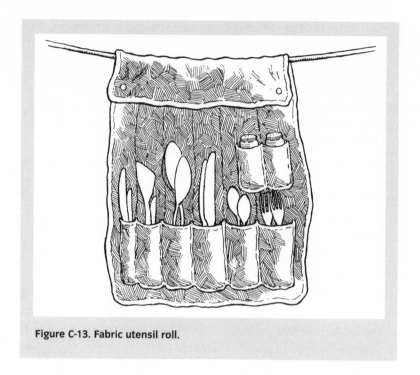

Figure C-13. Fabric utensil roll.

available from most gun shops. It is inexpensive. The product may also be used to darken the decks and rails of aluminum canoes and fishing boats.

Drying dishes: Pack a half-dozen sheets of paper toweling for each meal. The toweling is convenient for drying cookware, cleaning the stove, etc.

Food Ideas

For a gourmet treat, drop chunks of raw fish into boiling soup and cook for a maximum of five minutes. Sounds terrible but tastes superb and is the logical solution to preparing fish when vegetable oil or stove fuel is in short supply.

Making popcorn: If you're tired of trying to season popcorn in a pot that's too small, try this: Carry some large grocery sacks on your next campout. As you complete each batch of popcorn, pour it into the paper bag (don't use a plastic bag—hot popcorn will melt right through it). Season the popcorn and shake the bag to mix. When the popcorn's gone, burn the bag . . . or fold and store it in a plastic bag for future use.

Making biscuits and cakes: Mix batter in a plastic zipper-lock bag. Add the water, knead the bag with your hands until the consistency of the mix is correct, then punch a hole in the bag bottom and force the gooey mess into your awaiting oven. Burn the plastic bag. No mess or fuss.

Quick 'n' easy trail suppers can be prepared by adding any or all of these items to boiling soup mix: instant rice, dry noodles, elbow macaroni, Bisquick dumplings (use a plastic bag to mix), or Potato Buds.

Bagels for lunch: Bagels are an ideal trail bread. Buy the frozen kind, which keep nicely for about a week after thawing. Pile bagels high with sausage, cheese, or peanut butter and jelly for a nutritious lunch. Bagels are tasty and they pack well.

Pita (Mediterranean pocket bread) is another alternative to trail crackers. Pita contains preservatives (bagels do not) and will remain fresh and tasty for at least two weeks in typical summer weather. One pita bread per person is substantial lunch fare when combined with the usual noontime extras.

Tortillas contain preservatives and last as long as pitas. Add beans, cheese, hamburger, etc., and you have a complete meal.

Cheese in soup? You bet! Sprinkle dried Parmesan cheese on soup for a gourmet treat. Chunks of cheese (any kind) add spark, flavor, and calories to trail spaghetti and chili.

Peanut butter on pancakes? Sounds awful but tastes divine. The peanut butter melts into the hotcakes and provides a rich taste.

To make good-tasting boiled camp coffee: Bring water to a boil, then remove the pot from heat. Add one tablespoon of ground coffee per cup, plus an extra tablespoon for the pot. Stir coffee into the water, put on a lid, and set the pot aside for five minutes to allow the grounds to settle. Do not boil pot-brewed camp coffee; you'll destroy the delicate flavor and introduce a muddy metallic taste.

For classy coffee, add cinnamon or almond extract and you'll draw raves from everyone. A quarter teaspoon of almond extract or powdered cinnamon per eight cups of coffee is about right.

To make delicious camp mocha, use one packet of hot chocolate mix per cup. Fill cup with fresh-brewed coffee and top with some mini-marshmallows. Teenagers love this drink!

Hot pancakes for a big crew: Mix pancake syrup and margarine or butter in a small pot and heat. This will help keep pancakes really hot when they are prepared in advance for a large group.

A Thermos bottle is a practical accessory, even on strenuous hiking trips. Boiling water poured into a vacuum bottle that is not used for beverages may provide the nucleus for hot dishwater later. Saves running the stove (using precious gas) to heat dishwater.

Prepackaging saves time! Prepack everything you need to prepare a given meal in a zipper-lock plastic bag. Everything should be premeasured and mixed so that you don't have to fuss on the trail. For added simplicity, I traditionally pack my plastic-bagged breakfasts in green nylon bags, my lunches in blue, and my suppers in red. This saves considerable groping at mealtimes and provides abrasion resistance for the tear-prone zipper bags inside. Adhesive-tape labels identify the specific contents of each nylon bag.

A few last tips:

- Place fresh vegetables, crackers, cookies, and other breakables in your teakettle to keep them from being crushed on a strenuous backpacking or canoe trip.
- A stainless-steel Sierra cup is a lousy drinking cup but is a great ladle for soup and stew.
- An empty cardboard milk carton makes a handy "safe" for crushable foods like cookies and eggs. Use the wax-coated milk carton to mix powdered soft drinks and as an emergency fire starter on a rainy day.
- Dried foods are generally bland unless they're heavily spiced. I carry oregano, garlic powder, seasoned salt, black pepper, cayenne, thyme, and cumin inside small film containers, which are kept in a nylon "spice bag."
- Farm-fresh eggs will keep for weeks without refrigeration! Small- and medium-sized eggs have thicker shells than large eggs, so they're less apt to break on a hiking or canoe trip. You can check the freshness of eggs by floating them in a bowl of water. The deeper they sink, the fresher they are. Discard any eggs that float to the top.

Some Breakfast Favorites
Bacon/Cheese McPita/McTortilla
Option 1: Fry and set aside two thin slices of Canadian bacon per person. Scramble or fry one egg per person and set it aside. Now, lightly fry an open-face Mediterranean pocket bread (pita) or a tortilla in a teaspoon of cooking oil. When the bottom of the pita or tortilla is brown (twenty seconds), flip the bread over and lay thinly sliced cheese on top. Pile on the bacon and egg, add a dash of your favorite salsa (optional), and immedi-

ately toss a dash of cold water into the sizzling skillet. Cover and steam for fifteen seconds then serve immediately. In one minute you'll have a wholesome, delicious sandwich.

Option 2: Same as above, but omit the egg.

Option 3: Cut pita bread in half and fill the pockets with any fresh thin-sliced or grated cheese. Generously sprinkle garlic powder and oregano (optional) over the cheese. Fry each pita half in a well-oiled, covered skillet for about twenty seconds. As soon as you flip the pita, add a dash of cold water—and cover—to steam the cheese.

Tortillas are less filling than pitas but they have a more delicate, toasty flavor. Cook each tortilla flat in a well-oiled skillet for about ten seconds, then flip it over and add cheese and garlic powder to the toasted side. Immediately roll the tortilla into a burrito shape, add cold water to steam, then cover and simmer for twenty seconds.

Cinnamon Tortillas, Stewed Fruit, and Canadian Bacon

Make a tortilla burrito as described above, but substitute margarine, cinnamon, and white or brown sugar for the cheese and garlic. Tastes just like a cinnamon roll!

Boiled dehydrated apples and brown sugar, with a side of Canadian bacon, round out this perfect meal.

Note: Freshly baked pita bread and tortillas will keep at least two weeks without refrigeration if they are well sealed when you leave home.

Swift Suppers

Here are some things to consider as you plan your suppers.

- Most freeze-dried and dehydrated entrees consist of three parts—pasta or rice; freeze-dried chicken, beef, or shrimp; and spices. Remember this, and you can mix and match a variety of foods to suit your tastes.
- The meat is the most expensive part of any dried meal. One-quarter pound of freeze-dried hamburger (essential to make spaghetti, stroganoff, or chili) costs three times as much as a Big Mac! Chicken and shrimp are even more pricey.

However, you can easily dry these meats yourself in an inexpensive home dehydrator. Several excellent vacuum-sealing machines are available.

I've had good luck with a powerful home unit called the FoodSaver by Tilia (see appendix B). *For example, here's how to dehydrate hamburger:*

1. Fry the hamburger, drain the grease, then pour boiling water through the meat to remove as much fat as possible.

2. Line each dehydrator tray with three sheets of absorbent paper toweling and spread the hamburger out on the trays. Allow no more than 1 pound (¼-inch thickness) of hamburger per tray.

3. Turn the dehydrator to high (140 degrees F) and wait twenty-four hours. Vacuum seal (best) the dried hamburger or double-bag it in zipper-lock bags. Use a drinking straw to remove as much air as possible from the zipper-lock bags. Vacuum-sealed, dehydrated hamburger will keep about a year at room temperature; carefully zipper-bagged meat should last a month. As a safety precaution, keep dehydrated meats frozen until just before your camping trip. Use dehydrated hamburger in spaghetti, chili, soups, and stews.

Hamburger/Cheese Vegetable Soup

Add 1 pound (about ¾ cup) of dried hamburger to instant vegetable soup. Toss in a heavy handful of wide egg noodles or instant rice and add some dried mushrooms and a few slices of cheese. A dash of red pepper and garlic powder complete the recipe.

Spaghetti and Chili

To prepare spaghetti, you'll need dehydrated hamburger, pasta, spices, and tomato paste. Chili requires dehydrated beans, which are easily made by drying canned beans: Dump the canned beans (after pouring off the liquid) on the dehydrator tray and turn the heat to high. The beans will be dried and ready to pack in about eight hours.

To make spaghetti sauce, line the dehydrator trays with plastic cling wrap and spread any commercial sauce evenly on the trays. In twelve hours you'll have a thin, rubbery mass that resembles a fruit roll-up. Peel the dried sauce off the plastic wrap, roll it up, and freeze it. Later, break chunks into a plastic poly bottle. Add water to the chunks to rehydrate the sauce.

If you don't want to mess with making your own sauce, order tomato powder at your local co-op. Add a little water to the powder and you'll have paste; add more water for sauce or soup.

Pita Pizza

This is everyone's favorite meal!

Ingredients: One or two pieces of pita bread per person, dried tomato powder, fresh mozzarella cheese (hard, fresh cheese keeps nearly a month if it's vacuum sealed), oregano, garlic powder, salt, cayenne pepper. Add any or all of the following: dried pepperoni, summer sausage, hard salami, Canadian bacon, fresh onion, green pepper, dried or canned mushrooms .

Procedure:

1. Slice and fry the meat and drain off the grease on paper toweling. Thickly dice the vegetables and mushrooms, fry them in light oil, then drain off the grease and set the veggies aside.

2. To make the pizza sauce, pour ½ cup of tomato powder into a bowl and add water to make a thick paste. Sprinkle in oregano, garlic, salt, and cayenne.

3. Fry an open-faced pita at low heat in a well-oiled, covered skillet. When the bottom of the pita is brown (about twenty seconds), flip over the pita and thickly spread on tomato sauce, cheese, meat, and vegetables to taste. Immediately add a dash of water (to steam melt the cheese) and cover the pan. Allow the pizza to cook at very low heat for half a minute, or until the cheese has melted.

Add Fresh Vegetables to Your One-Pot Meals!

Fresh onions, tomatoes and green peppers will keep about five days on a camping trip, if they are properly packed.

Place onions in a cotton or paper bag. Stow the bag inside a rigid container.

Here's how to prepare and pack green peppers and tomatoes:

1. Wash the vegetables, then float them in a sink full of drinking water that has been treated with about ⅛ cup (the amount isn't critical) of chlorine bleach. Allow the vegetables to soak for several minutes in the treated water before you dry and pack them away. The bleach will kill the surface bacteria that promotes spoilage. A similar procedure is used in some of America's finest restaurants to keep vegetables fresh.

2. Separately wrap each vegetable in clean paper toweling. Pack the towel-wrapped veggies in a paper or cotton sack and set the sack inside a

teakettle or other crushproof container. Do not wrap vegetables in non-porous plastic!

Tip: When you're ready to cook, wash in fresh water only the portion of vegetable you need. Do not wash the entire vegetable! Doing so will introduce water-borne bacteria, which may accelerate spoilage.

Two Slick Cooking Tips

1. As mentioned, a dash of cold water in a hot, covered skillet will quickly steam-cook foods. You can also use this method to restore the freshness of week-old bagels, pita bread, and tortillas. Simply "steam grill" the bread in a covered skillet for a few seconds.

2. If you insist on carrying loaves of bread, here's an old woodsman's trick that guarantees perfect toast: Distribute a heavy pinch of table salt on the surface of a hot, dry (no grease!) skillet. Set a slice of bread on the salt. Do not cover! When the bottom of the bread is toasted to a golden brown, flip the bread over and toast the other side. The salt won't burn or stick to the bread or skillet.

How to Prepare Freeze-dried Foods So They Always Taste Good

Freeze-dried foods are fickle. Prepare 'em according to directions one day and they're great. Repeat the procedure another time and . . . *ugh!*

Take heart. Here's a foolproof cooking method that works regardless of the weather, the zodiac, or a cranky stove.

Step one: Read the cooking directions but don't take them too seriously. What works at home on the range often fails on a flat rock in a nor'wester.

Step two: Separate the component parts of the food. Generally, there are three parts—a meat portion; a noodle, rice, or vegetable portion; and a spice packet. (See the first example under "Why Some Meals Fail," below, for the specifics of preparing cook-in-the-bag meals.)

Typical directions say: *Add contents of all packets to x cups of boiling water. Reduce heat, simmer fifteen to twenty minutes or until noodles [or whatever] are tender.*

Step three: Put 20 percent *more* water in your cooking pot than the directions call for, and add the meat portion only to the cold water. Bring the water to a boil and add a healthy dash of "all-spice," which you make by mixing approximately equal amounts of the following spices:

Oregano
Onion powder
Marjoram
Thyme
Seasoned salt and pepper mixtures (I buy a commercial blend.)

Step four: When the water is at a rolling boil, add contents of the spice packet (if there is one). Reduce heat to slow boil and let spices and meat stew together for a full five minutes. If there is no spice packet, allow meat to stew for five minutes before you proceed to step five.

Step five: Add contents of noodle, rice, or vegetable packet to the boiling water. Reduce heat, cover, simmer, and stir occasionally for the amount of time indicated in the package directions.

Step six: Eat and enjoy. All portions of the meal are thoroughly cooked and the taste has been fully developed.

Why Some Meals Fail

You haven't cooked the meat long enough. Half-cooked reconstituted meat spoils the whole stew. Except in very warm weather, cook-in-the-bag foods just don't get done enough. It's best to place the cooking bag in a covered pot of near-boiling water for ten minutes. Add about 10 percent more water to the cooking bag than the directions call for.

You burned the pasta! This is easy to do on a one-burner trail stove, especially if you plop the contents of all food packets into the boiling water simultaneously. If your stove's turned high, you may burn the meal quicker than you can say "Turn the heat down, Jack!"

Insufficient water. Remember, you can always boil out too much water, but there's not much you can do with a stew that's so thick it's burned and glued to the pot bottom.

Not enough spices. Don't underestimate the value of spices when preparing freeze-dried foods. Most quick-cook products are unacceptably bland unless they're well spiced. The suggested "all-spice" above works wonders on everything from spaghetti to shrimp Creole.

Spoilage: Dehydrated foods come packed in plastic and have a shelf life of about one year. This is because plastic is not a complete water barrier. Freeze-dried foods come packaged in aluminum foil, which is an absolute vapor barrier. Consequently, these products have an unlimited shelf life.

This should tell you something about end-of-season food sales. Don't buy dehydrated foods in September if you plan to use them the following July. Your autumn "bargain" may turn out to be summer indigestion.

It's important to realize that many products contain both freeze-dried and dehydrated components (for example, spaghetti with freeze-dried meatballs). While the foil-wrapped meatballs won't spoil, the plastic-wrapped spaghetti and spices might. Only foods that are completely sealed in foil are immune to spoilage. Unfortunately, you almost never see these products offered at sale prices.

Introduction of bacteria and/or water vapor during repackaging. Don't handle dried foods or expose them to air any longer than necessary when you repackage them. This will reduce the chance of bacteria and water vapor getting into the food.

Tip: Slice meat and cheese with a knife that's been dipped in boiling water for a full minute. This will reduce transfer of bacteria into the food.

Cold-Weather Cooking Tips

Stoves used on snow must be set on a support or they'll melt the snow beneath and quietly sink out of sight. Fires built in snow must also have suitable support.

Don't set stoves on pieces of closed-cell foam (so the fuel tank will retain heat . . . and pressure) as is recommended by some authorities. A hot stove will melt the foam and stick solidly to it.

Pot covers are essential for winter cooking. Open pots lose too much heat; in subzero temperatures, water may not reach boiling unless it is placed in a covered pot.

Snow provides a natural windscreen. Dig in your stove so it's completely protected from the wind. Subzero temps and a good wind will lengthen cooking times considerably.

Insulate your water bottles so they won't freeze: Carry water bottles in an inside parka pocket so they won't freeze. In camp, store them upside down in the snow. The frozen interface will then be at the bottle's bottom and you'll be able to pour the liquid from the capped end. Snow is a marvelous insulator: Water bottles stored overnight this way will be "pourable" come morning.

Light for the kitchen: Winter nights come early; often there is insufficient light to cook by. Traditional flashlights lose power in cold weather and are awkward to hold. Select instead a powerful headlamp with a conventional bulb or a LED. Lithium batteries—or a separate battery pack that you can keep warm inside your parka—are essential when it's bitterly cold. *Tip:* to preserve your night vision, place a red plastic filter over your light.

Securing drinking water in winter may require that you bore through the ice of a frozen lake. For this, an ice chisel is better than the traditional cumbersome auger. Fit a short length of threaded pipe to the tail of the chisel so you can screw on a pole to provide weight when chopping. Don't use a hand ax for chiseling; it is awkward and dangerous.

How to wash dishes in subfreezing temperatures: Heavy rubber gloves will protect hands from the cold. Dishwater should be near boiling. A copper sponge or 3M nylon pad is all you need to remove food particles from pots and bowls. Detergents aren't necessary, as there is no bacterial growth in subfreezing temperatures. In fact, dishes need not be washed at all. Some authorities recommend that you clean dishes with snow—a particularly inefficient practice. Boiling water and rubber gloves work much better!

Foods that don't work well in winter: Frozen cheese looks and tastes like candle tallow. Peanut butter and jelly are sure to be frozen; there is no way to keep these items thawed unless you carry them in your pockets.

Gasoline is dangerous in cold weather! Gasoline, naphtha (Coleman fuel), and kerosene freeze at very low temperatures. If these fuels contact exposed skin in subzero temperatures, instant frostbite will result. Always wear rubber gloves when fueling stoves in cold weather. (See STOVES, page 171, for a thorough discussion of safety and troubleshooting procedures.)

CORD AND CORD LOCKS (see also ROPES, for knots and hitches)

The best camp utility cord is ⅛-inch-diameter nylon parachute cord. Nylon cord should be "hot cut" (use a butane lighter) rather than sliced, so its core and sheath won't separate.

Figure C-14. Secure your stuff sack with a quick-release loop.

Singe (melt) the ends of nylon and polypropylene cord and rope to pre-vent them from unraveling. Nobody whips the ends of ropes anymore.

Nylon cord locks are small, spring-loaded nylon clamps used to secure the cords of sleeping bags, parka hoods, and stuff sacks. Every camping shop carries a good supply of them for the do-it-yourselfer who wants to add versatility to his or her camping outfit. A less-expensive solution that works as well is to purchase nylon hose clamps from scientific supply houses. You can buy a dozen rubber hose (tubing) clamps for the price of one cord lock.

You don't need cord locks to secure the thongs of nylon stuff sacks if you learn the simple knot illustrated in figure C-14.

Now comes the hard part—threading the pair of ⅛-inch-diameter nylon parachute cords through the tiny cord-lock hole. One cord goes through easily; the second dies a slow death in mid-push. Ultimately frustration reigns and the "good idea" is disgustedly thrown into a drawer for use later.

Here's an easy way to thread the paired cords through the cord-lock hole: Place the tips of the cords side by side, one tip ⅛ inch below the other. Then tape the two tightly together. Press open the cord-lock button, and voilà, the cords go through instantly—simple and fast.

COZIES

It's a cold, blustery day and you're anxious for a hot meal. You boil water on your gasoline stove, then place spaghetti noodles in your largest pot, taking care to stir constantly so the noodles won't burn. You know that if you stop stirring and cover the pot, the pasta will boil faster. However, it may also burn and stick to the pot bottom. But if you continue to stir the uncovered food, heat will escape into the air and the spaghetti will take much longer to cook. What to do?

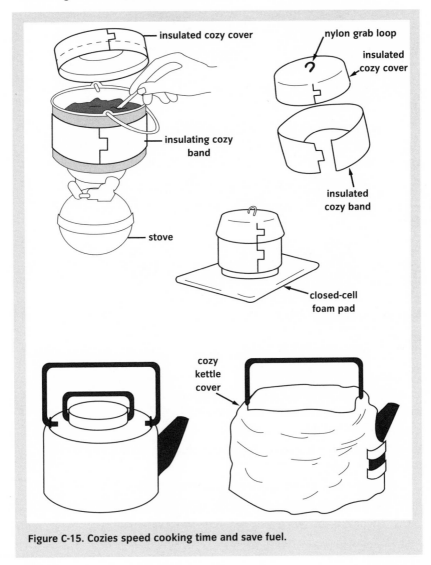

Figure C-15. Cozies speed cooking time and save fuel.

1. Bring the water to a rolling boil and add the uncooked spaghetti. Turn down the heat to medium and stir until all the noodles are absorbed into the water.
2. Turn off the stove. Cover the pot and set it on a closed-cell foam pad.
3. Immediately cover the pot with an insulated tea cozy or a sweater or jackets (not nylon—it melts!). Pile additional clothes on top to keep the heat in.
4. Entertain yourself for twenty minutes while the spaghetti slow cooks in its own heat. "Cozy cooking" saves time, stove fuel, and a burned pot bottom! Use this procedure whenever you make rice, soup, or hot cereal.

Tip: Make insulated cozies to fit all your pots. I prefer a two-piece model (top hat and pot band) like the one illustrated in figure C-15, because it's more versatile and energy-efficient than a one-piece model. The encircling band keeps the pot from losing heat to a cold wind when you remove the cover to stir your food. This saves considerable cooking time and fuel on cold, blustery days. Fitted cozies are essential for winter camping, camping trips above the tree line, and whenever you must cook a lot of food for a large group. A skillet-cover cozy keeps heat in when you steam-cook pita pizza, bagels, and tortilla burritos.

I also make a fitted cozy for my teakettle. The spout pokes through a slit that's controlled by a Velcro tab. Fresh coffee will stay hot for about an hour in a cozy-covered kettle if you place the kettle on an insulated foam pad or fabric pot holder.

Cozy fabrics: Nylon or acrylics catch fire or melt! Cotton and wool work well. Insulated ironing board material is satisfactory. An old welding blanket is the best material of all because it won't melt or catch fire.

DENTAL FLOSS

Dental floss is the toughest "thread" you can buy. I use it to mend tears in packs, tarps, and other heavy-duty camping items. *Tip:* You'll need a heavy-duty sewing needle with a large eye to accommodate the thick dental floss.

If you crack a canoe seat, thwart yoke, or tool handle, try this: Apply instant epoxy to the crack then tightly and evenly wrap the crack with dental floss. Spread instant epoxy over the wrap and allow it to dry. Your repair will never let go!

DENTAL TOOL

A pointed dental tool is useful to remove a stubborn gasket from your trail stove, clean a fuel jet, or pick out a spring. Dentists throw out these tools when they get dull. Ask your dentist to save some for you!

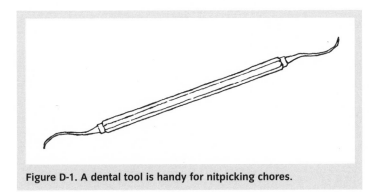

Figure D-1. A dental tool is handy for nitpicking chores.

DIAPERS AND DIAPER PINS

Diapers (cloth) make excellent camp towels. They're lightweight, compact, and absorbent.

Diaper pins are much more rugged and visible in dim light than other safety pins. Uses are endless: They can serve as clothespins—pin *through* the line and wet clothes won't slide together—and as an emergency replacement pin for eyeglasses. Use them to secure pockets in packs and clothes when zippers fail, pin money and credit cards inside pockets, attach a whistle to a life jacket, hang a flashlight from a tent, etc. A dozen diaper pins are not too many to bring along on a camping trip.

DUCT TAPE

Duct tape is the most useful repair item you can have. The hard-to-find olive drab "army" tape sticks better than the common gray tape found in hardware stores. 3M brand silver duct tape is the best!

Be sure to include some nylon filament (strapping) tape in your repair kit: It beats duct tape for mending broken canoe paddles, boat seats, and tool handles. *Tip:* Remove tape from its bulky roll and rewind it on a short pencil. Now you can "write about what you fix." Everything should be multipurpose in a camping trip!

ETHICS IN THE WILDERNESS

This section is about the imperfect science of sanitation and ethical camping procedures. It is no longer acceptable to build beds of green pine boughs (or dead ones, for that matter), lash log furniture, trench tents, hack green trees, and otherwise disturb the natural environment to suit our whims. There's just too little wilderness and too many of us. If we are to preserve the remaining backcountry for future generations, then each of us must adopt a solemn "I care" attitude. We must unfailingly practice ethical use of our natural resources, and we must teach—indeed, preach—ethics to all who will listen. And for those who turn the other ear, there must be laws . . . and penalties. The alternative is regulation upon regulation and a lessened quality of experience for everyone. Here are the recommended land- and water-use procedures:

Disposal of human and food wastes: Bury these wastes in mineral soil (if possible) 2 to 6 inches deep. The upper foot of soil contains the majority of decomposer organisms and so ensures the fastest rate of decay.

Toilet paper should be burned. Unburned tissue may take a season or more to degrade. Human waste will be gone in a matter of days if the weather is warm. When camping on the granite rock of the Canadian Shield, or anywhere soil cover is at a premium, simply follow the recommended procedure for shallow burial and cover the waste with whatever soil cover is available.

Caution: Do not burn toilet paper unless you have a water bottle and can put your fire dead out! A number of forest fires have been caused by burning toilet paper.

Please do not leave leftover food around camp "for the animals." This will upset their ecology and make them dependent on man—not to mention the aggravation they'll bestow on campers who will later occupy the site.

Fish entrails: It is illegal in most states to throw fish entrails into a lake or river, and for good reason. Bacteria consume the viscera and multiply, which raises germ levels to possibly dangerous proportions. Bacteria also use vast amounts of oxygen, which in turn robs fish and aquatic organisms of this essential element. Since food scraps react similarly, they too should never be tossed into a body of water.

Bury fish remains as you would food wastes—100 feet from water and well away from the campsite area. If you are camping in a remote area where seagulls are common, you may leave viscera on a large rock—well away from human habitation—for the gulls. This procedure is not acceptable on heavily used lakes!

When not to bury fish remains: Don't bury fish remains if you are camping in the heart of bear country. The rotting viscera will attract bears to you! Alaskan and Canadian guides prefer to toss fish remains well out into the lake or river, where they will be consumed by predator species. This procedure is recommended only for remote areas where bears are a problem. Popular parks have their own regulations.

Cans and bottles should always be packed out of the wilderness. Tin cans should be burned out and crushed flat with the back of an ax or your boot, then packed out. The typical steel can requires about 75 years to decompose completely; aluminum cans may need 500 years! A glass bottle could last a million years in the environment. We do not bury cans and bottles today. PACK THEM OUT!

Your garbage detail will be easier if you make a strong nylon bag, with drawstring, for this purpose.

Dish washing: Dishes should never be washed in a waterway. Food scraps encourage bacterial growth, and even biodegradable detergents kill essential microorganisms. Dishes should be washed on land and in a large cooking pot. Dishwater is best disposed of on mineral soil, 100 feet from a lake or river.

Swimming is fine, but bathing in waterways is not. If you use soap to wash your hair and body, please rinse on the shore (with a bucket of water), well away from the water's edge.

A word about biodegradable products: It's fashionable today to extol the virtues of biodegradable products over those that do not break down by bacterial action. Certainly, you should choose biodegradable detergents, tissues, and toilet paper whenever possible. Be aware, however, that even the best biodegradable products depend upon bacteria, moisture, and time for decomposition. And this means increased germ counts, lowered levels of oxygen, and visual pollution for some time. There's no such thing as a free ride!

Bough beds: Cutting evergreen branches to make bough beds is illegal, immoral, and damaging to the trees. An air mattress or foam pad works better. The use of dead evergreen boughs or mosses should also be discouraged, as this material provides a surface cover that blots out sunlight and consequently kills vegetation below. Campsites should always be left as natural as possible so that nature can effectively do its thing.

Cutting green trees is, of course, illegal and damaging. Since green wood burns poorly, there's no sense cutting it for firewood. You'll find plenty of good dead firewood in the backcountry if you look for it (see FIRE MAKING, page 85).

Graffiti: It's always shocking to see initials and names carved or painted on trees and rocks in the backcountry. But it does happen, even in the most remote wilderness. The cause is certainly ignorance and insensitivity, neither of which can be tolerated by those of us who know and care.

Noise: Most people take to the backcountry to experience peace and quiet. Loud, man-made disturbances are obviously unwelcome and, in state and national parks, usually illegal. Please keep radios at home or use a personal Walkman or iPod.

Color: Some campers are offended by brightly colored camping gear and clothing. Consequently, the trend is toward gentle earth tones—greens, browns, and grays. However, there's no denying the safety (and photographic) advantages of brightly colored tents, canoes, and clothing in remote areas. Despite much hoopla, the color issue is exaggerated. There are more pressing environmental concerns in the backcountry.

Lugged hiking boots: Chunky-soled mountain boots churn up much more soil than nonaggressive footwear and are therefore discouraged in popular hiking areas. Primitive people got along quite nicely without Vibram lugs and you will too, not to mention the freedom of foot you'll enjoy by selecting lighter, more flexible shoes. Nonetheless, the damage that results from use of Rambo-style boots is probably overrated. Like color, there are more pressing concerns.

Fire site: Fire sites should always be left as natural as possible. In military terms, everything that's not growing or nailed down should be removed from the premises. Every scrap of paper and every shred of aluminum foil, down to the tiniest speck, should be picked out and hauled home. Ideally, there should be no partially burned wood left in the grate—absolutely everything should be consumed by flame before you pass on.

It is permissible, but no longer traditional (or even desirable), to leave cut firewood for those who will later occupy the site. Some modern campers consider the sight of a woodpile an affront, something that detracts from the wildness of the area. So cut only the wood you need and put your fire dead out—check it with your hands to be sure it is DEAD OUT—before you leave.

Education: Unfortunately, there are not yet enough of us who care and who will carry the banner for ethical land use. We must spread the word as gospel, but quietly, sensibly, and in a nonintimidating way, with full realization that you can always get more bears with honey than with guns. Studies show that the majority of campers mean well even though they often do what is improper. Most abuse occurs out of ignorance. The majority of people will willingly follow your lead if properly taught.

FABRIC SOFTENER

An auto mechanic who loves camping recommends placing sheets of fabric softener inside sleeping bags and packs and in vehicles that will be stored in country garages where vermin can get in. The fabric softener repels bugs and rodents and keeps things smelling fresh. It really works!

FIRE MAKING

Anyone can start a fire on a bone-dry day or when they're armed with dry newspaper, kerosene, or charcoal lighter. But let the day deteriorate to persistent rain, and where there's smoke there won't be fire! Here's how to make and maintain fire when foul weather comes to stay:

Tools: You'll need a sharp knife, hand ax, and a saw (folding saws are highly recommended). Contrary to the ravings of some "authorities," it is nearly impossible to make fire in prolonged rain without all these tools.

Finding Wood

In an evergreen forest: Collect several handfuls of the dead lower branches of evergreen trees. Wood should range in size from pencil-lead thickness to no bigger than your little finger, and it should break with a crisp, audible snap. If you don't hear the positive "snap," the wood is too wet, in which case look for a downed, dead tree as discussed on the next page.

If the wood is suitably dry, it will burst into a bright flame the moment a match is applied. Use a small candle to provide sustained heat to your tinder ball if the bark of the wood is wet. From this point on, it's simply a matter of adding more wood and protecting the developing blaze from rain. (See "To maintain fire in a driving rain" later in this section.)

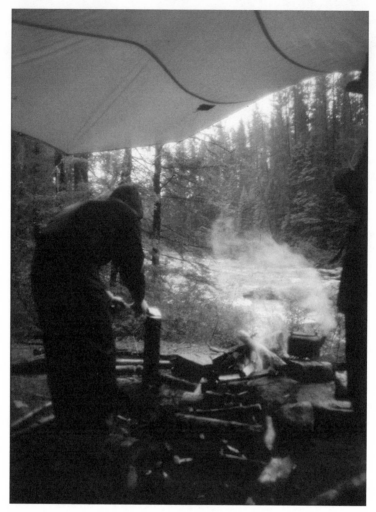

Figure F-1. Making fire in the rain. Along the Gull River, northern Ontario.

Look for resin blisters on the outside bark of balsam fir trees. Break a few blisters with a sharp stick and collect the highly volatile resin. Use the resin as a "chemical fire starter" to propel your tinder to flame.

Locate a dead, downed tree and saw off a portion that does not touch the ground. Grounded wood rots quickly and is apt to be unsound. Especially search for deadfalls that overhang a sunlit clearing or waterway. These are almost certain to be rotfree, as sunlight kills microorganisms that cause decay.

If you cannot find a dead, downed tree to saw up, look for any floating log. If the log floats, the center is dry. Splittings taken from the heart will burn.

When you have completed your first saw cut through the deadfall, check the center of the cut log with your hand. Is it bone dry? It should be. Even a monthlong rain will seldom soak through a 6-inch log!

Next comes the "smell test." Smell the cut end of the log. Damp or rotten wood will smell moist and musty. If there is no odor, saw the deadfall into 12-inch sections, then split each chunk with your hand ax by the method illustrated in figure A-2 earlier in this book. It should require only a few minutes to reduce each log chunk to ½-inch-diameter kindling by this procedure.

Cut wafer-thin tinder from a few splittings with your knife. The key to producing long, thin shavings rather than little squiggly ones is to use a sawing rather than a whittling action. Even a small, dull knife will produce nice shavings if you persistently saw the blade back and forth.

Figure F-2 shows a much more powerful way to cut long, thin shavings. Simply *reverse* the knife edge and smartly pull the knife and stick apart, as illustrated. Before you "pull," be sure the stick is located *outside* of the knife (not in front of it) and the sharp edge has a good bite on the wood.

Figure F-2. An efficient way to cut shavings.

Another knife trick is illustrated in figure F-3. You can easily split kindling up to 2 inches thick with this method. *Important:* You need a sheath knife or lock-blade folding knife for this procedure. A pressure-spring folder could close on your hand when you pound! Even the strongest lock-blade folder, however, will eventually be damaged by continued pounding

Figure F-3. Here's a safe and powerful way to split thick kindling with your knife. *Caution:* Don't use a folding knife for this unless it has a locking blade.

on the spine. Get a sheath knife if you adopt this procedure.

Tip: Stumps and roots are rich in volatile resins. Conifers, especially, have so much pitch that they will burn on their own for hours—a reason why fires in evergreen forests are so devastating. If you can find an old broken-down stump, save some of the fatwood for starting fires.

Fire-Building Procedures

Build a well-ventilated platform fire according the three steps below.

Step 1

Establish a fire base of 1-inch-diameter sticks as illustrated in figure F-4. Place pencil-thin support sticks at right angles to the fire base.

Step 2

Meticulously stack wafer-thin shavings on top of the kindling to a height of about 1 inch. Place the shavings so that plenty of air can get between them. Smoke is nature's way of saying you're smothering the flame!

Figure F-4. Fire-burning procedures.

Pencil-thin kindling

6"

1-inch-thick sticks

Step 1: Establish base.

Put ½-inch diameter sticks here

Step 2: Stack shavings.

Add fine-split kindling above the tinderbox to lock the tinder in place.

Step 3: Add kindling.

Next, put two ½-inch-diameter support sticks at right angles to the fire base. These will support the heavier kindling you'll add over the tinder in step 3.

Step 3
Now pile on fine-split kindling above the tinderbox to lock the tinder in place. Again, leave space between the splittings so your fire can breathe.

Your fire is now ready to light. Apply flame directly below the tinder (shavings). A small candle will furnish the sustained heat necessary to ignite damp wood.

Hand-feed shavings (not kindling) one at a time into the developing flame. Don't heap kindling on until you have a bright, reliable blaze.

Fire-Starting Tips

Carry strike-anywhere matches in addition to a butane lighter and candle. Keep matches in a plastic jar with a cotton wad on top. A spent 16-gauge shot shell nested inside a 12-gauge case makes a tough watertight match safe. Some campers waterproof matches by painting on nail polish, but this causes match heads to deteriorate. A waterproof match case is a better idea.

An effective method of drying matches is to draw them briskly through your hair. Don't use your clothes; they are too abrasive.

Fire Ribbon—a semiliquid fire-starting paste is available at most camp stores. Just squeeze it on like toothpaste. A summer's supply will fit in a 35-millimeter film canister.

You can make your own fire starters by soaking miniature "logs" of rolled newspaper in paraffin.

Cotton balls dipped in Vaseline make wonderful fire starters!

Emergency fire-making kits: You'll need a flattened half-gallon milk carton, a handful of wood shavings (cedar is best), some splittings of scrap wood, Fire Ribbon, and a small candle. Store everything in a zipper-lock bag. When emergency strikes, rip up the milk carton, splash tinder with Fire Ribbon, and light your match. Materials will burn reliably for at least five minutes—enough time for you to search the woods for additional fuel.

Witch's broom is a blue gray lichen that grows on the branches of some evergreen trees. It is extremely flammable when dry.

Paper is hydrophilic (loves water). It absorbs moisture on damp days. Don't depend on paper to start your fires!

In an emergency, you can always burn money!

One or two sticks robbed from a beaver's house make good kindling and tinder. Beaver wood has been de-barked so it is apt to be rot free. For the sake of the beaver, please take only one or two sticks, and then only in an emergency.

Emergency ignitors: You can't beat a butane lighter and dry matches! The chemically impregnated magnesium rods sold as survival tools will ignite dry tinder but are next to worthless when things are damp. And magnifying glasses must be very large (at least 2 inches in diameter) to reliably ignite tinder.

Steel wool makes excellent emergency tinder.

Flour (any kind) will burst into potent flames if sprinkled lightly over a blaze.

Cooking oil (vegetable oil) will enrich a flame only if the fire is already very hot. Brazil nuts, potato chips, and corn chips burn brightly. Try trick birthday candles—the kind you can't blow out—to ignite damp wood. Some campers store a few popsicle sticks inside their stove fuel (gasoline or kerosene) bottles. The fuel-saturated sticks make powerful fire starters.

Make a tubular fire blower (figure F-5)! You'll need a 6-inch-long piece of narrow diameter copper or aluminum tubing and 18 inches of plastic or rubber Bunsen-burner hose. Most hardware stores have these materials.

Figure F-5. Tubular fire blower.

Use your blower to nurse a fickle flame and whenever wood is too thick or damp to burn well. The concentrated air turbocharges hot coals and turns them into willing flames.

An unused rain jacket or small square of plastic will provide all the overhead protection you need to start a fire in a driving rain. So will an overturned canoe, propped up by paddles shoved through the seat braces.

To maintain fire in a driving rain: Build a loose "log cabin" around your fire with whatever wood is available. Construct a two-tier flat "roof" for your cabin from newly cut kindling and fuel. The roof will deflect rain and the fire below will dry out the lower level of wood and bring it to flame. If you maintain a two-tier roof, you'll have a continuous supply of dry wood no matter how much it rains. *Note:* Since you're robbing the fire of oxygen, expect smoke . . . lots of it!

Banking the fire to preserve fuel: Use this procedure when you have a good hot fire but little wood to maintain it. Bank your fire by setting small logs, parallel to one another, across the top. The rule of thumb for a smoke-free flame is to allow a radius width between parallel pieces of wood. Thus, a pair of 2-inch-thick logs should be separated by a full inch to ensure adequate ventilation. Banking will reduce this distance to a mere (though identifiable) slit, which will naturally diminish use of oxygen and slow combustion. You should also eliminate any breeze coming into the fire. A large flat rock or a tier of logs will work fine.

Extinguishing the fire: Throwing water on a fire is not good enough. You must ascertain it is out by checking the once-fiery bed with your hands. If water is in short supply, use the "sprinkle/stir" method outlined below.

1. Sprinkle a handful of water on the flames with your hands. Continue to sprinkle until the fire has gone out.
2. Stir the fire with a stick and sprinkle some more. Repeat as needed until the fire is DEAD OUT!

FIRST-AID KIT AND PROCEDURES

The following recommendations are from the pen of my friend William Forgey, M.D., the guru of wilderness medicine. "Doc" Forgey is the past president of the Wilderness Medical Society, an assistant clinical professor of family medicine at Indiana University School of Medicine, and a national consultant for the Student Conservation Association and other nonprofit organizations. He is on the national health and safety committee of the Boy Scouts of America, and in 2005 this organization honored him at the national jamboree by naming a subcamp in his honor. Dr.

Dr. Bill Forgey.

Forgey has authored more than a dozen popular outdoor titles. His flagship book, Wilderness Medicine: Beyond First Aid, *is the ultimate medical resource for those who venture afield (see appendix A).*

—CJ

When facing a medical emergency in a wilderness location, you would ideally have a medical kit with exactly the right ingredients and the knowledge of how to use them. Well, let's face it—it probably ain't going to happen that way. Medical kits can be bulky, heavy, expensive, and hard to obtain. Even physicians can feel inadequately trained when faced with unfamiliar emergencies, especially in remote areas. So what to do? How do you decide what to take on the trail?

When choosing items for an emergency or survival kit, I always apply the chocolate rule. I look at the item I'm thinking of including and compare it to a piece of chocolate of equal size. I look at one, then the other, thinking all the time: "Which would I rather have in the bush with me?" Generally chocolate will win.

So it's obvious that even as a physician, I do not want to lug in a heavy medical kit, especially if I must choose between carrying it and something really useful and preferably edible. My solution to this dilemma is to make up a medical kit with multifunctional and cross-therapeutic components.

A multifunctional component is an item that has more than one use. Cross-therapeutic components mean that several different items in the kit can be used to treat the same problem. Such a kit has few components that generally handle many problems, and because of their versatility, the kit does not exhaust easily.

Nonprescription Oral Medical Kit

12 Percogesic tablets (pain, fever, muscle spasm, sleep aid, congestion)

20 ibuprofen 200 mg tablets (pain, fever, bursitis, tendonitis, menstrual cramps)

12 diphenhydramine 25 mg capsules (antihistamine, antianxiety, cough, topical anesthetic, sleep aid, muscle cramps, nausea and motion sickness prevention)

5 bisacodyl 5 mg tablets (constipation)

5 loperamide 2 mg tablets (diarrhea)

12 cimetidine 200 mg tablets (heartburn, certain allergic reactions)

Percogesic tablets. Relieve pain, fever, and muscle spasm. Each tablet contains 325 mg of acetaminophen and 30 mg of phenyltoloxamine citrate. Ideal for injuries of joints and muscles as well as aches from infections. Phenyltoloxamine is also a decongestant. It induces drowsiness and can also be used as a sleeping aid and to calm a hysterical person. Dosage is generally two tablets every four hours as needed. It's one of the most useful nonprescription drugs obtainable.

Ibuprofen 200 mg tablets. Brand names are Advil, Nuprin, and others. Ibuprofen relieves pain, fever, menstrual cramps, and inflammation. Overuse syndromes such as bursitis and tendonitis are common in wilderness-related activities, and ibuprofen is an ideal treatment. The nonprescription dosage is two tablets, four times a day. It should be taken with food to prevent stomach irritation or heartburn. The prescription dosage is four tablets taken four times daily; this dose may be necessary for severe inflammation.

Diphenhydramine 25 mg capsules. The brand name is Benadryl, but many variations of medication are sold under this brand name, and the variations contain ingredients other than just the diphenhydramine. For antihistamine action, one or two capsules can be taken every six hours. To use as a powerful cough suppresser, the dose is one capsule every six hours. For muscle spasm relief, use one or two capsules at bedtime alone or in combination with two ibuprofen 200 mg tablets. For nausea or motion sickness, one capsule every six hours as needed.

Bisacodyl 5 mg tablets. This laxative works on the large bowel to form a soft stool within six to ten hours. Use one tablet as needed.

Loperamide 2 mg tablets. An antidiarrheal with the brand name of Imodium, this medication can treat intestinal cramping and, to a lesser extent, nausea. Dosage for persons twelve or older is two tablets after the first loose bowel movement, followed by one tablet after each subsequent loose bowel movement, but no more than four tablets a day for no more than two days. The prescription use of this medication is usually two tablets immediately and two with each loose stools up to a maximum of eight per day. Follow the package instructions for children's dosages.

Cimetidine 200 mg tablets. The brand name is Tagamet. This medication suppresses acid formation. It may be used to treat certain allergic reactions. The nonprescription dosage is two tablets four times daily. Prescription use goes as high as four tablets four times daily for acid suppression. There are many alternatives to using this drug, such as Zantac.

Nonprescription Bandaging Kit

5 packages Spyroflex 2"x2" wound dressings (or carry 2 packages for each person)

5 packages Nu-Gauze pads, high-absorbent, sterile, 2 ply, 3"x3", 2 per package

10 Coverlet bandage strips, 1"x3"

1 waterproof tape, 1"x15'

1 Sam splint, 36"

1 elastic bandage, 2"

1 elastic bandage, 3"

1 elastic bandage, 4"

1 Hibiclens surgical scrub, 4 oz. bottle

1 tetrahydrozoline ophthalmic drops, 0.05%, 15 ml bottle

1 maximum-strength triple-antibiotic ointment with pramoxine, 1 oz. tube

1 hydrocortisone cream 1%, 1 oz. tube

1 clotrimazole cream, 2%, ½ oz. tube

1 pair protective gloves

1 irrigation syringe

Spyroflex 2"x2" wound dressing by PolyMedica Industries is a multiuse bandaging system that replaced wound closure strips *and* coverings. It accelerates blood clotting, holds lacerations closed, is a barrier dressing to protect the wound from the outside, treats abraded skin as well as leaking and dry wounds, and is an excellent cover for first- and second-degree burns. Most important, it establishes a local environment that speeds up wound healing. The dressing is a "smart" dressing that absorbs and evaporates the correct amount of vapor to produce the proper healing condition. This dressing can be left in place for up to ten days, thus decreasing the need for large quantities of bulky dressings. *Alternative improvisation:* Cellophane and duct tape. Cellophane, plastic food wrappers, or plastic sheeting of any kind makes an excellent wound covering. Taped plastic dressings don't adhere to the wound and are therefore easy to remove. Seepage leaks from the unsealed edges of the dressing and moisture that is contained within the dressing speeds healing. The clear dressing also allows you to watch the wound as it heals.

Nu-Gauze pads. J&J Company has developed a gauze that is 2 ply, yet it absorbs nearly 50 percent more fluid than conventional 12-ply gauze pads. This may not seem important until a rapidly bleeding wound needs care. For years J&J has made a Nu-Gauze strip packing dressing—the Nu-Gauze pads are a completely different material. They are a wonderful advance in gauze design. *Alternative improvisation:* cotton T-shirts or other clothing, bandannas.

Coverlet bandage strips. A Beiersdorf product, Coverlets are common 1"x3" bandage strips, but they are the best made. They stick even when wet, last through days of hard use, and stretch for compression on a wound and conform for better application. *Alternative improvisation:* duct tape, climbing tape.

Waterproof tape. A tough tape that can be used for splinting or bandage application. There are no brand advantages that I can determine. A 1"x15' roll on a metal spool is a usable size. *Alternative improvisation:* duct tape, climbing tape.

Sam splint. A padded, malleable splint that provides enough comfort to be used as a neck collar. It is adequately rigid to splint any extremity and universal so that only one of these need be carried for all splinting needs. This item replaces ladder splints, etc. I never recommended the inclusion of splints in wilderness medical kits until this product was developed. It weighs less than five ounces. *Alternative improvisation:* Malleable splints can frequently be made from stays found in internal backpack frames. Other stiff materials can be used, such as strips of Ensolite foam pads or inflatable pads, held in place with tape or wraps of torn cloth.

*Elastic bandages, 2", 3", and 6".*Obtain good quality bandages that stretch without narrowing and that provide firm, consistent support. *Alternative improvisation:* Elastic bandages can be replaced with almost any cloth that is firmly wrapped in place. The most stretchy form of cloth usually available is the cotton T-shirt.

Hibiclens surgical scrub. This Stuart product (chlorhexidine gluconate 4%) far surpasses hexachlorophene and povidone–iodine scrub in its antiseptic action. Its onset and duration of action is much more impressive than either of those two products. *Alternative improvisation:* Many surgical scrubs are available without prescription and are ideal for wilderness use, but they can all be replaced with potable (drinkable) water irrigation (see "irrigation syringe" discussed on the next page).

Tetrahydrozoline ophthalmic drops .05%, 15 ml bottle. These eyedrops are used for allergy relief and to remove red color and discomfort due to smoke, eye strain, etc. It will not cure infection or disguise the existence of a foreign body. Place one or two drops in each eye every six hours. These drops can also be used to soothe an earache. Use three or four drops every six hours for this purpose. *Alternative Improvisation—eyes:* Rinse eyes with clean water. A wet, cold compress relieves eye itch and pain. If there is a possible foreign body and the irritation is significant, sometime blinking with the eye under water provides relief. This process may have to be repeated every thirty minutes. *Alternative Improvisation—ears:* Warmed cooking oil is a soothing eardrop that relieves itching and pain. However, an infected ear should be treated with prescription antibiotics.

Maximum-strength triple-antibiotic ointment with pramoxine, 1 oz. tube. Each gram of this ointment contains 500 units of bacitracin, 3.5 mg of neomycin sulfate, 10,000 units of polymyxin B sulfate, and 10 mg of the anesthetic pramoxine hydrochloride. Use the ointment as a topical antibiotic in the prevention and treatment of minor infections of abrasions and burns. This formulation is also an anesthetic that numbs the skin. A light coating should be applied twice daily. Neomycin can cause skin rash and itch in some people. If this develops, discontinue use and apply hydrocortisone cream to counter this effect. *Alternative improvisation:* Honey or granulated sugar placed on wounds is painless and kills germs by dehydrating them. A strong sugar solution draws the fluid from the bacteria, but human cells are able to actively avoid the dehydration process and are not injured by this technique.

Hydrocortisone cream 1%, 1 oz. tube. This nonprescription steroid cream treats allergic skin rashes, such as those from poison ivy. A cream is ideal for treating weeping lesions, as opposed to dry scaly ones, but it will work on either. To make this medication more effective, apply an occlusive dressing (plastic cover) overnight. *Alternative improvisation:* Blistery rashes can be soothed and the leaking fluid dried by applying a cloth made wet with concentrated salt solution.

Clotrimazole cream 2%, ½ oz. tube. This is one of the most effective antifungal preparations available for foot, groin, or body fungal infections. Brand names are Lotrimin and Mycelex (vaginal cream). The vaginal cream in a two-ounce tube is less expensive per ounce and works well on the skin surface as well as vaginally. *Alternative improvisation:* Dry, itchy lesions of any type respond to a soothing coating of cooking oil.

Protective gloves. Due to concerns about hepatitis B and C and with AIDS, it is prudent to carry protective gloves for first-aid use. These can be nonsterile (they are easily sterilized by boiling or treating with antiseptics). Vinyl gloves will last much longer in a kit than latex gloves, but the best to obtain are the nitro or new barrier gloves. *Alternative improvisation:* Use an empty food bag or waterproof stuff sack as a glove, or wrap your hand in the most waterproof material available.

Irrigation syringe. Required for forceful irrigation of wounds. The best would have a protective spray shield, such as the Zerowet shield. Otherwise, wear glasses to protect your eyes from splash contamination. *Alternative improvisation:* The solution to pollution is dilution. Forceful irrigation is the best method to clean a wound and dilute the germ count to the point that the body's immune system can kill the remaining germs. Without a syringe, augment the volume of water that you are pouring on the wound with a brisk scrubbing action using a soft, clean cloth.

I have not included any prescription medications in the suggested medical kit, as you can generally manage all problems that you will encounter with the above items. For expeditions into very remote areas, you will probably want to add a few prescription items—such as a powerful pain medication, an antibiotic, and an eye anesthetic agent.

The best pain medication would be nasal inhaled Stadol (butorphanol). The drug is five times stronger than morphine on a milligram-per-milligram basis. One spray up a nostril should relieve pain of a major broken bone. If not, spray the other nostril in about fifteen minutes. If you spray too much medication into the patient's nose, it will run down his throat into his stomach and be deactivated by stomach acid.

A good all-purpose antibiotic to carry would be the Zithromax tri-pack. This antibiotic is great for treating traveler's diarrhea and many upper respiratory infections.

An eye anesthetic agent, such as tetracaine ophthalmic drops, allows you to more easily examine an injured eye and remove a foreign body by flicking it out of the eye with the edge of a bandanna. It provides instant pain relief to spark burns and branch lash-back injuries. But these compounds delay healing and their use must be restricted. They usually need to be refrigerated, which is certainly a drawback for wilderness use. A few weeks in a pack will not be a problem, but this medication needs to be discarded after the trip.

It's no secret that wilderness first-aid skills require improvisation and basic knowledge of wound care and illness management. Ideally you will be able to take a course in wilderness first aid or even a Wilderness First Responder class.

(*Note:* Dr. Forgey's book *Wilderness Medicine,* fifth edition, describes a more extensive first-aid kit and, more importantly, explains how to diagnose and treat injuries and illnesses in remote areas.)

FIRST-AID TIPS FOR COMMON PROBLEMS

Fishhook Removal (String-Pull Method)

A hook in the cheek will kill the planned trip. You must be able to treat this injury if you have anglers along. A hook through the skin is one of the most common wilderness injuries.

Treatment: The common advice is to work the embedded barb through the skin, cut it off, and extract the hook. But this won't work if the hook is embedded to the curve. You may have to back the hook out partially and reset the angle so the tip will clear the skin rather than work deeper into it. In any case, you'll have a messy situation with lots of pain. Here's a painless way to extract the hook (figure F-6):

1. Loop light cord or heavy fishing line around the curve of the hook.

Press shank of hook against skin surface.

Strong cord or fishing line

A

Vigorously jerk hook along skin surface.

B

Figure F-6. String-pull method of removing fishhooks.

2. Push the eye of the hook firmly against the surface of the skin.

3. While holding the shank down, firmly jerk the cord.

Dislocated Shoulder

A dislocated shoulder is one of the most common and painful ailments. Relocation is easy if you use the Stimson method illustrated in figure F-7.

Procedure: Place the victim face down on a flat, elevated platform, like a rock face or an overturned boat. Place an approximate ten-pound weight inside a fabric stuff sack and tie the sack to the wrist of the fully extended arm with a soft handkerchief or padded belt. As the muscles tire, the victim will relax and the shoulder will relocate. The method is foolproof.

Other Neat First-Aid Tips

Don't use freshwater from a lake or river to flush wounds. Surface waters contain microorganisms that can cause infection. Wounds should always be cleaned with boiled or chemically treated water.

Earaches are often related to a change in the pH (acid-base balance) of the ear canal. A recommended field cure is to flush the ear with dilute vinegar (acetic acid), which lowers the pH. No vinegar? Try urine (uric acid). It works!

Figure F-7. Stimson maneuver.

Warning: Don't assume you can handle all emergencies with the few items and skills suggested here. When serious injury threatens, your best bet is to evacuate the victim immediately. The items and methods outlined in this book are not a substitute for the skills of a competent physician and the controlled environment of a hospital.

FLASHLIGHTS AND CAMP LIGHTING DEVICES

Any light used for camping should be waterproof and have a lanyard ring so it can be hung in a tent. It should also have a positive rotary switch that won't accidentally turn on in your pack.

Conventional flashlights: Most popular flashlights are AA-cell models with alkaline batteries and high-intensity bulbs. These tiny flashlights burn out batteries and bulbs quickly but are nice if you want maximum brightness and minimum size.

LED flashlights: These are the hot new lights in town, and for good reason. They don't burn out and the LED bulbs are much tougher than normal bulbs. But all LEDs are not the same. Some are much brighter than others—they are graded like diamonds, and the brightest ones demand a premium price. You get exactly what you pay for!

LEDs are very efficient so their run times are much longer than bulbs—but not as ridiculously long (like hundreds of hours!) as some flashlight companies profess. Yes, LEDs do produce barely discernible light for a great many hours, but this light is usually too dim to be useful. Remember this before you leave extra batteries at home!

Tactical lights: In 2004 I had a dicey bear encounter along a river in Saskatchewan. The sky was dark gray when this bad boy came into camp. We tried to shoo him away, but he was persistent. One man activated his Surefire tactical light (www.surefire.com; see appendix B), which put out 120 lumens of light (that's about eight times brighter than a double D-cell flashlight!). Seconds later the bruin was gone.

Tactical lights are so bright they will momentarily blind an attacker. I ordered a Surefire light as soon as I got home!

Bulb and battery basics:

- Other things being equal, the bigger the battery, the longer it will last.
- Alkaline batteries cost much more than zinc-carbon batteries but last about five times longer. Lithium batteries last longest (up to ten years!), but they're frightfully expensive. Anne Bancroft was the first woman to travel across the ice to both the north and south poles. She carried an MSR headlamp and a small Tekna flashlight that she wore on a string around her neck. Both lamps were powered by lithium batteries—essential in the minus 70-degree Fahrenheit cold.
- Zinc-carbon batteries can be recharged and used in any flashlight, but the charge won't last as long as it will with expensive nickel-cadmium (NiCd) batteries.
- Gas-filled bulbs are much brighter and more expensive than vacuum bulbs, but they don't last as long. Generally, the brighter a bulb, the faster it will burn out.

Candle lanterns are more cutesy than functional. Batteries burn for about the same length of time as quality candles of similar weight, and artificial light is much brighter than open flame. Nonetheless, candle lanterns are fun toys, and they add some warmth to a tent on chilly nights. They are best at home for winter camping, where every BTU of heat is appreciated.

Mantle lanterns: The minisize Coleman Peak 1 lantern puts out nearly as much light (for half the size and weight) as its traditional big brother.

Mantle lanterns are considered essential equipment for auto camping but are viewed as gauche by the self-propelled camping crowd. However, they are strong enough to withstand the abuse of rugged canoe or horse-packing trips if you pad the globes and pack them well. The new mantles are much stronger than those of decades ago.

Caution: Never inhale the fumes from a newly lit (previously unburned) mantle. The gases released are highly poisonous!

If your lantern won't generate pressure, the leather pump gasket may be too dry (needs oil). Trail stoves also suffer from this malady. Most of the new pump gaskets are synthetic; the traditional leather models work better. Some leather stool washers (check the plumbing section of your hardware store) fit some lanterns and stoves perfectly!

Don't fill a mantle lantern more than three-fourths full of gas. You need air space to generate pressure.

FOREST FIRES

As a forester in Oregon many years ago, I fought several good-size forest fires. And I have been canoeing when the woods were ablaze all around me. Here's what to do if you're camping and see a forest fire heading your way:

- Fires often move in a predictable direction, so try to outflank a blaze by moving perpendicular to its path. Try to stay on or near water. If you're on a lake and the fire has reached you, move to the opposite shore and stay near the water's edge. If the shoreline is burning all around, get into the center of the lake and stay there. Wet down your clothes and hat. Remove all nylon and polypropylene clothing—these synthetics produce terrible burns!

  Note: Intense heat can turn the water in wet clothes to steam, which will burn you badly. Wet down your clothes only if there's a nearby water source where you can cool off.

- If sparks are flying and you have a boat, capsize the boat in the middle of the lake and get under it for protection. The craft will act as a spark shield. The large air bubble trapped inside the craft will enable you to breathe and speak normally.

- An intense ground fire generates its own winds, which may reach speeds over 100 miles per hour! If this happens, you may be in big trouble whatever you do. Generally, you'll survive even very large fires if you're at least 100 yards from a burning shoreline.

- Fires die down at night and flare up with the morning winds. So rest during the day and travel from evening through dawn. And remember, heat rises—the closer you are to the ground, the less smoky the air.

- Winds generally drive fires uphill. Seek out a valley to rest or camp.

- Fires may jump half a mile or more—don't think you are safe just because you're near a large body of water.

FRISBEE

A giant Frisbee is more than a toy. Here are some practical uses: pot cover, serving platter for food, cutting board, camp seat, windbreak for your stove, tool for fanning a reluctant fire, containment tray for tools.

G

GPS (GLOBAL POSITIONING SYSTEM)

The hottest new navigational device is the handheld GPS (global positioning system) receiver. With a GPS unit, you can determine an accurate position anywhere on Earth in a matter of minutes. Or you can enter a set coordinates of a place you want to go and the GPS receiver will provide a compass bearing and distance that will be updated by satellite information as you progress. Press a button and you get a speed readout and an estimated time of arrival. You must be moving faster than about 11 miles per hour to get an accurate measure of your speed. Hikers and canoeists *should not* take GPS speed readings too seriously!

Without a map, GPS can be used to track your location. Enter your starting position into the unit and save it as a waypoint. Establish other waypoints as you proceed, then, like Hansel and Gretel, follow your electronic bread crumbs home. GPS accuracy is 3 meters or less!

You must know how to read and interpret topographic maps in order to master GPS technology. You must also have—and know how to use—an accurate compass. The one built into a GPS has limited capabilities. Be aware that all handheld GPS units operate on small batteries that could fail when you need them most. And few civilian GPS models are waterproof, which means you must be careful how you use them in rain.

It is not practical to leave a GPS unit on for continuous positioning unless you have battery recharging capabilities or an unlimited supply of batteries. The most useful GPS feature is its ability to verify your location on a map—possible *only* if your map has a reference system to which your GPS unit can relate. Not all maps have appropriate reference lines. Those that do include all U.S. and Canadian topographic maps that are marked with degrees of latitude and longitude. Canadian maps and U.S. military maps also provide decimal-based Universal Transverse Mercator (UTM) coordinates, which are much easier to use than latitude/longitude. Any

GPS receiver can be set to read lat/lon or UTM coordinates, as you prefer. (See page 130).

Maps that don't have a coordinate system to which the GPS can relate include nearly all public road maps, most state and national park hiking and boating maps, and special-purpose recreational maps like those drawn for the Boundary Waters Canoe Area of Minnesota. If you use one of these special-purpose maps, you'll also need to carry a GPS-compatible topographic map.

The bottom line is that your map must have integral GPS coordinates or you won't be able to plot the fix your GPS unit calculates! Topographic maps are hard to find in most towns, but you can order them from the government sources listed in the MAPS section, page 127.

Some things to consider when choosing a GPS unit:

• Learning how to use GPS is like mastering a computer; if you don't use it, you'll lose it! The best plan is to buy a unit that will mount in your car. Get a dashboard mount and a cigarette-lighter plug-in so you can practice setting waypoints, save track data, and master other operations without running down batteries. You won't become proficient if you use your GPS receiver just a few times a year!

Figure G-1. Learning to use a GPS unit is like mastering a computer. If you don't use it, you'll lose it! Note the reading on the unit, which indicates that we have just crossed the arctic circle.

- Large GPS units are generally more user-friendly than small ones. Miniature GPS receivers often have awkwardly placed controls, and their tiny antennas don't access satellites as fast or reliably as bigger antennas.
- Not all "waterproof" GPS units have waterproof battery compartments!
- Every GPS should have a simulator mode so you can learn the intricacies of operation more quickly.

Things you don't need in a GPS unit:

Electronic compass: An electronic compass is no more accurate (most are *less* accurate!) than a good needle compass. Unlike a needle compass, an electronic compass must be recalibrated every time you change batteries or move very far from its previously calibrated location. To recalibrate, you rotate the instrument (usually twice) 360 degrees—full circle. The compass must be held dead level during rotation. Sound bizarre? It is! If you go out of calibration range and forget to recalibrate, you're lost! Running by e-compass also consumes some battery power. Needle compasses "point for free."

Barometer: A barometer must be frequently recalibrated to provide accurate air pressure readings. Yes, you will get a relative readout without calibration, which is useful to determine weather trends. But you can probably buy a watch with this feature for less money than what it will cost you in a GPS unit.

Thermometer: Electronic thermometers are slow to register readings. They're just one more thing to drain battery power.

Color display: Color is nice, but it consumes battery power and it doesn't add accuracy or utility.

Sometimes, simple things are simply best!

HAND CREAM AND LIP BALM

Moisturizers are among the most important—and forgotten—items on a camping trip. I double up on tubes and keep them in different places in my pack. Healing Badger Balm (www.badgerbalm.com; see appendix B), is the best hand cream I've found. It acts like an extra pair of gloves and reduces wind chapping. Its olive oil and aloe formula doesn't sting cracked skin.

HONEY AND SUGAR—GOOD MEDICINE FOR WOUNDS

Honey will sweeten your tea and heal your wounds. It is slightly acidic so it effectively kills microorganisms. The University of South Florida in Tampa used honey on patients who were undergoing abdominal surgery. Doctors there found that the honey was more effective than some expensive antibiotics! If honey works well, sugar works better. Why? Because bacteria require moisture to survive, and sugar has none!

Dr. Avashalom Mirzrahi, a microbiology professor at Hebrew University in Israel, discovered that honey is also good medicine for treating burns and ulcers. Medical reports show that people who took two to three ounces of honey each day over several months cured their ulcer.

HYPOTHERMIA

Hypothermia (commonly called "exposure sickness") is the most common and dangerous of outdoor ailments. No one is immune to its icy grip. You can suffer hypothermia while climbing a mountain in Tibet or biking across Chicago. Dozens of people die from it each year.

Hypothermia occurs when body temperature drops below about 95 degrees Fahrenheit. As blood is rushed to the vital organs, chilling spreads throughout the body. This is accompanied by clumsiness, slurred speech, and loss of judgment. Coma and death may result within a few hours if body temperature is not raised.

Hypothermics usually cannot identify their problem. They will maintain (often until death!) that they are "okay." You must observe symptoms, diagnose correctly, and treat quickly. Your friend's life may depend on it. Check these symptoms:

- Slurred speech, stiffness in limbs (difficulty walking), an irrational view of reality. Victim acts irresponsibly—loses hat, mittens, or other equipment along the trail. Loss of short-term memory.
- Victim can't walk a straight line.
- Victim was shivering before and now shivering has stopped. *Note: Mild* shivering is nature's way of rewarming the body. It does not indicate hypothermia. Hypothermia begins with violent shivering. Be aware, however, that some people—especially those who are over-tired—do not exhibit a shivering reflex. So do not rely on shivering to ascertain hypothermia!

Treatment:

1. Provide shelter at once! Any place out of the wind and wet is good.
2. Replace wet clothing with dry. Be sure the victim's head and neck are covered with warm clothing (hat, scarf, etc.).
3. Apply moderate, even heat. If a fire is available, use it. If there are several people in your party, have them loosely "hug" the victim to keep him or her as warm as possible.

    If the victim can swallow, hot soup (or water) will re-warm spirits and insides. Do not administer stimulants like alcohol, coffee, or tea.

    For serious cases (where the victim is unable to walk, suffers amnesia, etc.) administer the "sandwich" treatment. This consists of stripping the victim's clothes and sandwiching him or her between two nonhypothermics. Cover the threesome with sleeping bags and clothing. Be sure to insulate everyone from the cold ground (use a foam trail pad, additional clothing, leaves, grass, branches, etc.).

    Hypothermics must be handled gently: Roughhousing may initiate a heart attack!
4. Hypothermia drains both body and spirit. Considerable rest is warranted after the danger subsides.

KNIVES

The primary use for any camp knife is preparing foods. You'll slice vegetables, meat, and cheese; spread jam and peanut butter; and cut your supper steak. Rambo survivalists will insist on a stiff-backed sheath knife with a blade at least 6 inches long, while more gentle souls will argue the merits of a penknife. Between the two extremes are scores of expert campers who will agree that at least one knife in the camping party should have these two characteristics:

1. Enough length (4 to 5 inches) to slice meat and cheese and to reach deep into the peanut butter can without getting gunked up.
2. A thin, flat-ground blade for effortless slicing.

Nearly all knives sold for outdoor use have blades that are too thick. One-eighth of an inch across the spine is the maximum thickness permissible for a utility knife, no matter how delicate the edge. Try slicing a tomato with the typical hunting knife and you'll see why!

Your favorite kitchen knife would probably be perfect for camp use if it had a bit less length, more backbone, and better steel. In fact, the most popular knives on the frontier were the famous Green River models, which were nothing more than solidly built kitchen knives.

The primary camp knife may be a fixed blade or folding model. You'll pay much more for a good folder than for a sheath knife of similar length.

If your taste runs to folding knives, select a model with a 3- to 4-inch-long thin, preferably flat-ground blade. Lock-blade knives are safer than those with traditional pressure springs, and their blades can be opened single-handedly while you are wearing mittens. However, lock blades tend to loosen with time as the lock mechanism wears. Pressure-spring folders usually stay tight much longer.

Which knife for you? If you've read between the lines, you'll conclude that you need two knives for camping: a thin-ground, kitchen-style model for preparing foods and a substantial multipurpose folder of some sort. I carry a sheath knife with a 4⅓-inch blade and a multipurpose Leatherman tool. There's also a Swiss Army knife hidden in my pack. The nail file and scissors are very useful.

Stainless or carbon steel? Stainless is much more difficult and expensive to work than carbon steel. It's also harder to sharpen, especially to the supersharp shaving edge I prefer. My experience suggests that most people—particularly those who are not expert at sharpening knives—will be happier with a high-grade carbon-steel blade than a stainless one. Granted, carbon steel rusts, but so does a fine ax or gun. If you're serious about the outdoors, you'll take joy in maintaining your knife. *Note:* If you need to make fire with flint and steel, a carbon-steel blade will produce sparks. A stainless-steel blade won't.

Steel hardness: The Rockwell (Rc) test is the standard by which the hardness of steel is measured. The higher the number, the harder the steel. Generally, hard steels take and retain a better edge than soft steels. There's a limit, of course—steel that is too hard may be too brittle for knives. There's a common agreement that a rating of Rc 56–59 is ideal for good edge holding with minimum brittleness (assuming that quality steel is used). Most cheap pocketknives run much less than Rc 56, while nearly all high-quality knives fall into the 56–59 range. Some special steels, hardened to Rc 60 and beyond, are used on a limited basis for expensive custom knives. Only diamonds are harder than zircon-oxide (ceramic) blades, whose Rc ratings approach 100. However, ceramic knives are much too brittle for serious outdoors use.

Smooth edge or serrated? A lion's share of today's outdoor knives have serrated edges, which are great for cutting through wrist-thick rope and metal doors. But how do they slice salami and pine? Not very well. And they are difficult for the average person to sharpen! A folding saw, hand ax, and thin-bladed knife, in combination, will outperform *any* Rambo-style survival blade on the planet. Believe it!

Here are my preferences, along with some specific knives I can recommend:

Fixed-blade knives: In 1967 I purchased a fixed-blade Gerber Shorty. Its thin (0.080-inch), flat-ground tool-steel blade had enough heft to split kindling and sufficient flex to fillet fish. It applied peanut butter to pita bread

Figure K-1. Cliff's favorite knives, from left to right: The Gerber Shorty (4.5-inch blade, M2 tool steel; Rc 60-62; no longer manufactured). The Cliff Knife (4.3-inch blade, L6 tool steel, Rc 56-58, from Idaho Knife Works). Grohmann #1 Original, a flat-ground camper (carbon steel, Rc 56-58). Cliff encouraged the flat-ground blade design. Grohmann #2 Trout and Bird (stainless steel only).

with the efficiency of a professional spreader. I resharpened the old Gerber till it couldn't be sharpened anymore, so in 1996 I set out to find a replacement. I began my search for a Shorty look-alike by studying every knife catalog in the land. I figured a knife as practical as the Shorty must have keen competition. Wrong! There wasn't a good "user" in the lot. Every blade I saw was either too short, too thick, hollow ground, too wide, or had dumb serrations. I wondered if the designers of these knives ever spent any time in the woods!

Ultimately, the choice came down to regrinding an old carbon-steel butcher knife or designing my own. I chose the latter option and asked Mike Mann—a full-time custom knife maker living in a log cabin in the mountains of Idaho—to build my dream knife. Mann mostly forges award-winning blades for historical reenactments, but he also builds modern hunting, fishing, and kitchen knives. He flat-grinds all his blades and he doesn't use stainless steel. I was thrilled to discover that his prices were well below his competitors.

I used the Gerber Shorty as a working pattern and added more belly and a sharp, dropped point. I specified a 0.078-inch-thick blade and full-tang handle with polished wood (Mike used curly maple) scales. My new Cliff knife, as Mann calls it, is lighter, better balanced, and much prettier than the old Gerber. You can get one outfitted to your tastes from Idaho Knife Works (www.idahoknifeworks.com; see appendix B).

Note: I have no financial affiliation of any sort with Idaho Knife Works. I simply suggest the Cliff knife to you because it works so well for me.

The Grohmann #1 Original, flat-ground camper model, is another fine knife—and a great value (www.grohmannknives.com; see appendix B). I'm proud to say I encouraged its development. The #1 Original comes in carbon and stainless steel. I much prefer the carbon model.

Folding knives: Schrade carbon-steel Old Timer knives are an outstanding buy. Old Timers come in a variety of styles from tiny penknives to big twin-blade lock backs. Most discount stores have an assortment of these knives. There are also some practical sheath knives in the Old Timer line. I only wish Schrade would see fit to use thinner steel for the blades.

How to Care for Your Edged Tools

I occasionally spray working saws and axes with WD-40. I wipe kitchen knives with digestible canola oil or occasionally cut salami or cheese. *Caution: Do not* use petroleum oils on knives that will be used to cut food!

Flitz and Wenol are terrific metal polishes if you like a mirror-bright finish on your knives. RIG Universal—a Vaseline-like product that is available at gun shops—provides superb long-term protection (even against salt water) for carbon-steel tools. And plain old petroleum jelly (Vaseline) also keeps rust away.

Sharpening: Don't ever sharpen a knife on an electric sharpener or one of those mechanical wheeled gadgets sold at supermarkets. You'll ruin the knife beyond repair. Instead, use sharpening hones.

You'll need a coarse hone and a fine hone. The quality of the abrasive is more important than whether the stone is natural or synthetic. Indeed, Amazon natives still use water-worn rocks to sharpen their machetes— and they obtain whisper-sharp edges. My favorite stones are the ones sold by Razor Edge Systems (www.razoredgesystems.com; see appendix B). I also like DMT diamond hones (www.dmtsharp.com; see appendix B), and natural Wachita and Arkansas oil stones. The cheap carborundum stones you buy in hardware stores are about the only stones I dislike. But even these will produce a superior edge if you know what you're doing.

The jury is out on whether you should lubricate your hone with oil or water or use it dry. I lubricate fine stones, not coarse ones. Final lubrica-

FIGURE K-2. Maintain a 15- to 20-degree angle, and cut into the stone. Use plenty of cutting oil and clean the stone (and blade) frequently.

tion seems to produce a smoother, more polished edge. I use light oil (WD-40 or kerosene) with natural stones, water with diamond hones. Don't use conventional oils—they gum up the stones.

This procedure produces a wickedly sharp razor edge:

Use the coarse stone first, without lubrication. Keep the back of the blade raised 15 to 20 degrees (the shallower the angle, the better the geometry of the final edge) and cut *into* the stone. A trick to maintain the proper angle is to adjust an overhead light so that it casts a shadow along the back of the blade when the blade is laid flat on the stone. Raise the blade until the shadow just disappears and you'll have the recommended angle. If you can't maintain the proper sharpening angle, try using a circular motion of the blade instead. A circular motion isn't recommended, however, because it makes it harder to keep the same angle (blade bevel).

Hone one edge until a burr appears on the opposite side—you can feel the burr with a fingernail. Then hone the other side until a burr again appears. Now switch to the fine hone. Maintain a film of very thin oil to float away steel particles that otherwise clog the pores of the stone. Clean the stone (wipe off the surface and apply clean oil) after every twenty strokes or so. This prevents suspended grit from dulling the knife edge.

Exotic-looking tools that clamp to the knife blade are sold for the purpose of maintaining the proper sharpening angle. These tools work great for people who don't know how to sharpen knives by hand.

If you want a polished razor edge, finish by honing on a superfine Arkansas or straight razor stone, then strop the sharpened blade on a piece of leather that's impregnated with jewelers' rouge. Strop the edge *away* from the leather—one stroke per side.

Clean your sharpening stones: With use, grit builds up inside the pores of your sharpening stones and the stones become "finer" (smoother) over time. You'll prolong their life if you occasionally "boil them out." Simply submerge the stones in a pot of boiling water (with a few drops of detergent added) for a few minutes.

To check for blade sharpness: A knife is considered sharp if it will shave hair from the back of your hand. A less barbaric method is to shine a bright light on the sharpened edge. You should see no flat spots, no inconsistencies . . . nothing!

Sharpening (butcher's) steels do not sharpen a knife; they merely realign the microscopic teeth of the blade edge. A steel is handy for touching up a knife (it's simply a coarse version of a leather strop), but it can't take the place of a genuine whetstone.

Tip: If you dip the blade of your knife in boiling water for about thirty seconds, it will be much easier to sharpen.

Best way to carry a hefty folding knife is in a pocket sewn into the back of your field trousers. Sew a line of stitches through the pant leg and pocket as illustrated (figure K-3) and attach a snap flap or Velcro tab at the top.

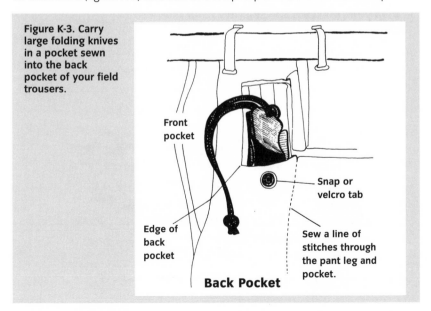

Figure K-3. Carry large folding knives in a pocket sewn into the back pocket of your field trousers.

Front pocket

Snap or velcro tab

Edge of back pocket

Sew a line of stitches through the pant leg and pocket.

Back Pocket

Equip your knife with a nylon lanyard so you can pull it out with one hand.

This system is more secure, less obtrusive, and more comfortable than a leather sheath worn on the belt.

To make a sheath for a fixed-blade knife, you'll need: sole leather (the thicker the better), contact cement, two-piece rivets, paper, scissors, and a sharp utility knife. Leather and rivets may be ordered from any Tandy leather company store.

1. Make a pattern for your sheath from paper or thin corrugated cardboard.
2. Transfer the paper pattern to the leather.
3. Soak the leather in lukewarm water until it is soft, then cut out the sheath pattern with a sharp knife.
4. Contact cement a ¼-inch-wide "edge guard" of leather around the sheath perimeter.
5. Rivet a belt loop to the back of the sheath, then contact cement the sheath edges together.
6. Insert the knife into the glued sheath and painstakingly form the wet leather to fit. Work the hilt area carefully until you get a perfect fit.
7. Withdraw the knife from the sheath (the leather will remain formed) and rivet—or ask your shoemaker to sew—the sheath together.
8. When the sheath is dry, apply many coats of shoe polish. Do not use boot greases on sheaths; they will soften the leather.

Figure K-4. Make your own case-style leather sheath.

Figure K-5. You can easily make one of these knife sheaths in one to two hours.

KNOTS, HITCHES, AND LASHINGS

While canoeing Manitoba's North Knife River in the summer of 1991, my crew experienced three days of wind-driven, icy cold rain. Temperatures in the 30s and wind speeds of 30 miles an hour threatened to shred our paired (12-by-12-foot) nylon rain tarps. I used every trick—and length of cord—to keep the shelter tight and well drained.

When the skies cleared, we had one last admiring look at our storm-defying roof before we began its disassembly. I'd used 200 feet of parachute cord, 100 feet of nylon rope, and two prussik knots to keep things taut, and it resembled Charlotte's web. "Nice rig," remarked one man, "but how'll we ever get it down? Wet knots are murder to untie!"

"Just watch," I replied with a knowing grin. One pull of each "slippery" loop severed the lines in a matter of seconds. In all, barely five minutes were needed to coil ropes and cords and to stuff the flies into their awaiting sacks.

Fabric shelters must be tightly stressed to withstand high winds and prolonged rain. Guylines and hemlines must be drum tight yet release easily (with a single pull!) when the storm subsides. The alternative to quick-release knots is to pick, swear, and cut them apart. Experienced outdoors people always end their knots with the "slippery" loops illustrated in this chapter. In figure C-14, a quick-release knot is used to secure the mouth of a nylon stuff sack.

Outdoor handbooks define dozens of knots. But for camp use, the half hitch, power cinch, sheet bend and bowline are enough. Occasionally, you may find use for the prussik loop and the two common lashings illustrated here.

Use two *half hitches* to anchor a rope or cord to an immovable object like a tree or rock. This is a good hitch to use when mooring a boat. You'll be able to untie the knot more easily if you end the second half hitch with a quick-release loop as illustrated in figure K-6. Simply pull the line on through if you don't want the quick-release feature.

Figure K-6. Two half hitches.

The *power cinch* (a modification of the trucker's knot, see figure K-7) provides the block-and-tackle power you need to snug tent and tarp guy-lines and keep them tight. The hitch ties and unties in a flash and is much more powerful, secure and versatile than the tautline hitch, which is touted in old-time camping books. Use the power cinch for rigging a clothesline, tying canoes on cars, securing a package on cartop carriers, and any place you need a tight lashing that won't slip. See my book *Basic Essentials: Knots for the Outdoors* for other practical uses of this ingenious hitch.

Begin the power cinch by forming a simple overhand loop, as shown in step 1. Pull the loop through as in step 2, forming the loop exactly as shown.

If the loop is formed as in step 2, a simple tug on the rope will eliminate it. This is preferable to the common practice of tying a knot in the loop, which after being exposed to a load is almost impossible to get out.

If you are tying a boat on top of a car, tie the long single line (shown attached to the tent) to the boat's bow or stern (use two half hitches or a bowline) and run the double line through a steel S hook on the car's

Figure K-7. Power cinch.

bumper. Now apply power, as illustrated. You have a tough pulley with a 2:1 mechanical advantage!

If you want a reliable knot, complete the hitch by tying a double half hitch around the body of the rope. If you want the hitch to release with a single pull, end it with a single half hitch and quick-release (slippery) loop as illustrated.

The *sheet bend* (figure K-8) is the knot of choice for tying two ropes together. Ropes tied with a sheet bend won't slip under a load, and they come apart easily even after being pelted by heavy rain. When rope sizes are dissimilar, use the smaller-diameter rope to make the bend and quick-release feature. If you want absolute security, as in rescue work, use the double sheet bend!

The *bowline* (figure K-9) is an absolutely secure knot that won't slip. Use it any place you need a nonslip loop at the end of a line. Mountain climbers use the bowline for securing climbing ropes around their waists. If you require absolute security (especially with slippery polypropylene ropes), secure the tail of the finished knot around one arm of the loop with a couple of half hitches.

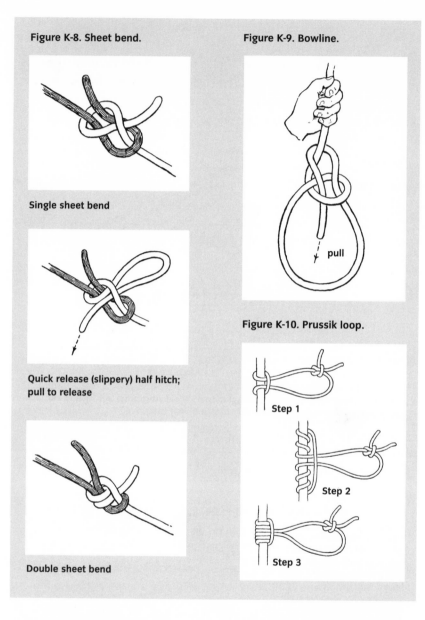

Figure K-8. Sheet bend.

Single sheet bend

Quick release (slippery) half hitch; pull to release

Double sheet bend

Figure K-9. Bowline.

pull

Figure K-10. Prussik loop.

Step 1

Step 2

Step 3

Scenario: Rain is pooling on a portion of your nylon cooking tarp. An aerial guyline would solve the problem, but there is no place to anchor it. You could run a rope between two poorly situated trees, then secure your guyline to it, but the pull would be parallel to the rope and the knot would slip down it. What to do?

Why, rig a *prussik loop* (figure K-10), of course! Use the prussik whenever you want an absolutely secure loop that won't slip along a tight line. Mountaineers use this knot for footholds to climb a vertical rope. The prussik loop slides easily along a tight rope, yet it jams solidly when a horizontal or vertical load is applied. Make the loop from an 18-inch length of parachute cord, completed with a sheet bend.

Lashings

Use a modified *shear* lashing (figure K-11) to connect short spars together to achieve the pole length (around 6 feet) you need to heighten the roof of a rain tarp. A *diagonal* lashing (figure K-12) will connect spars in an X configuration and allow you to erect a tight ridgeline when rope is in short supply.

Figure K-11. Modified shear lashing. Place the poles parallel to one another and tie a *clove hitch* around one pole. Then wind your cord tightly around both poles several times and finish with a clove hitch.

Begin with a timber hitch.

Figure K-12. Diagonal lashing. Begin with a very tight *timber hitch* around both poles. Take three or four turns side by side around one fork, and three or four more, side by side around the other. Then tighten the lashing with two frapping turns and end it with a clove hitch around one of the poles.

End with a clove hitch.

LIGHTNING

Lightning is a more serious threat than most campers are willing to admit. Next to hypothermia, it is the most dangerous "thing" in the outdoors. Realities of backcountry travel necessarily expose travelers to some risk of being struck by lightning, but this risk may be sharply reduced if you religiously follow these guidelines:

1. Lightning ordinarily strikes the highest object in its path, so if you pitch your tent in an open field or plateau, be certain there are trees or rock formations of significantly greater height nearby.

2. A cone of protection extends from the tallest trees or landmass (as the case may be) about 45 degrees outward. Pitch your tent or walk, canoe, etc., within this cone of protection, but stay far enough from its source so that lightning can't jump from the object to you. Lightning may jump a dozen feet or more across water, so don't snug against the shoreline if you're canoeing or boating in an electrical storm. Instead, keep within the cone of protection offered by the shoreline trees.

   A note about the cone of protection: A new guideline from the National Outdoor Leadership School (NOLS) questions the cone-of-protection theory. NOLS advises hikers to avoid stands of trees and instead seek rolling terrain. The theory is that strikes are most common near tall, lone trees and that the ground surrounding these trees becomes highly electrified. NOLS says lightning doesn't often hit rolling regions that are sparsely treed, so you should be safe there. This makes sense, but only if there's cooperative topography nearby. Consider this example from my own experience canoeing the Gull River in northern Ontario:

   My friend Al Todnem was in the lead when lightning suddenly lit up the sky and rain fell so furiously that I could barely see my bow partner. The river was maybe 200 feet wide at this point and trees choked the shoreline to the water's edge. There was no safe landing in sight.

The distance of a lightning strike can be estimated by dividing the number seconds between the flash and thunderclap by five. At the 2.5-second strike (meaning lightning was half a mile away), Al turned sharply toward shore and poured on the coal. I stayed near the middle of the river and hollered for him to come back. But he couldn't hear me above the roar of the rain.

When Al was just offshore, lightning struck the top of a tall birch at the river's edge. The top exploded into flame and showered cinders in all directions. The burning top—which probably weighed several hundred pounds—splashed down an arm's length from his canoe! Al back-paddled furiously as burning embers showered his boat. Fortunately, no one was injured.

Yes, boaters should get to shore as quickly as possible when lightning strikes, but only if there's a safe landing spot away from tall trees. Often there isn't. Unforgiving topography—a steep, slick, or vegetation-choked beach—is one reason why; another is that the sunlit opening of river valleys encourages tree growth near the water's edge. The result is that the tallest trees often grow right next to the river—at the precise place you plan to land. Go there, and as the above case illustrates, you're asking for trouble!

3. Lightning may travel along tree roots, which may extend dozens of feet outward. If roots are close to the surface of the ground, as in rocky areas where there is little soil cover, sufficient energy may be transmitted along subsurface roots to pose real danger to anyone standing on the ground above them. Keep this in mind when pitching your tent.

4. If you're caught outside the cone of protection and suddenly feel electrical energy building (dry hair will stand on end), immediately get as low as possible to reduce the human-lightning-rod effect.

5. The notion that nonmetal boats are safer than metal ones in a lightning storm has no basis. A lightning strike generates millions of volts, enough to fry anything in its path. Steel ships are occasionally struck by lightning, usually with no ill effects. This suggests that aluminum boats and canoes may in fact be safer than nonmetal ones, simply because they more readily dissipate current around the hull into the surrounding water.

If lightning flashes all around, get down low in your boat (below the gunnels) to reduce the lightning-rod effect. Again, try to maneuver into

45°

Stay within the cone of protection but not so close to shore that lightning may jump from shore to canoe.

Lake

Figure L-1. The cone of protection.

the cone of protection offered by the shoreline.

6. Always check your campsite for tall, leaning trees, especially dead ones, which may come crashing down on you in lightning or wind storms.

7. *If you're in a tent and lightning strikes all around:* Sit up immediately and draw your legs to your chest so that only your buttocks and feet contact the ground. A foam sleeping pad (preferably doubled) placed beneath you may provide enough insulation to keep you from being grounded. If you have no foam-rubber sleeping pad, substitute any material that will insulate you from the current.

   It is absolutely essential that you maintain the recommended "sitting" position during an electrical storm. In the unlikely event you are struck by lightning while in this position, only your feet and buttocks are apt to burn. But if you're lying flat, electrical energy may pass through your heart and cause death.

Note: Use of a ground cloth inside your tent is highly recommended as it ensures you'll have a bone-dry tent. All your preventive efforts to outwit lightning will be dashed to the winds if your bedding gets wet. See, TENTS, page 194, for a thorough discussion of the importance of an interior ground sheet.

After the Strike!

Lightning strikes a tree at the opposite end of your campsite. You run to your friends, one of whom is unresponsive and not breathing. One of his shoes is missing and there is a small deep burn on the sole of his foot. You check for a pulse; there is none.

Treatment: Lightning usually kills people by producing cardiac arrest. It may also paralyze the respiratory system. If your friend is alive, the burns are probably minor and you can attend to them later. Right now, you've got to get the heart and respiratory system working.

Begin CPR immediately! If you can restore heart rhythm and breathing, you can probably save your friend.

Keep the patient warm and send for help immediately. Electric shock may cause disorientation, coma, seizures, and spinal-cord injuries. It may also rupture the eardrums. All you can do until help arrives is to keep your friend immobilized and warm and convince him that he'll be okay.

LYME DISEASE

According to wildlife experts, there are now more white-tailed deer in Minnesota, Michigan, and Wisconsin than existed in the entire United States at the time of Columbus. Good news to hunters perhaps, but not to hikers who may contract debilitating Lyme disease, which is carried by deer. In 2004 alone, nearly 20,000 cases of Lyme disease were reported to the Centers for Disease Control and Prevention. That's 27.4 cases for every 100,000 persons.

Several species of ixodes (deer/bear) ticks carry the disease. Ixodes ticks are very small, about the size of a sesame seed. Their color is dark brown to black; the female often has a rusty brown appearance.

You must be bitten by an infected tick to get Lyme disease. Other insects can carry the Lyme-producing bacteria, but they can't spread it to humans. Pregnant women *can* transmit the disease to their unborn infants.

Symptoms: You won't feel the tick bite—it's painless. Symptoms may appear days (or years) after being bitten. In the early stages, there's a red rash or lesion that may migrate to other areas of the body or spread in size. The lesion can be solid red or look like a bull's-eye. The rash is usually about 4 inches across but can be much smaller or larger. You may experience fatigue, headache, fever, and muscle or joint aches. If Lyme disease goes untreated, it can cause arthritis, meningitis, and facial palsy. The disease has caused miscarriages, birth defects, and other health problems.

Prevention

There's no vaccine for Lyme disease, so prevention is everything. Here are the most practical recommended field procedures:

1. Wear long-sleeved shirts and long pants. Tuck your pants into high socks or rubberband or tape the cuffs to keep ticks from crawling up your legs. I prefer to tuck my pants into 12- to 16-inch-high boots.

2. Ticks generally crawl upward, so a shirt collar may prevent ticks from crawling down your neck. Spray the collar with insect repellent.

3. Wear light-colored clothing. It's easier to see ticks on light-colored clothes than on dark ones.

4. Select tight weaves. It's harder for ticks to hold onto tightly woven fabrics than loosely woven ones.

5. *Apply insecticide!* An insecticide plus repellent is your best protection.

    An insecticide that contains 0.5 percent permethrin will kill ticks on contact. Spray permethrin on your boots, pant cuffs, and shirt sleeves but *do not* get any on your skin. Permethrin should be sprayed on clothes and tent openings at least three hours before use, then allowed to dry in a well-ventilated area. Dried permethrin will kill ticks for up to two weeks and will last through several rains and washings. Permethrin kills slowly; affected ticks may live an hour or more, which is not enough time for them to posture and dig into your skin. When used as directed, permethrin is safe and effective. Most sporting goods stores carry it.

    Use skin-safe repellents that have a high concentration of N,N-diethyl-meta-toluamide (DEET) on the exposed parts (avoid lips and eyes) of your body. Spread spray-on repellents *by hand* so you don't miss any spots. Treat arm and leg holes in clothing (tick entry points) with both repellents and permethrin.

    See page 32 for instructions on how to remove an embedded tick.

MAPS AND MAP TRICKS

Topographic maps, in the largest scale you can get, are best for finding your way in the backcountry. The smaller the denominator of the map scale fraction, the larger the scale and more useful the map. The numerator of the fraction indicates map units; the denominator equals ground units. Thus, a scale of 1/24,000 would be interpreted as "one unit of distance on the map equals 24,000 units of distance on the ground." Some representative comparisons are shown below:

1:24,000	1 inch on the map equals 2,000 feet on the ground.
1:50,000	1¼ inches equal 1 mile.
1:62,500	1 inch equals approximately 1 mile.
1:250,000	1 inch equals 4 miles.

For average field use, American maps in 1:62,500 scale or Canadian maps in 1:50,000 scale are most versatile.

To order United States maps:
U.S. Geological Survey (USGS)
Box 25286, Federal Center
Denver, CO 80225
(888) ASK USGS
(303) 202–4693 (fax)
www.usgs.gov
The USGS is your complete source of U.S. topographic maps and aerial photos. Ask for a free index and the UTM (Universal Transverse Mercator)

fact sheet. The USGS accepts checks, money orders, and popular credit cards.

To order charts and tide tables of U.S. coasts, the Great Lakes, sections of major rivers, and contoured fishing maps:
National Oceanic and Atmospheric Administration (NOAA)
Communications and Education Division
SSMC4, Room 13317
1305 East–West Highway
Silver Spring, MD 20910
(301) 713–3060
www.nos.noaa.gov
Search for maps and charts on NOAA's Web site.

To order indexes to Canadian maps and locate dealers who sell Canadian maps:
Canada Map Office
615 Booth Street
Ottawa, ON, Canada K1A OE9
(800) 465–6277, (613) 952–7000
www.maps.nrcan.gc.ca
Order indexes to topographic maps (but not maps) from the Canada Map Office. The Canada Map Office will provide a list of U.S. and Canadian dealers who sell topographic maps.

Map index: Request a free index to topographic maps if you do not know precisely what to order. The index will tell you what maps are in print, in what scale, and at what cost. If you roughly define the area of your interest (to the nearest state or Canadian province), you'll receive the correct index from the U.S. Geological Survey or the Canadian map distributor.

Colored or monochrome maps? Some 1:50,000 scale Canadian maps may be ordered as monochrome (black-and-white) editions. Monochrome maps are as accurate and easy to understand as colored versions but are less expensive. They also photocopy perfectly—something to consider if you want to provide low-cost maps for a large number of people.

Aerial photos: All maps today are drawn from aerial photos. Photos are available for nearly every inch of land surface and are useful when you need the finest possible detail. Aerial photos are sometimes available as stereo pairs. With them, you can accurately identify features as small as a boulder or tree. Inexpensive stereoscopes may be purchased from surveying companies and hobby shops.

The same agencies that supplied your maps can tell you how to get aerial photos. There are millions of photos on file, so be sure you accurately identify the location you need. The best way to get the right pictures is to box in the area of your interest on a large-scale topo map. Send this map, with instructions, to the air photo library. They'll return your map with your order. You can also identify the photo location with precise latitude and longitude coordinates.

Aerial photos can also be accessed and downloaded online. For U.S. photos just type in "aerial photos U.S." on any search engine; for foreign images type in "aerial photos" followed by the country name. The active interface will do the rest. Be aware that the quality of your downloaded photo depends on the resolution of your printer and the paper you choose. If you need high-resolution images, you should probably order them.

Land Use Information Series maps are available for some parts of Canada. They're standard 1:250,000 scale colored maps that have information about wildlife, fishing, geology, ecology, climate, and places of interest, overprinted on their surface. Land Use Information maps will tell you the precise location of lake trout, the migration route of caribou (and the time of migration), the nesting region for peregrine falcons, etc. These maps are wonderful for planning trips or for dreaming! They cost no more than conventional topographic maps and they're available from the same place. Specify Land Use Information Series maps when you order. A special index to these maps may be obtained free from any Canadian map distributor.

Provisional maps (white prints): Most topographic maps are old; some were last field checked decades ago. Topographic features won't change, of course, but man-made ones—roads, trails, buildings, power lines—will. If, for example, you're going fishing in Canada, you'll want a map that indicates the location of recently built roads that service the area. Only the most recent topographic maps will indicate the features you want.

However, there may be provisional or white-print maps available that have the information you need. Logging and mining companies and provincial Ministries of Natural Resources (MNR) use provisional maps in their daily work. If these current if unspectacular maps are available, the MNR or the logging or mining company that services the area will know where to find them. The tourism office in the province of your interest will supply the addresses of MNR area offices. You may also call or write the Canadian Consulate for this information.

Four Ways to Waterproof Your Maps

1. Insert them in zipper-lock plastic bags. Giant 12½-by-16-inch bags are available from most office supply stores.
2. Cover them with clear contact paper—makes maps waterproof but you can't write on them.
3. Paint on Stormproof or one of the special waterproofing treatments manufactured by Aquaseal or Nikwax. Every camp shop has them.
4. Apply Thompson's Water Seal—an industrial-strength chemical used for sealing concrete block. "TWS" is available in hardware stores in aerosol cans and tins. Apply it with a foam varnish brush. TWS makes maps water repellent, not waterproof. You can write over it with pen or pencil.

Tip: Use a felt-tip highlighter to mark your course of travel on your map. Highlighter ink won't run or bleed, and you can see topographic features through it.

Learning to Use Map Features

UTM (Universal Transverse Mercator) Coordinates

If you have tried to plot a location on a map to the nearest 100 meters using degrees, minutes, and seconds of latitude/longitude, you know it isn't easy. That's because latitude/longitude is not a rectangular grid.

Enter the UTM grid. It is perfectly rectangular, and coordinate values are in meters. UTM coordinates are referenced or overprinted on all U.S. and Canadian topographic maps. Every GPS unit can be set to read them.

Very briefly, here's how UTM works: The Earth is divided into sixty zones. Lettered bands of latitude divide the zones. This creates a rectangular grid. The UTM coordinate designation for the church in figure M-1 is: 357400E, 5476200N. You always read "right, up"—that is, you read the easting coordinate first, then the northing one.

If you enter the above coordinates as a waypoint into your GPS unit,

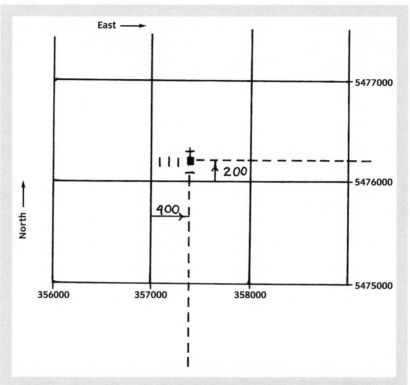

Figure M-1. The UTM coordinate designation for the church is 357400E, 5476200N. If the church were located in zone 16T, a GPS unit would read 16T 0357400E, 5476200N. Note that the GPS unit places a 0 before the first number in the easting coordinate.

you must specify the *zone* in which you are located (example: 16T), and the map *datum* (example: NAD27). The datum is the "Earth model" that was used to make the map. Datum and zone information are printed in the margin of every topographic map.

If the church were located in zone 16T, your GPS unit would show these coordinates: 16T 0357400E, 5476200N. Note that the GPS places a 0 before the first number in the easting coordinate so that both northing and easting numbers each have seven digits.

The details of using UTM are much too complicated to detail here. For a complete treatise on the subject, see Michael Ferguson's excellent book *GPS Land Navigation* (see appendix A). Canoeists and kayakers have special needs and thus may want to read the UTM section in my flagship book, *Expedition Canoeing*.

Contour Lines

The light brown lines overprinted on topographic maps are called contour lines. They indicate the elevation (above sea level) of land features and thus permit you to view the topography in three dimensions rather than two. Entire books have been written about contour lines and their interpretation. However, you'll get along quite nicely if you master these basic rules:

- Contour lines connect points of equal elevation. You will gain (or lose) elevation only when you travel from one contour line to another. If you walk along a contour line, you will be "on the level."
- Closely spaced contour lines indicate lots of elevation change (drop), whereas wide-spaced lines show the opposite (figures M-2 and M-3).
- The contour interval (CI) is the vertical distance between contour lines. Its value in feet or meters is stated in the map margin. If the CI is 50 feet, each successive contour line on the map increases or decreases (as the case may be) in elevation by exactly 50 feet.

Figure M-2. Basic contour of a long sloping hill indicating the significant drop on the right side of the hill and the gentle slope at left.

- The contour interval is not the same for all maps, so look closely. Convert meters (all the new Canadian maps are metric) to feet (1 meter equals 3.3 feet) if you're confused by the metric system.
- The larger the contour interval, the less clear are the characteristics of the area. In short, a map whose CI is 10 feet gives a clearer picture of the topography than one whose CI is 100 feet.
- Where contour lines cross or run very close together, you'll find an abrupt drop—a falls or canyon (figures M-3 and M-4).
- The closed or V end of a contour line always points upstream (figure M-4).

Figure M-3. Contour lines that run very close together and parallel the banks of a waterway indicate canyons.

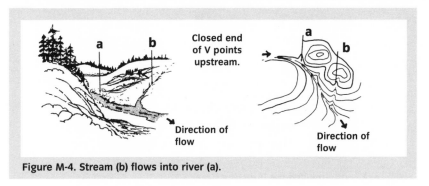

Closed end of V points upstream.

Direction of flow

Direction of flow

Figure M-4. Stream (b) flows into river (a).

Using contour lines to determine the drop of a river:

For safety's sake, you should know the drop per mile or kilometer of any river you boat. Drop figures suggest the nature of rapids that lie ahead. By comparison, a drop of:

- 3 to 5 feet per mile is easy canoeing—suitable for novices.
- 6 to 10 feet per mile indicates easy rapids—some canoeing experience is desirable.
- 10 to 15 feet per mile is real white water—best know what you're doing!
- More than 15 feet per mile—watch out, big rapids! You may have to portage.

Caution: These are *rough* indicators only. Other factors, like the volume of water, exposed rocks, and how the drop occurs (whether gradually or all at once), determine whether you will paddle or portage a particular rapid.

To compute drop:

1. Draw an arrow wherever a contour line crosses the river. Write the ele-

Figure M-5. Determining the drop of a river.

vation in feet or meters next to the contour line, as illustrated in figure M-5. Circle the number so you won't confuse it with other map data.

2. Determine the difference in elevation and the distance in miles or kilometers between the contour lines you've marked. Some canoeists prefer to make a table like the one illustrated in figure M-5.

3. Divide the difference in elevation (vertical distance) by the horizontal distance between points. In the example: From *a* to *b*, the river drops 100 feet in 5 miles, or 20 feet per mile—a probable portage. From *b* to *c*, the drop is 100 feet in 10 miles, or 10 feet per mile—fun canoeing! My book *Expedition Canoeing* provides more sophisticated examples for those who are canoeing in harm's way.

MONOFILAMENT FISHING LINE

If you're camping out and lose the screw that holds the rim of your glasses to the bow, here's how to fix it. Tie a knot in a piece of monofilament fishing line and thread it through the screw hole. Knot the other end, then use a cigarette lighter to melt both knots to form a tight rivet. The repair will hold for quite some time.

NALGENE BOTTLE TRICK

The plastic leash that secures the plastic cap to a Nalgene bottle acts like a spring when the cap is open. You must hold the cap firmly away from the bottle when you take a drink or the tensioned leash will cause the cap to snap shut in your face. The solution is to remove the cap with its attached leash and reverse the leash on the mouth of the bottle. This twists the leash and holds the open cap away from the bottle and your face! (Thanks to Pat Padden, of BP Associates in Minneapolis, for this clever tip.)

NETTED BAGS

Strong, netted (mesh) nylon bags with draw cords are popular because you can see what's inside. Here are some uses for these bags on a back-woods camping trip:

- Put dirty clothes inside and "rinse wash" (no soap) the bag in a nearby waterway. Or loosely pack wet, newly washed and rinsed clothes in the mesh bag and tie the bag to your hiking pack. Clothes will dry in a few hours in the hot sun.
- As an anchor for your boat or canoe: Put a rock inside the mesh bag and attach the bag to an anchor rope. This is not as strong as a basketball net anchor.
- To weight the end of a rope that will be tossed over a high tree limb.

PACKS AND PACKING METHODS

Care of packs: Abrasion (dirt!) is the major enemy of the polyurethane coatings used to waterproof packsacks, so wash your packs with a good detergent at least once each camping season. Tree sap (pitch) may be removed with a small amount of cleaning fluid or gasoline. Don't overdo it though; harsh chemicals may dissolve waterproof coatings!

Allow packs to dry thoroughly before you store them. Wet canvas will mold and damp polyurethane coatings will mildew and peel.

Extending the closing flaps of packsacks: Some packsacks have closing flaps that are too short. The easiest way to extend them without cutting leather or nylon fittings is to sever the flap just behind the closing straps. Sew in a flap extension and reattach the severed piece.

To improve the abrasion resistance of a soft pack, install a double bottom of the same or heavier fabric. An upholstery shop or shoemaker can do this for you quickly and inexpensively.

The bottom corners of packs are subject to considerable abrasion. An early (and still excellent) solution was to crown them with glove leather. You can sew small pieces of lightweight leather to abrasion-prone spots or simply paint these areas with epoxy resin. Epoxy will stiffen the fabric and make it virtually tearproof. Use epoxy to stabilize frayed threads and small holes that are awkward to patch with a sewing machine.

How to pack a soft pack: Now that nearly all packs have internal or external frames, many campers discount the importance of proper packing. This is unfortunate, for any pack—and your back— will benefit by doing it right. Here's the proper procedure:

1. Set the pack on its back. Insert along its length all the soft items that won't gouge your back.
2. Weight should be kept as high as possible. Pack lightweight gear (except

crushables) on the bottom; heavyweight items go on top.

3. For ease of identification and speed of packing, everything should be stored in nylon bags. For example, I commonly keep my extra clothing in a lobster red nylon stuff sack. My lightweight camp mocs go in an orange bag, stove in a yellow bag, repair kit in a zippered canvas case, rain gear in a powder blue sack, etc. The nylon material of stuff sacks may be waterproof, but the stitching

Figure P-1. Tent pole bag secured beneath modern packsack flap.

and mouth of the bags are not. So don't depend on waterproof nylon bags to rainproof your outfit. Instead, line your pack (in summer or winter) with a plastic bag and waterproof important items by the double-bag sandwich treatment outlined below under "reliable waterproofing."

4. Most tents have poles that are too long to fit the confines of a packsack. Consequently, tents and poles should be packed separately, as follows:

a) Stuff your tent (don't roll it—rolling takes too much time and identically creases the fabric) into its nylon tent bag. Pack poles and stakes into a special heavy-duty pole bag with drawstring closure. Sew a loop of nylon webbing to each end of the bag and attach lengths of parachute cord to the loops.

b) Place your stuffed tent inside your pack and set the pole bag horizontally under the pack flap (figure P-1). Snake the closing straps of the pack through loops in the cord end. Now your poles can't possibly fall out of your pack!

Reliable waterproofing: Most camping technique books recommend that you waterproof your gear by placing it inside a nylon stuff sack (or pack) that has been lined with one or two plastic garbage bags. If you've ever tried this procedure, you know what happens—the thin plastic liner destructs within a few uses. Of course, you can always carry along "a few" extra plastic bags. . . .

Here's a better way—one that won't fail three days into your camping trip:

1. Stuff your sleeping bag, clothing, or other articles into a nylon sack (an abrasion liner), which need not be waterproof.
2. Place this sack inside an absolutely watertight plastic bag. Twist, fold over, and secure the mouth of the plastic bag with a loop of shock cord.
3. Set this unit inside a second nylon bag, which need not be watertight. Your articles are now completely protected against rain and a canoe capsize. Note that the delicate plastic liner is sandwiched between two layers of tough nylon, out of contact with abrasive materials. Use this sandwich-bag method to pack everything you must keep dry. This is the best way to protect a sleeping bag that rides obtrusively on the outside frame of a backpack.

Hip belt and tumpline: Most backpackers know the advantages of a hip belt, but few appreciate the worth of a tumpline. A tumpline consists of a wide leather or fabric strap that is secured to the "ears" (sides of the pack at shoulder level) of a packsack. The packer places this strap just above her forehead, grabs the tumpline near her head, leans forward, and trucks confidently down the trail. The early voyageurs carried hundreds of pounds of furs by this method; packers in undeveloped countries still rely on this system.

Tumplines are most useful when ascending steep hills, as they take considerable weight off the pack straps. To make a tump strap for your pack, simply sew a D ring to each side of your pack at shoulder height or below, and mount the tumpline across them.

Tip: Place awkward bundles like day packs, fishing rods, and canoe paddles under the tump strap in the hollow of your back, as illustrated in figure P-2. When your neck and head begin to ache, cast

Figure P-2. Packing with a tumpline.

off the tumpline and shift the load to the shoulder straps. Change back to the head strap when the pain is gone.

Pack pockets: Sew up some small envelope-style pockets and attach them to the outside of your pack with heavy-duty glove snaps or Velcro strips. These pack pockets will add versatility to your hiking outfit. If you attach mating strips of Velcro to the inner walls of your tent, sidewalls, or thwarts of your canoe or boat, etc., your pack pockets can be quickly remounted to provide added convenience.

Pack padding (figure P-3): You can soften the back of any pack by inserting a closed-cell foam sleeping pad inside. Just

Figure P-3. You can soften the back of any pack by inserting a closed-cell foam sleeping pad inside.

slip the rolled mat into the pack and let it unroll against the sides. Hard objects, like stoves and saws, won't gouge your back, and foods and beverages will stay cool in the midday sun. The pack will stand upright by itself, which will make it easier to pack.

PILLOW

Everything should be multipurpose on a backcountry camping trip, even your pillow. A practical pillowcase can be made from a lightweight terry cloth towel. Fold the towel lengthwise and sew up the two long sides. Set a Velcro tab or snap in the open end. Stuff your down or polyester vest into the pillow case. Add more clothes if you want more thickness. Terry cloth breathes and it won't slide on the slick floor of your tent. You can use your pillowcase as an emergency sponge, bathing towel, dirty clothes bag, or stuff sack. One friend made a luxurious polyester pile pillowcase and sized it to fit his head so he would have an extra hat!

RAIN GEAR

Rain gear has become quite stylish. Some parkas now feature hoods with integral bills that turn with your head, underarm zippers for better ventilation, drip-proof pockets, waist and hem cords, and much more. These niceties are nice, of course, but they won't keep you dry. What will is a sensibly designed garment that is constructed of genuinely waterproof material.

Fabrics: There are those that work and those that don't. Some work sometimes. And the difference between fabrics is not necessarily a function of price. In fact, some of the best (most watertight, that is) rainwear costs less than some of the worst!

If you want reliable rain gear at a reasonable price, see what the professionals are wearing. Foresters, wildlife management people, and construction workers all require tough garments that are absolutely waterproof. Rain garments like these are available at every industrial supply store. The new industrial rain suits are constructed of fabrics that are similar or identical to those used on the best foul-weather sailing suits. But because there are no pockets, no underarm zippers, and often no hoods to boost the price, the cost is much less.

Until recently I was convinced that a bulky foul-weather sailing suit was the best protection one could buy for camping in prolonged rain. Every lightweight suit I'd tried failed minutes into a major storm. Still, I yearned for something lighter and more compact. So I tried an experiment: I replaced the bulky sailing jacket with *two* lightweight, unlined Gore-Tex raincoats. Together they were much lighter and more compact than my killer raincoat.

Jacket 1 goes on at the first sign of rain. If the storm picks up, I add jacket 2, which slips easily over the first. Water that gets past the first jacket is stopped by the second. I stay dry in any rain. And I have two quick-drying garments that can be worn alone or layered for warmth. If I'm canoeing, I wear one raincoat under my PFD (portable flotation device) and one over it. This encourages ventilation and discourages condensation—and my PFD stays dry.

Gore-Tex is relatively cool and comfortable. It breathes under most conditions, even on hot muggy days. Modern Gore-Tex rainwear is quite reliable, even in showers that last for days. Leaks are usually due to bad design, not to failure of the Gore-Tex substrate. Pay particular attention to the closures at the wrist, neck, and waist. Zippers should be covered with double-overlapping flaps to seal out blowing rain, and double cuffs help stop dribbles. Slash pockets *must* have protective rain flaps or they'll become ponds. And beware of armpit zippers; I haven't found one yet that doesn't leak in hard rains!

Naturally, heavy-duty two-ply construction is more rugged, reliable, and expensive than lightweight single-ply construction. You can buy several conventional rain parkas for the price of a good Gore-Tex one—something to consider if cost counts.

Style: Whether you hike, canoe, motorcycle, backpack, or sail, you'll be happiest with a generously sized two-piece rain suit. Ponchos provide inadequate protection and may be dangerous in a boat upset. Below-the-knee rain shirts are ideal for casual fishing and auto camping but are otherwise impractical.

You'll put on and remove rain gear frequently between showers, so select garments that are easy to slip on and off. Pants that have an elastic or corded waistband are much more versatile than those with bibs.

Tip: Remove the elastic waistband of rain pants and substitute a fabric cord and cord lock. Elastic loses its strength in time, and rain pants will fall down. A cord provides quick, positive adjustments.

Avoid pants with snaps or Velcro tabs at the bottom. These restrict ventilation. Besides, primitive man learned long ago that water doesn't flow uphill! Ankle closures are only useful for mountaineering above the timberline.

Pant legs should be oversize so you can easily slip them on over heavy trousers or boots. Some expensive rain pants feature baffled zippers at the ankles. Straight-cut pant legs go over boots just as easily and are less costly to manufacture. Zippers eventually gum up with debris and fail—they're just another gimmick to drive up costs.

Tip: If you want to learn all there is to know about good rain gear, check out the best foul-weather sailing suits. The only frills you'll see on these garments are ones that work. Now compare your observations to rain garments in camping shops!

Jacket fit: Buy your rain parka a full size larger than you think you need, large enough so you can wear several layers of clothes beneath. Rain gear that looks trim in the store will be hot and restrictive in the field.

Color: Color is a personal choice, though navy blue garments outsell all others by a wide margin. And that's unfortunate, for this color attracts mosquitoes, which invariably come out between showers!

Hoods: A traditionally styled sou'wester hat is much more functional than a restrictive hood. However, if you select a hooded parka, be sure the zipper comes right to your nose. Those that stop at the chin must have a throat strap to seal off the neck area or they'll admit cold air and rain.

Pockets, seams, and zippers: Two covered pockets are more than enough in any rain jacket. Additional pockets add weight, bulk, and cost and threaten the integrity of the waterproof construction. The fewer the seams in any rain garment, the more watertight it will be. Except to close the front of a jacket, the value of zippers is overrated. Underarm zippers (which are added for ventilation) keep out rain only if you don't raise your arms. And zippered flies in rain pants usually leak within a few seconds.

Waterproofing standards: The U.S. Army requires a garment to withstand a minimum of twenty-five pounds per square inch (PSI) water pressure in order to earn the title of waterproof. At first thought, this industry-accepted minimum seems adequate, that is until you realize a person may exert that much pressure (or more!) simply by sitting on the edge of a boat seat. Kneel down or plant your elbows firmly in the duff and you may experience similar results. In all likelihood, minimally rated rainwear will not keep you dry!

Good rain clothes will withstand two or three times the amount of water pressure specified by the military, but even this may not be enough for strenuous field use. Then there's the matter of abrasion. Every time you put on or take off your rain parka, or move while wearing it, a microthin layer of waterproof chemical is scraped off the fabric. In time, leaks develop.

One answer to the abrasion problem is to sew a liner into the garment. But liners add weight, cost, and bulk. They also absorb sweat and are slow to dry. A better solution is to insist on a fabric with a minimum 100 PSI waterproof coating. And for really severe applications (like foul-weather sailing), you may want to consider the merits of a fabric that boasts a 150 PSI (or greater) rating.

Unfortunately, manufacturers of rainwear do not usually advertise the PSI ratings of their products. For comparison: A Kenyon Industries light polyurethane coating (Light K-Kote, as specified on the garment label) will average 25 to 50 PSI on the Mullen hydrostatic test, which is used to determine waterproofness of fabrics. But a Super K-Kote (double) treatment will run 100 PSI or more, which makes it suitable for all but the meanest applications.

Tip: You'll increase the effectiveness of your rain gear if you double the thickness of abrasion-prone areas—knees, elbows, and especially the seat. All you need is a sewing machine and some matching fabric. And don't forget to seal the seams you've sewn!

Rain gear for children: See the section CHILDREN, page 52.

When not to wear rain gear: Some authorities suggest you eliminate a windbreaker from your clothing list and instead rely on your rain parka for wind protection. Frankly, I think this is bad advice. Every time you lean against a tree or scrape a rock, abrasion takes its toll. In no time leaks develop. If you want your rain gear to last more than a season or two, use it only for its intended purpose and switch to a wind shell when the need arises.

Tip: If you wear your raincoat over your nylon wind shell, you'll reduce abrasion to the waterproof inner coating (the shell acts as a liner). Twin jackets will also keep you warmer and drier than a single waterproof garment.

What to wear under rain gear: Don't wear cotton! It absorbs perspiration and supercools the body. Since perspiration cannot escape through a waterproof covering, a wet, clammy feeling is guaranteed.

If you wear a pure wool shirt over a wool, polyester, or polypropylene undershirt, you'll stay dry—or at least comfortably dry.

Tip: Store rain clothes in a nylon stuff sack between uses. This will keep them clean and eliminate the abrasion that results from stuffing clothing into packs.

Care and repair of rain gear: Hand wash in detergent. Air-dry thoroughly before storing. Store rain gear on hangers so air will circulate. Don't keep these items in confining stuff sacks—polyurethane coatings will mildew!

Patch holes and tears with matching material. One way to get matching fabric is to cut up the stuff sack that came with the garment. Be sure to seal the seams you sew.

Thrifty Outfitters in Minneapolis (www.thriftyoutfitters.com; see appendix B) is one of the few certified Gore-Tex repair facilities in the country. If Thrifty can't fix it, no one can!

ROPES AND ROPE TRICKS

To most campers, a rope is a rope, and they make no distinction between manila, polypropylene, Dacron, and nylon. That's too bad, because different rope materials and weaves excel in different applications. What works best as waterski towline is completely inappropriate for rigging a rain fly. Here are three points to consider when choosing ropes:

1. *Flexibility:* Flexible ropes accept knots more willingly than stiffer weaves but are more likely to snag in their own coils. Choose flexible ropes for tying canoes on cars and for any place a proper lashing is essential. Stiff ropes are best for throwing lines (lifesaving), boat mooring and tracking lines, and general use around water.

2. *Slipperiness:* A slippery rope is always a nuisance. Some ropes, notably those made from polypropylene, are so slippery that they will not retain knots.

3. *Diameter versus strength:* Modern synthetic lines are very strong. Even ⅛-inch-diameter parachute cord has more breaking strength than you will probably ever need. However, large-diameter ropes are easier to handle and less likely to snag than small-diameter ones. Quarter-inch-diameter rope is about minimal for heavy-duty camping applications. One-eighth-inch-diameter parachute cords are the recommended camp utility cord.

Note: There are several grades of parachute cord. Avoid the cheap stuff that's commonly sold at hardware stores.

Types of Rope

Nylon: This is the most popular fiber for utility rope, and for good reason. It's strong, light, immune to rot, and inexpensive. On the negative side, it stretches considerably when wet and shrinks when dry. This makes it a bad choice for mooring boats, for canoe-tracking lines, and anywhere you need a rope that won't change dimensions. Nylon also degrades in the sun. A nylon rope may lose half or more of its strength in a single season if it's continually exposed to the weather.

The two most common weaves are the three-strand braided and the sheathed core. Braided rope is very soft and flexible but it cannot be flame whipped after it's cut. The ends of nylon and polypropylene ropes are usually sealed after cutting by melting them in the flame of a cigarette lighter. Three-strand braided rope simply unravels when heat is applied. It must be whipped the traditional navy way by winding the ends with waxed string or by dipping them in plastic whipping compound (available at marinas).

Sheathed nylon ropes (there are many variations) feature a central core surrounded by a woven nylon sheath. This construction is slightly less flexible than the braided type but is pliant enough for camp use. Sheathed ropes flame whip easily and do not unravel. Quarter-inch-diameter stock is ideal for rigging clotheslines, tying gear on cars and trailers, and other utility applications.

Polypropylene: The choice lies between round, three-strand stiff-braided line and the cheap flat-woven stuff sold in hardware stores. It's no contest; the stiffer line excels in every category. Sailors prefer polypropylene to nylon because it floats and it doesn't stretch when wet. It also comes in bright colors.

Ropes for mountaineering: Some types of mountaineering rope make excellent utility line. The choice lies between the three-strand hard lay construction or the kernmantle type (a core of braided or twisted strands, the kern, is covered by a protective braided sheath, the mantle). Three-strand rope is much cheaper than kernmantle, and it has a stiffer hand, which makes it ideal for lining canoes, mooring boats, and anywhere you need a snag-free rope that won't fail.

Dacron line is the material for sailboat sheet and mooring lines. It's wonderfully strong, beautifully soft, and frightfully expensive. If you're a sailor you know all about Dacron line. Advantages of Dacron over nylon include 1) very little wetstretch/dry shrinkage and 2) immunity to the degrading effects of sunlight—a feature important on boats exposed to the weather.

Manila and hemp have almost gone the way of the passenger pigeon. These natural-fiber ropes (manila is far superior to hemp!) have a nice hand; they coil beautifully, offer a textured grip, and even smell nice, but they rot easily and for their weight aren't very strong. I can think of no reason to use natural-fiber ropes when better synthetics are available for about the same price.

Tip: Abrasion is the major enemy of rope, so occasionally wash your ropes with detergent to remove ground-in grime. You'll prolong the life of your ropes considerably.

Coiling Tricks

Nylon utility ropes are best coiled and bound by the old navy method, indicated by the four steps discussed below:

Figure R-1. Coiling a rope— old navy method. Step 1: Coil the rope and hang it from your thumb.

Figure R-2. Step 2: Pinch the waist and coil the free end around it.

Figure R-3. Step 3: Make a loop and insert it through the eye of the coils.

Figure R-4. Step 4: Snug the collar. Note the handy loop for hanging.

1. Coil the rope and put your thumb through the coils to hold them in place. Leave about 3 feet of rope uncoiled (figure R-1).

2. Grasp the rope in one hand and pinch it at the waist to form an "eye." Coil the free end (tail) around the rope and upward toward the eye. Overlap the first coil to lock it in place. Wind evenly and tightly (figure R-2).

3. Form a loop near the end of the tail and pass it through the eye (figure R-3).

4. Grasp the collar (wound coils) in one hand and the rope body in the other. Slide the collar up to the rope to lock the loop in place. (It may be easier to hold the collar firmly in one hand and pull downward on the body of the rope.) The rope is now secured; a pull on the tail will release it (figure R-4).

The Throwing Coil: Use this method for large-diameter ropes and throwing lines. The old sailing method is faster to wind and release, but the coils are more likely to snag when the line is tossed.

1. Coil the rope carefully, taking care to rotate your coiling hand downward so as to give each coil a half turn before you lay it in place. The half turn keeps the strands of the rope aligned and prevents the coils from twisting. It is the secret to coiling a rope so it won't snag when you throw it.

2. Wind the tail tightly around the coiled rope. Overlap the first winding to lock it in place.

3. Make a loop near the tail and work it under your last winding. Pull the loop to tighten the winding. A pull on the tail will release the rope.

You can carry the coiled rope over your shoulder, hang it on a nail or cleat, or secure it around a rod or canoe thwart as illustrated in part d of figure R-5.

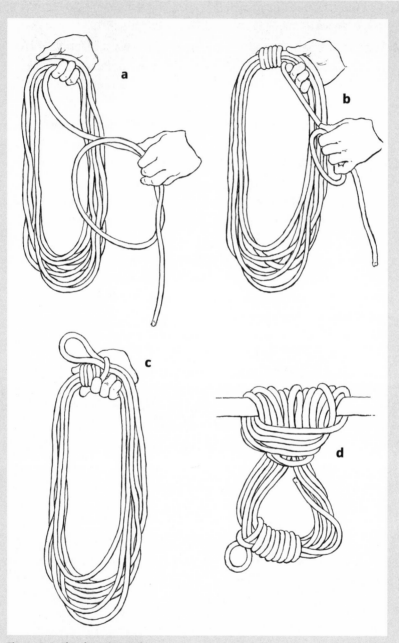

Figure R-5. The throwing coil.

S

SAW (FOLDING)

A folding saw is one of your most useful camp tools. On a rainy day you may be unable to get a fire going without one! Triangular metal saws are flimsy and they won't cut big logs. The best camp saw I've seen is a full-stroke rectangular model called the Fast Bucksaw (www.fastbucksaw.com; see appendix B). It's constructed of hard maple and has an easily replaceable 21-inch blade (refills are available from the manufacturer or at any hardware store). When assembled, it's so rigid you'd swear it was a one-piece model.

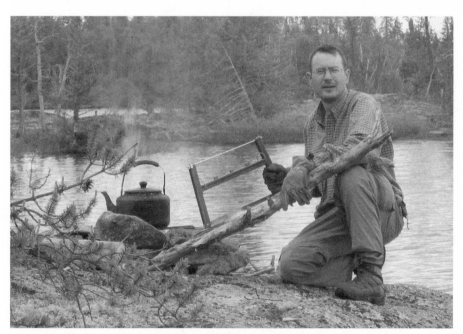

Figure S-1. The Fast Bucksaw is the best folding camp saw I've found.

If you want to go light and can get by with a less-efficient saw, I recommend the ten-ounce all-aluminum Sawvivor, which assembles in seconds. It comes in 15- and 18-inch blade lengths. (Visit www.trailblazerproducts .com; see appendix B.) For an ultracompact saw, choose one of the many jackknife pruning styles available at camp shops and garden centers.

Some saw thoughts:

- Long blades are more efficient than short ones.
- Lightweight saws feel great when you pick them up, but they lack the heft to run easily through wood.
- The more space between the blade and the frame, the larger the diameter of the logs you can saw.
- A folding saw that assembles fast is a blessing.

Saw blades: Some saw blades have rakers, others don't (figure S-2). Rakers don't cut—they just remove resinous sawdust that becomes trapped in the saw kerf. You need more rakers to cut green softwood than to cut green hardwood, and you need no rakers at all (for example, a carpenter's saw) if the wood is dead and dry and nonresinous. A blade that

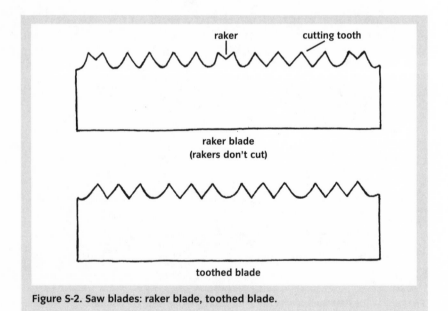

Figure S-2. Saw blades: raker blade, toothed blade.

has one raker for every four teeth (fairly standard on a multipurpose blade) will lose 20 percent of its cutting efficiency. You don't need rakers on a camp saw that is used to cut dead, dry wood. Indeed, cutting green wood in most campsites is a crime! But rakers look cool, so saw makers offer them. The good news is that you can buy rakerless replacement blades at most hardware stores.

Tips: Keep your folded saw in a fabric bag with drawstring closure. This will keep the parts cleaner and speed assembly time. Occasionally wipe tree sap from saw blades with a rag dipped in gasoline, alcohol, or WD-40. This will improve cutting efficiency and keep the blade from rusting.

SHOVEL

A ¾-inch-diameter, footlong aluminum tube, flattened at one end, makes an ideal camp shovel. Use it for burying fire remains, fish viscera, and human wastes where proper disposal facilities do not exist. (See ETHICS, page 81, for the proper way to dispose of wastes in the backcountry.)

SHOWER

You can make an effective portable shower by attaching a light plastic hose and showerhead to a folding plastic water jug. Use a long hose and drive the system with foot pressure. If stove fuel or wood (to heat water) is in short supply, consider bringing along a commercial Sun Shower, which is similar to the above system except for its special heat absorbing fabric. Sun Showers can be purchased at most camp shops and marinas. They are quite popular with yachtsmen.

SIGNAL GEAR

Only those who are going in harm's way really need signal gear (figure 5-3). A minimal kit would include a whistle, signal mirror, fire starters, and maybe a few orange smoke distress signals (available at marinas). Naturally, you should include a cell phone if you have coverage. Flares are valuable on water but are very dangerous on land—they can start a forest fire!

A more advanced kit might include the following:

Satellite phone: Iridium and Globalstar are the major companies that

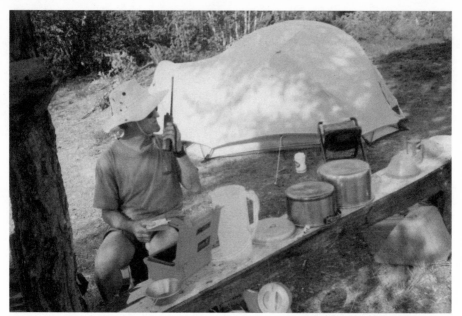
Figure S-3. Signal gear is essential if you're going in harm's way. Here Cliff is talking to a bush pilot on his VHF aircraft radio. Along the MacFarland River, northern Saskatchewan.

serve civilians. Iridium has complete world coverage; Globalstar has some blackout zones. If you're going where help is an airplane ride away, a satellite phone is the best protection you can buy. Satellite phones operate just like regular phones, except that calls must be dialed in international mode. In the United States and Canada, you dial 001, followed by the area code and number.

VHF aircraft transceiver: Even on remote trips it's not uncommon to see an airplane every day. Any plane you can see is probably within 10 miles of you—close enough to be reached on a handheld VHF aircraft transceiver. The typical VHF transceiver has a 15-mile range—enough for about eight minutes of talk time at propeller plane speeds, or less than a minute for jets.

In a life-threatening situation, you may broadcast on the restricted emergency frequency (121.5 megahertz). But for other concerns you must stick with the frequencies that are assigned to local companies. Be aware that transmitting without an FCC license isn't strictly legal! In the bush, however—and given the short range of handheld transceivers—everyone looks the other way.

VHF marine radio: Looks and works just like an aircraft model but operates at a lower frequency. Boats on the coasts and Great Lakes all have them. Channel 16 is the emergency channel.

CB radio: People in Alaska and the Canadian north converse mostly on CB radios. Most power boats have them. Channel 9 is reserved for emergencies.

PLB (personal locator beacon): A PLB emits a distress signal that allows rescue personnel to hone in on you. Some units use a GPS chip to provide precise positioning. A PLB is strictly a signaling device—you can't talk or receive messages on it.

The best bang for the buck is probably a satellite phone and a GPS. With these you can report your problem and your GPS location coordinates. And you can obtain on-the-spot medical advice. Don't know whom to call? Just dial 911!

SKIS (CROSS-COUNTRY)

Under certain conditions, the surface of cross-country skis will load up with crusty snow and impede performance. To prevent this ice buildup, occasionally apply a paste wax to the top of your skis.

SLEEPING BAGS

This is your most important item. With care, a good sleeping bag will last half a lifetime, even with almost regular use. Serious backcountry travelers choose from these popular sleeping-bag fills: goose and duck down, Polarguard, Quallofil, Hollofil II, and Primaloft (a downlike synthetic). Any of these products will serve you well if they're properly sewn into a well-constructed bag.

Principles of Sleeping-bag Design

1. The smaller the bag, the less area it will have to insulate. Translation: Confining mummy bags are much warmer for their weight than roomy rectangular ones.

2. Most heat loss from a sleeping bag occurs through the open head end. It's nearly impossible to seal the open end of a rectangular-style sleeping bag so that warm air won't escape. (One solution is to install a collar—

see figure C-9 for details.) For this reason integral hoods are mandatory on sleeping bags that will be used for cold-weather camping.

Tip: An effective makeshift collar can be tailored from a sweater or scarf. Drape the garment across your chest and bunch the fabric around your neck and shoulders. This will eliminate drafts and increase warmth.

3. Inexpensive mummy-style sleeping bags and all rectangular models are built with a flat foot, which means the material is simply folded in half at the foot end and a zipper is installed around the edge (as in a typical station-wagon sleeping bag). A boxed-foot design, though more costly to manufacture, is much more comfortable. Here, a foot-high circular panel is sewn in at the bottom (like the end of a tin can), which allows you to maintain a comfortable toes-up position without bearing against tight material.

4. A full-length zipper running from foot to chin is a must. Bags with half-length zippers become impossibly hot in warm weather.

Categories

Down and synthetic sleeping bags are generally categorized as:

- *Summer weight*—comfortable in temperatures to freezing.
- *Three season*—warm to about 10 to 15 degrees Fahrenheit.
- *Winter*—good to 20 below zero or more. There are some special arctic bags that go much lower than that.

Note: "Comfort ratings" are speculative. Few sleeping bags are as warm as their manufacturers suggest.

Which Sleeping Bag for You?

Most people select three-season models, thinking they represent the greatest value of the money. Wrong! The typical three-season sleeping bag becomes too warm when temperatures rise above 50 degrees Fahrenheit, which means they are next to worthless for average summer use.

Only if you do considerable primitive camping in the spring and fall should you buy a three-season bag. Otherwise, a lighter, less-costly summer bag will be a better buy. Tent temperatures commonly run about 10 degrees warmer than the outside environment, so a good summer bag will keep you toasty well below freezing. In really cold weather, you can mate your summer bag with an outer or inner liner or with a blanket.

Which is best, down or synthetics? Down bags are lighter, warmer, more compact, and have a more "gentle hand" than any of the synthetics. If you've ever slept under a down comforter, you know what I mean. Good down is also much more resilient and long-lived than synthetics. For an equivalent weight of fill, down has a lower and wider temperature comfort range. This means down will keep you warmer when it's cold, and cooler when it's warm, than will a synthetic.

For example: Consider two three-season sleeping bags, one down, one Polarguard or Quallofil. Both bags are rated to 10 degrees Fahrenheit. The finished weight of the down bag will be at least a pound less than either synthetic and it will compact into a much smaller space. The synthetic bag will become too warm when the temperature reaches 50 degrees Fahrenheit, while the down bag will remain quite comfortable even at 60 degrees.

However, good down sleeping bags are more expensive than equivalently rated synthetic ones, and you can't beat them around as much. Wet down is almost impossible to dry under typical field conditions. Because down is a natural fiber, it absorbs body moisture, which in damp winter conditions can be a serious problem. For this reason, experienced winter hikers usually select synthetic-fill sleeping bags.

Question: If down dries so slowly, shouldn't we eliminate it from consideration for summer use too? Absolutely not! If you sandwich pack your sleeping bag as I recommend in the PACKS AND PACKING METHODS section (page 136) and stormproof your tent accordingly (see page 206), you will never get your bedding wet. I guarantee it!

Buy what you can afford; but whatever you buy, make sure it has a hood to keep your head warm, a full-length two-way zipper to keep your feet cool, and a temperature range that matches the environment in which you'll camp. If you choose a mummy bag—and most experienced campers do—try it in the store before you buy it. Mummy bags come in different lengths and girths; some are quite restrictive while others are surprisingly roomy. If a bag feels tight in the store, you won't like it in the field.

Winter sleeping bags are more generously sized than summer ones to allow dressing space inside. Winter campers usually take their clothing and canteens to bed so they need space for all these "rummage sale" items. The typical polyester-fill winter bag weighs five pounds or more. Summer-weight bags may weigh half that.

Packing the sleeping bag: Sleeping bags (discounting station-wagon types) should be stuffed, not rolled. Zippers should be closed to prevent galling of the material. Just grab the foot end of the bag and stuff it, handful by handful, into its nylon sack. This is easier on the fabric and fill than traditional rolling.

Do not store sleeping bags in stuff sacks; you'll wear out the filler in no time. Instead, keep sleeping bags in a breathable cotton sack (a pillowcase works fine) or store them flat or on hangers.

When to Clean Your Sleeping Bag

Once every year or two is often enough, even if you use your bag a lot. A down bag will lose some loft and resiliency with the first washing. Additional washings seem to have no adverse effect.

Some campers never wash their sleeping bags; they believe that washing will ruin them. But body oils and dirt will accumulate and the insulative value of the bag will decrease accordingly. It's a catch-22. My advice? Keep your bag as clean as possible and wash it carefully when the occasion demands.

How to Clean Your Down Sleeping Bag

Hand washing is the best way to clean any down-filled item. Nonetheless, manufacturers usually recommend dry cleaning on down product labels simply because so many down items have been ruined by improper machine washing. Make no mistake: Dry cleaning with powerful perchlorethylene solvents will reduce the loft and warmth of a down bag. But it will not destroy it. Improper washing will! Here's the recommended procedure for hand washing:

1. You'll need a huge basin to wash your sleeping bag. A bathtub is ideal.
2. Use lukewarm water and any mild soap. I've had good luck with Woolite, Ivory Snow, Ivory Liquid, Basic-H, and other liquid dishwashing detergents. There are also some special down soaps that may or may not be worth their high price.

3. Place the sleeping bag into the soap solution and sponge the shell thoroughly. Rub gently at stubborn spots. Do not use Spray 'n Wash or stain removers! The shells of sleeping bags are tightly woven to contain the down, so it may require many hours for wash water to work through them.

    Allow the bag to soak in the wash water for an hour or so, then squish the bag gently with wide-spread hands. Carefully work wash water well into the down. A couple hours of additional soaking and frequent "squishing" should remove most of the dirt.

4. To rinse the bag, drain the tub and gently press soapy water out of the article with both hands, fingers spread wide. Don't lift or wring out the article. A water-filled sleeping bag is very heavy, and the delicate baffles may tear if you roughhouse the project.

    A minimum of two rinse cycles is recommended. You absolutely must get all the soap out or the down will mat when it dries.

5. Gently place the thoroughly rinsed sleeping bag into a large plastic clothes basket for ease of handling. Now, it's off to your Laundromat with several dollars of change in hand.

6. Place the incompletely rinsed bag into an extractor (a high-speed centrifuge) and spin out the remaining water. If your Laundromat does not have one of these machines, a large washing machine set on spin dry will work. One pass through the extractor machine or two passes through the washing machine will safely exhaust nearly all the water.

7. Next, place the bag in a large commercial clothes dryer set on very low heat. Be sure the dryer puts out low heat! If it does not, run it with the door ajar (jam a magazine through the door hinge over the safety button so the machine will continue to run) to bleed heat. Check the progress of the bag every ten minutes.

    Some people place a terry-cloth towel into the dryer to absorb the static electricity. This seems to speed drying.

It will take you a full day to wash your sleeping bag!

Warning: Do not attempt to dry a sleeping bag in family-sized clothes dryers. The heat is concentrated over too small an area. You may, however, safely spin dry your sleeping bag in your home washing machine if a commercial extractor is not available.

How to Wash Polyester-Fill Sleeping Bags

Polyester-fill sleeping bags and garments cannot be dry-cleaned. The cleaning fluid will destroy the fill. These garments are best hand washed in the same manner as down bags. Yes, you can machine wash them successfully. However, most sleeping bags are too large to be safely washed in family-size washing machines—some abrasion, stretching of stitches, etc., is sure to result. If you must machine wash your bag, use one of the large front-loading commercial machines. Even then, my vote goes to hand washing.

Polyester-fill jackets, vests, and other small items may be safely washed in most home machines (gentle cycle only). But, they must be dried with low (under 120 degrees Fahrenheit) heat—or better yet, no heat!

Dos and Don'ts for Sleeping Bags

Don't roll sleeping bags; stuff them.
Don't yank sleeping bags out of stuff sacks; pull gently.
Don't leave sleeping bags stuffed for long periods of time.
Don't machine wash down sleeping bags.
Don't dry-clean polyester-fill sleeping bags.
Don't wash down bags with harsh detergents.
Don't pick up a wet down product without adequately supporting it.
Do air and fluff sleeping bags after each use.
Do store sleeping bags flat, on hangers, or in large porous sacks.
Do sponge clean the shell of your sleeping bag occasionally.
Do wash your sleeping bag when it gets dirty.

Tip: You can get along surprisingly well in summer without a sleeping bag if you fold a blanket or two in the manner illustrated in figure C-8. You an also increase the warmth of any station-wagon–size sleeping bag by applying the procedures outlined in figure C-9.

SLEEPING PADS, AIR MATTRESSES, AND SLEEPING SYSTEMS

Toddlers and teenagers can get along quite nicely without a foam pad or air mattress, but these items are a must for most adults. In general, air mattresses are more comfortable than foam pads, but they are cold to sleep on and they frequently fail. For this reason, most expert campers choose open- or closed-cell foam pads over more traditional air mattresses.

Air mattresses: Except for car camping, the traditional single-valved air mattress is extinct. Such mattresses require too much time to inflate and deflate to be practical on backwoods trips. The most popular system of air mattress for self-propelled outdoors people is the type that features multiple, replaceable plastic tubes, each of which has its own inflation valve. These air pads are less comfortable than traditional types but are more easily repaired (you just remove the punctured vinyl tube and replace it with a new one).

Except in the heat of summer, air mattresses cannot be used with down sleeping bags. Body weight compresses down to near zero thickness, and air mattresses do not have sufficient insulation to make up for this loss. In fact, the circulating air in an air mattress simply moves the cold from place to place. Even thick polyester-fill sleeping bags (polyester doesn't compress as much as down) may get cold when the temperature drops below freezing.

Tip: Place a thin closed-cell foam pad on top of an air mattress for the ultimate in warmth and comfort.

Hybrid air mattresses: A few companies produce air mattresses that are insulated with goose down or polyester. These mats are light, extremely comfortable, and very warm. The bad news is that oral inflation introduces moisture that can freeze or at best reduce the warmth of the mat. A special pump (provided) eliminates these concerns. Inflation is slow and a puncture renders the mat useless. I would never rely on this system for trips beyond the beaten path.

Closed-cell foam pads: You can choose PVC (polyvinyl chloride), polyethylene, EVA (ethylvinyl acetate), or a number of mix 'n' match types. EVA is so superior to other closed-cell foams that it defies comparison. EVA is unaffected by sunlight, heat, and most solvents. It is almost immune to abrasion. It's expensive and worth it!

A ¼-inch-thick closed-cell foam pad will provide plenty of insulation for summer (but not much comfort). For winter, you'll need at least a ⅜-inch thickness, more for subzero temperatures. Closed-cell foam pads are immune to water and mild abrasion so it is not necessary to cover them with materials.

Open-cell foam pads: There are dozens of grades of open-cell polyurethane foam. Some foams are soft and cushy, others are highly supportive. There is a difference in price! Select the most supportive foam you can find (try pads in the store); avoid pads that bottom out when you roll over.

Open-cell foam is delicate; it must be covered, preferably with a porous fabric that will pass imperceptible perspiration. Avoid covers made of waterproof nylon; you'll awaken in a pool of sweat!

Don't worry about getting your open-cell foam pad wet. If you storm-proof your tent and pack as I suggest, you won't have problems with wet gear.

Air-filled foam pads: The Therm-a-Rest began the revolution, now there's lots of competition. Basically, these units consist of a low-density (soft and cushy) open-cell foam that's sealed in an envelope of vinyl and nylon. An oversize plastic valve controls the air flow. Open the valve and the pad inflates itself. Close the valve to lock in the air. The result is a comfortable, incredibly warm (suitable for subzero use), and surprisingly reliable mattress. I've been using Therm-a-Rest mats for thirty years and have had few problems. My latest Therm-a-Rest is more than ten years old and there are no signs of a leak.

Tip: Make a fabric cover (one side cotton, one side soft wool) for your air-filled foam pad. The cover will protect the pad from punctures and keep it from sliding on the slippery tent floor. Most important, the cover will absorb the imperceptible perspiration that becomes sweat against your back. On hot nights, keep the cotton side up; turn the wool side up when it's cold. When it's too hot for any cover, sleep with your bare skin against the cool cotton cover and use your sleeping bag as a blanket.

A crinkly "space blanket" (every discount store has them), placed silver side up under your sleeping pad, will increase the efficiency of your sleeping system.

If you find yourself sleeping on an uncomfortable incline, level out your sleeping system

You sleep
"on the level"

Figure S-4. Sleeping comfortably on an incline.

by placing folded clothes beneath your air mat or foam pad. You can make an intolerable sleeping situation quite bearable by this method.

Tip: If you are stuck with an inclined site, pitch your tent *perpendicular* to the drop (one side lower than the other), rather than parallel to it with the entrance high, as suggested in most camping books. It's easier to level a sunken side than a lowered end. Figure S-4 shows why.

SNOW GLASSES

Dark sunglasses are necessary to prevent snow blindness in dazzling white conditions. You can make an emergency pair by applying parallel strips of electrical or duct tape to the lenses of standard glasses. Leave a narrow horizontal slit to see through.

SNOW SHELTERS

It's a well-kept secret that winter camping is a whopping good time. After all, when it's 20 below, only fools and "them's that knows what they're about" are apt to be out there. Along with predictable solitude comes exquisite beauty and awesome silence. Camped on a pristine blanket of white, there are no footprints or garbage to muck up the view. Touch the crispness of dawn, hear the harsh stillness of night. Like those who lived here millennia ago, you are part of the land, not meaningless passersby. What was in summer is no more. Everything is covered by sterile white.

Getting around in 4-foot snowdrifts requires new technique. You shuffle along on snowshoes or glide on skis. Equipment is carried in special back-packs or on classic toboggans, polyethylene sleds, or fiberglass pulks. Fire building becomes an art as well as a lesson in tedium. First you establish a base of logs so flames won't sink into oblivion, then you split dry kindling from the heart of a snow-drenched log. A folding saw and ax and a good sharp knife are essential tools in the winter woods.

And if you go above the tree line, there are new challenges and equip-ment. Instead of fires there are gasoline and butane stoves, low-slung mountain tents with cook holes and tunnel doors; baffled parkas, bala-clavas, and face masks; vapor-barrier liners, tinted goggles, and frost cream. And when tents fail—or for those who just disdain them—there are snow caves and trenches, quinzees and igloos. To the uninitiated, "sleeping out" in the dead of winter flirts with death. To those of us who know and live by nature's rules, it's hyacinths for the soul.

Ask an experienced winter camper if he or she prefers unheated tents to snow houses and you'll get ten to one in favor of the huts. That's because unlike tents, snow structures are warm inside. Sometimes too warm. Everyone knows that snow is a great insulator, but you won't believe how good until you've crammed three people into a snow cave built for two. Add a candle or two for light and warmth and watch the thermometer rise. Keep a close eye on the mercury level, for when water starts dripping from the inner walls, you've got problems. Snow is porous but ice doesn't breathe. And if your home freezes solid inside, air won't get in. Overheating a snow house is a very real concern—one that newcomers to winter sport don't take seriously enough.

Warnings aside, snow huts are comfortable and eminently safe, and as every kid will attest, they are fun and easy to build. Here are some ideas to get you started:

Quinzee Hut

A quinzee is the white man's version of the traditional Eskimo igloo. It's made by piling up snow then digging out the center, rather than by carefully laying snow blocks. Quinzees are as warm, as strong, and as spacious as igloos but they take much longer to build. Compared to igloos, they are terribly ugly. An Eskimo snow house is a work of art; a quinzee retains the appearance of a schlocked-together snow pile (which is exactly what it is). Nonetheless, quinzees are practical for base camp travel in winter and as emergency-survival dwellings. Kids build them just for fun and occasionally someone makes news by carving a garage-size quinzee from a giant snowbank. Quinzees are similar to snow caves, which are also built from packed snow. Snow caves, however, are hollowed out from an existing packed drift, which is faster and simpler than piling snow. Both structures serve the same function—that of keeping you warm and dry regardless of the weather outside.

You don't need a thick layer of snow to build a quinzee. You can simply haul in what you need or scrape a thin surface layer of snow to provide sufficient building material.

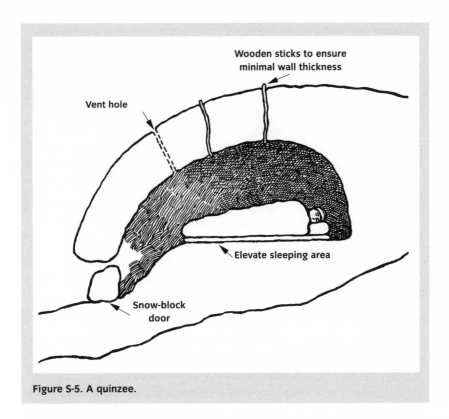

Figure S-5. A quinzee.

Building the Quinzee

1. First decide on the size. A 10- to 12-foot diameter is about right for two people. Most snow campers make their huts too small, so err on the large side. You can easily adjust the interior dimensions to a custom fit when you dig out the structure.

2. Pile up snow to a height of about 7 feet. This will provide comfortable sitting room inside for both occupants. You'll speed manufacture of the hut if you occasionally pack the snow pile with your shovel.

3. When the snow pile is complete, insert footlong sticks into the structure at approximate 18-inch intervals. "Porcupine" the hut with these sticks all around and on top. Don't stop until the quinzee resembles a medieval mace. These sticks provide a gauge by which you can judge the thickness of the walls when you dig out the center. It is essential to maintain a minimum 8-inch wall thickness. Without the "gauge," you'll

shovel right through the sidewalls, and once you've gone too far, repair is difficult.

4. If you want a tunnel entrance, now's the time to build it. Don't forget to porcupine the tunnel.

5. Now comes the hard part—finding something else to do for the next few hours. The structure needs time to settle, the snow must contract and harden. How long this takes depends on temperature, humidity, and age of the snow. If the snow is fresh and dry and it's very cold, the pile will take much longer to set. On warm days, the molecular change will occur much faster. Eight hours is usually enough time, regardless of the weather. Do not throw water on the hut to speed its cure; you'll wind up with an ice ball—one you can't dig out or breath inside of!

6. When the structure has hardened, prepare to dig. You'll need a small shovel and a friend. You'll get very wet from falling snow, so wear rain gear or highly water-repellent clothing. Dig out the tunnel entrance through to the center, passing carved snow to your partner outside. Now it's simply a matter of sculpting the interior to suit your fancy. Just remember to stop digging when you see the porcupine "hairs." You need to maintain an 8-inch minimum wall thickness! Do not remove the porcupine sticks from the structure; doing so will weaken the hut.

7. *Finishing the interior:* As everyone knows, warm air rises while cold air does the opposite. For this reason, you need to elevate the sleeping area a foot or so for additional warmth. While you're doing this you can also carve some "pockets" into the sidewalls, in which to place small items. Make a small shelf for your candle—a single candle will light the entire structure and raise its temperature considerably.

8. *Vent hole:* It's not absolutely essential to cut a vent hole in the roof, but it will make for a better exchange of air if you do. Simply punch a ski pole through the roof or pull out one of the porcupine sticks. Don't panic if the hole eventually fills with snow and closes. You'll get plenty of fresh air through the doorway, and the quinzee walls are porous.

9. *Doorway:* If you have a tunnel entrance to break the wind, you don't need a door. However, a snow block, angled across the entryway, will reduce heat loss without significantly affecting ventilation. Just be sure you don't close the snow-block door completely.

Tip: A length of nylon parachute cord makes an acceptable snow knife for cutting blocks. Just saw the cord back and forth through the snow until the block is free. This procedure will only work with "old snow," whose molecular structure has compacted.

Warning: The heat generated by two or three bodies in a small quinzee will easily maintain an interior hut temperature of 20 or more degrees Fahrenheit. In fact, temperature may rise above freezing if you're not careful. The danger is not in being too cold, it is in allowing the structure to overheat. If the temperature goes above freezing, the interior walls will melt and ice up, ventilation will cease, the structure will drip water, and you'll have an intolerable mess. So watch your thermometer—and your hut temperature—carefully.

Sleeping inside the Quinzee

As stated, interior temperatures are apt to maintain a balmy 20 degrees Fahrenheit even in subzero weather, so you don't need an arctic sleeping bag for comfort. Any three-season bag will do, providing you have plenty of insulation beneath you. You're sleeping on ice, remember?

Your first sleeping layer is a waterproof plastic ground sheet. Atop this place foam pads, carpeting, cardboard—anything that will insulate your body from the cold ground. If you have an open-cell-foam trail pad, a 2-inch thickness (or greater) will be required for comfort. A ⅝-inch-thick closed-cell foam pad may provide enough warmth. You need much more insulation below than on top!

Common fears: There are two. 1) "I'll die from carbon-monoxide poisoning," and 2) "The hut will collapse and smother me." Both concerns are unfounded. You'll get plenty of air through the entryway and vent hole, even in the unlikely event the quinzee freezes over. As to strength, there is no contest. Snow huts gain strength as they age. I doubt a polar bear could crush a week-old quinzee!

Tip: If you plan to use the shelter for several nights, chip away the ice buildup on the inner walls each day. This will maintain breathability of the structure.

Important: The entryway of a quinzee or snow cave should always be placed on the windward side of the structure. If wind-driven snow begins while you sleep, sufficient snow could pile up on the leeward side of the hut to seal a leeward entrance. This could be quite serious (deadly!) in a snow cave, especially in a blizzard. It's always wise to keep a small shovel in a snow hut, just in case you need to dig out in the morning.

One-Person Trench Shelter

You can use a nylon tarp in a variety of creative ways to construct a trench shelter. One plan is illustrated in figure S-6.

1. Make a snow pile 6 feet by 12 feet by 3 feet deep. Like the quinzee, let it set awhile before you begin the process of digging out. If you can find a snowdrift of these dimensions, you may begin digging immediately.
2. Dig a trench 9 feet long, 3 feet wide, and 2 feet deep. Make the entrance a foot lower than the sleeping platform so cold air will be drawn out of the structure.

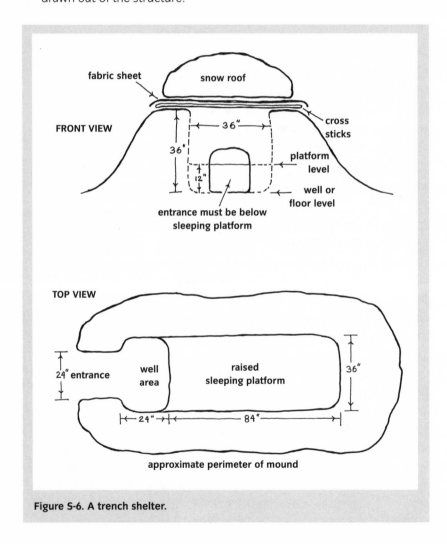

Figure S-6. A trench shelter.

3. Span the structure (side to side) with a couple dozen closely spaced sticks. Then set your tarp over the crossbars and cover it with an insulating layer of snow.

4. *Tip:* You won't need cross-sticks if you substitute two 7-foot-long aluminized space blankets for your nylon tarp. Merely overlap the cold-stiffened space blankets so they'll cover the 9-foot trench, then anchor the sides with snow. A real advantage of the space blankets over a conventional tarp is that they reflect much more warm rising air back to the sleeper below.

   Retrieving your tarp: If you leave snow on your tarp overnight, the snow will compact and make the tarp difficult to remove in the morning. One solution is to allow the snow to set for a few hours, then pull out the sticks and remove the tarp from inside the trench (better have smooth sticks or you'll tear the tarp). Expect some falling snow, but the roof should hold. Like a quinzee, the trench shelter will grow stronger with time.

Vaulted-Roof Snow Trench

If you have a snow knife (machete) and old snow, you can build a vaulted roof like that shown in figure S-7. Be sure to cut the blocks long enough so they'll butt at the peak. Fill cracks with loose snow.

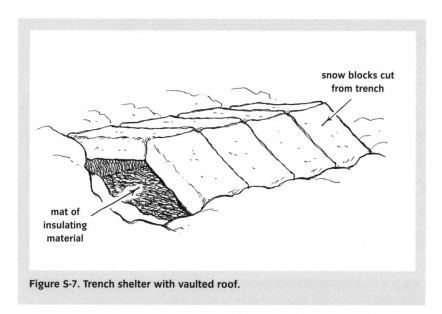

snow blocks cut
from trench

mat of
insulating
material

Figure S-7. Trench shelter with vaulted roof.

Sleeping on Snow

Sleeping on snow requires extra preparation. As mentioned, you need substantial insulation under your sleeping bag. Here are some other tricks that will add to your comfort:

- Place dry outer clothing in your sleeping bag before you retire. The clothes will absorb some of the bag's cold and reduce the size of the area your body must heat. Remove the clothing as the bag warms up.

- Wear long johns, a balaclava, and down or Polarguard booties to bed for extra warmth. *Don't* bring down parkas into your bag with you; they will absorb imperceptible perspiration and become damp. Use the parka as a pillow or as extra insulation to cover your feet.

- If you eat some high-energy food before you retire, your body will produce more heat as you sleep.

- Make a draft collar for your sleeping bag by placing a wool sweater or scarf across your chest and neck. Tuck the sweater sleeves around your shoulders to prevent air loss at the head of the bag.

- Don't cover your face with your sleeping bag if your nose gets cold. Your bag will not be able to eliminate the moisture from your breath. The moisture may even ice up on the outside—a dangerous situation! Instead, use a sweater or shirt as a face mask. You can easily breathe through this porous material.

- A midnight urination call at 20 below is no fun. Carry a special poly bottle for elimination. Women may want to try the proven Freshette device by Sani-fem, Inc.

- In winter your sleeping bag cannot easily dissipate all the moisture your body produces, so air out your bag in the sunlight for several minutes each day.

- A candle will raise the temperature of your tent or snow shelter by 10 or 20 degrees. *Reminder:* Batteries don't work well when they're cold, so insulate them until they are needed.

SNOWSHOES

For deep, open snow, select long, slender snowshoes with high-turned toes (the Alaskan or Pickerel style is best). Low-toed models plow deep under fluffy snow and double your work output.

For crusty snow or wooded areas, a small maneuverable shoe is best. My favorite "woods shoe" is the narrow cross-country model, which is basically a miniature version of the old Alaskan, though with a lower toe. The Sherpa bearpaw with its ingenious binding and integral traction device may be the best deep woods/mountain trail shoe of all. The common Michigan/Maine pattern is a good compromise style, though its low toe makes it a poor choice for fluffy snow. No one snowshoe will do everything well!

Snowshoe bindings: Leather bindings get wet and stretch; neoprene is much better. The standard Sherpa binding is among the most comfortable, rigid and easiest to use of all bindings. The Sherpa features a thick neoprene toe cup with stainless-steel hooks and wide nylon laces—and it goes on and off in seconds! All Sherpa brand shoes come standard with this unique binding, which can be purchased separately and installed on other shoes. You can even get special bindings that have quick-release straps and traction claws.

Plastic and aluminum snowshoes: Most of today's recreational snowshoes are made from aluminum and plastic. How do these perform when compared to traditional (and beautiful) wooden models? The answer is "better and worse." Synthetic shoes are better on groomed trails and in tight brush where speed and maneuverability are important—and their built-in claws are awesome on ice. They are also much lighter than wooden shoes, which makes them the clear choice for running or competition. Finally, they are maintenance free, something that can hardly be said for wood and rawhide.

There are downsides: The neoprene foot beds can load up with snow; you may get a painful "freezer burn" if you touch an aluminum frame with your bare hands in subzero weather; a broken neoprene lace may completely unravel; a cut rawhide lace won't retreat beyond the cut. Break an aluminum frame and you've got trouble. Broken wood can be pinned, spliced, and lashed—an easy field repair.

SOAPS

Backcountry soaps should be biodegradable and lather in cold water. They should also be highly concentrated for maximum efficiency. Bar soaps should not melt in the sun or crack in extreme cold. These are the traditional backwoods soaps:

- Kirk's Coco Hardwater Castile: Comes in bar form and lathers wonderfully in cold water. Very stable in heat and cold.
- Dr. Bronner's Peppermint Soap: The label provides hours of tireless entertainment. Surprisingly, a lot of the label's trivia is true. Dr. Bronner's formula works well for everything from washing dishes to hair. I've even used it for shaving and to brush my teeth. The nice peppermint smell is compelling. Every earth-friendly co-op and specialty store has it.
- A number of specialty liquid camp soaps are similar to Dr. Bronner's. One of my favorites is Huckleberry Finn's Peppermint Camp Soap, made by Sawyer Products. Sawyer also makes a delightful travel soap that is formulated with citronella (Citronella Travel Soap). It keeps mosquitoes away. Barely.
- N/R Laboratories No-Rinse shampoo and body bath (see appendix B) are among the most interesting products to come along in recent years. Just rub 'em in to create a rich lather, then strip off the floating dirt and oil with paper or cloth towels. No water—or only a very small amount of water—is necessary. For example, one ounce of the body bath in a quart of water is enough for a full sponge bath! No water is needed when you shampoo. There is no residue, so no need to rinse. No-Rinse cleaning products were first used on hospitalized patients who could not bathe normally. Now NASA's astronauts have discovered their merits. No-Rinse products are ideal for backpacking trips where clean water is hard to find.

SPONGE

A small sponge is one of the most useful and forgotten items on a camping trip. It will clean your tent floor, remove accumulated water from your canoe or boat, dissolve mud from your boots, mop up a tent leak, and more. A natural sponge is much more absorbent than the best synthetic.

STOOL (CAMP)

A camp stool is worth its weight and bulk on all but the lightest "go light" backpacking trips. Camp chores—cooking, washing dishes, sharpening edged tools, etc.—go easier when you don't sit on the ground. I most

Figure S-8. A folding stool is worth its weight on a camping trip. This one has a handy storage pouch and tube legs that won't sink into the ground. It folds flat and can be secured to a pack with a bungee cord.

appreciate my stool when I must wait out a storm under my rain tarp or endure a long tour of kitchen duty.

Friends scoffed when I first began to bring a camp stool on my wilderness canoe trips. Now they all follow suit. I've tried all manner of stool designs and have ultimately settled upon a simple collapsible model like those used at competitive shooting events. Be sure you get a stool that sits on two parallel aluminum rails. Avoid individual pointed legs that can sink into soft ground. My favorite camp stool weighs thirty ounces and has a canvas storage pouch beneath the seat. When not in use it folds flat and clips (with bungee cords) to my backpack.

STOVES

Camp stoves are pretty trouble free. Most will give a lifetime of good service if properly maintained. Here are some stove troubleshooting hints, priming tips, and maintenance dos and don'ts.

Troubleshooting

Problem: Flame sputters; stove won't reach normal operating temperatures.

a) Problem is likely due to dirt in the mechanism. Turn off the stove and pour about half the fuel out. Recap the tank and shake the stove vigorously for a few seconds to dislodge the clogged dirt particle. Then pour out the gas and refill the stove with fresh fuel. If this doesn't work, drain the stove and force high pressure air (from an air compressor) through the filler cap opening. If this fails, the stove must be disassembled and cleaned.

b) The safety valve, located in the filler cap, is damaged. Squirt a small amount of liquid detergent on and around the cap and look for air bubbles. If the valve is blown, replace the filler cap.

c) *Stove needs more pressure.* If additional pumping doesn't do the trick, check the leather washer on the pump stem. Lubricate the washer with oil or grease. Most new stoves have synthetic (plastic) pump washers that don't work as well as the old leather ones. Consider replacing a plastic washer with a leather one. Check the plumbing section of your hardware store. Some leather stool washers fit some stoves perfectly. *Note:* In subfreezing temperatures stoves must be insulated from the cold ground to maintain operating pressure.

d) *Check for improper fuel.* You cannot use lead-free automotive gasoline in white-gas stoves. Naphtha (Coleman fuel) is the cleanest burning of the stove fuels, and it is prefiltered.

e) *For Optimus/Svea stoves that don't have pumps:* The nipple may have become enlarged by improper cleaning (a bent cleaning needle will do it). The nipple (a low-cost item) must be replaced. Overpriming can burn the cotton wick and reduce its absorbent qualities. The remedy is to replace the wick—something that is best done by one who is familiar with the process.

Problem: Stove stays lit for about twenty seconds, then slowly goes out. Pumping it revives the flame.

Invariably this is the result of a slow leak in the tank-filler cap. Either the safety valve is blown or the silver solder around the filler neck has melted. Replace the pressure cap or resolder the neck.

Determine the exact location of the pressure leak by squirting liquid detergent around the pressure cap. If the safety valve checks out okay, the gasket in the filler cap is probably at fault. Replace the age-hardened gasket with a new one.

Problem: Butane (or butane-propane mix) trail stove loses pressure after it has run a while.

The burners of early butane stoves were mounted on top of their fuel canisters—the cooking pot reflected heat on to the canister below and kept it warm (and pressurized). The plus to this design was improved cold-weather performance; the minus was that an oversize pot could radiate enough heat to the canister below to cause it to overheat and explode!

To eliminate this danger (and potential lawsuits), most butane stoves now use a long armored fuel line to separate the canister and burner. This eliminates overheating but encourages supercooling of the tank and accompanying loss of pressure. The longer the stove runs, the colder the tank gets (frost may even form on the surface). When this happens, you must either live with the low flame or warm the canister to increase the pressure. One solution is to set the canister in a pot of hot (but well below boiling) water. Another is to make a "canister cozy"—simply fit a cylinder of closed-cell foam around the tank, add a foam bottom, and glue or tape the pieces together. If the flame drops while you're cooking, pour some hot water into the cozy. Keep the cozied canister in your sleeping bag at night so it will be warm in the morning.

Priming

Most white-gas and kerosene stoves must be preheated or primed with gasoline or alcohol to bring them to sufficient temperature to vaporize raw fuel. You don't need much heat to prime a gasoline stove. On a hot day, the sun or heat from your hands may generate enough pressure to cause fuel to stream from the nipple.

Pumps do not vaporize fuel; they simply allow you to maintain greater pressure in the fuel tank, which makes the stove easier to start and maintain, especially in cold weather.

Procedure for priming pump-equipped stoves:

1. Clean the nipple. Most stoves have a built-in cleaning needle.
2. Be sure the pressure cap is tight and the adjuster knob is closed. Then pump the stove a half-dozen times.

3. Crack the adjuster knob a quarter turn for about four seconds and watch fuel stream into the spirit cup below the burner head. Do not fill the spirit cup more than one-third full of gas!

4. Close the adjuster knob and ignite the fuel in the spirit cup. While the fuel is burning, give the stove another dozen pumps. When the flame has nearly died, crack the adjuster knob to permit the entrance of gas. An instant blue flame should result. *Note:* Overpriming (too much gas in the spirit cup) wastes gas, carbons up parts, and may overheat and damage stove parts. Underpriming makes stoves difficult to light. Learn to strike a compromise.

To prime stoves that don't have pumps:

1. Clean the nipple.
2. Remove the tank filler cap and withdraw an eyedropper full of gas from the tank. Replace the filler cap. Squirt the dropper full of gas into the spirit cup.
3. Ignite the gas in the spirit cup. When the flame has nearly gone out, crack the adjuster knob with a one-fourth turn. You should see a bright blue flame.

Note: The Optimus minipump, which is sold for use in cold weather, is unnecessary if you follow the eyedropper method of priming. Cupping stoves in hands, as is recommended by some stove makers, is slow, unreliable, and painfully cold in chilly weather.

Stoves: Dos and Don'ts

Do carry fuel only in recommended containers. Sigg aluminum liter bottles, or the original container, is recommended.

Do frequently check the temperature of your stove's fuel tank by feeling it with your hand. If the tank is too hot to hold, reduce pressure and/or pour water on the tank to cool it.

Do carry extra stove parts and tools. An extra pressure cap and leather pump washer is usually enough. Bring a small screwdriver and pliers.

Do empty the fuel in your stove after each trip. And burn the stove dry at the end of the camping season. Impurities in fuel left in stoves can cause malfunctions.

Do keep your stove protected in a rigid container when it's not in use.

Don't loosen or remove the filler cap of a gasoline stove when the stove is burning. This could result in an explosion!

Don't refuel a hot stove. There may be sufficient heat still available to ignite the fumes. Be especially careful in cold weather, as gasoline vaporizes much more slowly then.

Don't set oversize pots on stoves. Large pots reflect excessive heat back to the fuel tank, which may cause overheating of the stove. Run stove at three-fourths throttle if you use oversize pots.

Don't start or run a stove inside a tent or confined area or any place where there is insufficient ventilation.

Don't poke wire cleaning tools into burner jets from the outside. This pushes foreign matter into the vaporization barrel and clogs the valve.

Don't enclose a stove with aluminum foil to increase its heat output. The stove may overheat and explode!

Don't fill gasoline or kerosene stoves more than three-fourths full. Fuel won't vaporize if there's insufficient room for it to expand. Some stoves erupt into a ball of fire when they're overfilled.

End-of-Season Stove Maintenance

Once a year, fill the tank one-fourth full with fresh gas and add a capful (no more) of engine fuel-injector cleaner. Burn the tank dry. The injector cleaner will remove harmful deposits that could cause clogging. Lubricate the pump washer with nongumming high-grade gun oil or synthetic motor oil. Spray exterior stove parts with WD-40 to prevent rust. Wipe the stove dry with paper toweling and store the stove in a dust-free environment.

STUFF SACKS

Nylon bags with drawstring closures are useful organizers for food, clothing, and small items. Camping shops sell these bags in a variety of shapes and sizes. You can easily sew your own from nylon taffeta in a few minutes (see YARD GOODS, page 236).

Note: Ordinary fabric shops usually don't stock waterproof nylon, but the best camping shops do.

SURVIVAL

Anyone who has spent much time in the woods has, at one time or another, become lost. In his memoirs, Daniel Boone tells how he once became "mightily confused" for three days. As a young forester, I once shared a similar experience while working in western Oregon for the Bureau of Land Management. I did an incredibly stupid thing—one which I am naturally embarrassed to share with readers. But I was barely twenty-one at the time, so I'll blame my incoherence on youth.

I'd just finished marking a timber sale near Coos Bay when I was told the sale was canceled. My instructions were to remove from the trees the yellow plastic ribbons that denoted the cutting line. Now, most people of normal intelligence would simply follow the flagging to the end, *then* remove it. Not me. I began picking ribbons off the trees the moment I entered the woods. I realized the folly of this almost immediately, but I continued on. After all, I'd established the cutting line, which for the most part, followed a ridge. Yeah, there were some crossovers, but these were "obvious." I was certain I wouldn't get lost.

By noon that day, I was "mightily confused." By dark I was hopelessly lost. Sure, I knew the rules: "Stay put, build a fire, and someone will find you." But it was *Friday* and the government doesn't work on weekends. Monday was a holiday and I had Tuesday off for elk hunting. No one would even think of looking for me till Wednesday—five days from now! Besides, this was the Pacific Coast Range, where Douglas fir trees grow tall as skyscrapers. Crown cover here was close to 100 percent. Even a combat chopper pilot couldn't spot me beneath all that foliage. And making a signal fire in the persistent December rain was out of the question. Suddenly, "survival" became a meaningful word.

Space does not permit sharing the details of my ordeal. Suffice it to say that I set my compass for due west—the direction of the ocean and Highway 101—and struck off into the rain-drenched forest. Clothed in woolens and waterproof rain gear, I also had a knife, cigarette lighter, Thermos of coffee, and my lunch. Water abounded everywhere.

Three days later I walked into the sunlight of an unimproved logging road, which I followed to the whistle-stop town of Remote, Oregon. From there, I hitched a ride back to my jeep. I never told BLM about my adventure. Why? Because foresters *don't get lost!*

In this section we'll examine some personal survival shelters and techniques for coping with a wilderness emergency. You'll find no energy-draining thatched-roof lean-to's that take hours to build, for when you are lost, food is at a premium. Better to keep things simple by modifying natural shelters (caves, downed trees, brush piles, etc.) to meet your needs.

Frankly, a positive mental attitude is your most important survival tool. I vividly remember praising my Silva compass at the end of my three-day ordeal. Without it—and the knowledge to go west—I probably would have died in the Oregon woods, shelter or no. The tools of survival are less important than believing you'll get out alive!

Shelters

Possibilities are endless if you have a tarp. If not, the rule is to modify an existing shelter. Can you remove the lower branches of a downed tree to create a small nest? Or burrow into the hollow at a tree's base (figure S-9)? Perhaps you can stack some brush or logs along one side to block out the wind. A tiny reflector fire will help you weather the storm.

Before you move in, check for potential dangers—dead trees that may blow down on you, loose rocks, dry wash, etc. Make your crawlspace large enough to stretch out but small enough to conserve heat.

Next comes bark or boughs to insulate the floor and walls. If it's raining, divert the water with makeshift guttering. Otherwise, shingle fresh-cut browse. This is no time to think environmentally: Cutting vegetation and trenching your home are tenets of survival.

Figure S-9. It's best if you can modify an existing shelter.

Now crawl inside and try the fit. If you're cold, use evergreen boughs or leaves for a blanket. Perhaps if you rearrange the layering of your clothes you will add some warmth. For example, suppose you're wearing (from the skin out) a cotton T-shirt, cotton-polyester long-sleeved shirt, and wool sweater. Cotton wicks away body heat at a rapid pace, while wool does not. So wear your sweater next to the skin and the cotton garments over it. Don't overlook the value of nontraditional insulation like newspaper, leaves, a life jacket, or your packsack. Even rope, coiled about your body, will provide warmth.

If you have a vehicle, you have lots of options. All you have to do is dissect the expensive upholstery and sew the pieces into clothing. Any sharp object will function as an awl. Fabric ravelings and electrical wire provide thread (have you tried dental floss?), sticks become buttons. No formulas; just ingenuity.

Survival Kit

Most commercial survival kits have cutesy items—like wire, fish hooks, Band-Aids, and safety pins—that you will never use. The result is a heavy, bulky unit that's more likely to be left at home than carried to the wilds. At the other extreme are impractical belt-size kits whose miniaturized components defy productive use. For example, one enterprising company offers a wallet-size "survival card" that comes with a magnetized disk (compass?) that points north when you float it in water. How absurd!

The kit illustrated in figure S-10 is recommended by the Minnesota Department of Natural Resources. There is at least one documented case where quick thinking and some of its components saved a life. Here's the story:

A Minneapolis teenager was snowmobiling when a blizzard created whiteout conditions. Fortunately, the boy had recently completed an outdoor education class in high school, and he had a simple survival kit in his possession. When the young man could no longer see to drive, he used the coffee can to scoop snow from under the machine. Then he put on the plastic-bag "rain suit," wrapped himself in the space blanket, and spent the night inside the hollow. His snowmobile suit kept him warm, the "rain suit" kept him dry, and the reflective space blanket helped retain body heat. Here are the contents of his survival kit, along with some proven extras.

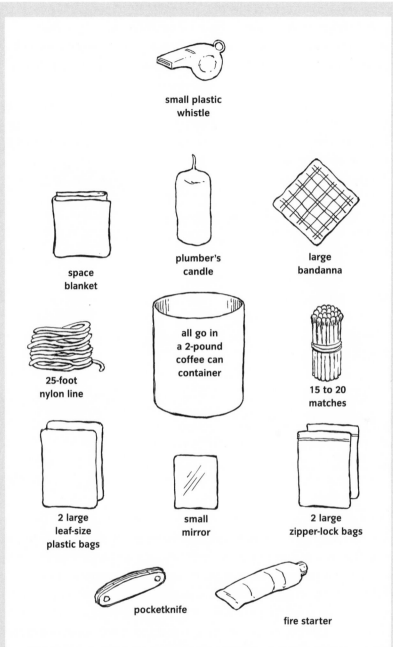

small plastic
whistle

space
blanket

plumber's
candle

large
bandanna

25-foot
nylon line

all go in
a 2-pound
coffee can
container

15 to 20
matches

2 large
leaf-size
plastic bags

small
mirror

2 large
zipper-lock bags

pocketknife

fire starter

Figure S-10. A survival kit.

Suggested survival-kit contents:

- Two large leaf-and lawn-size plastic bags. Cut out the bottoms and duct tape them together to form a continuous tube that can double as a tent and rain suit.
- Space blanket. Get one of the compact versions at any outdoor store. Don't open it; you'll never fit it back into the container! These space blankets are actually too small to cover an adult. Best use them to supplement your trash bags or to help warm a victim of hypothermia.
- Fifteen to twenty wooden stick matches, a large plumber's candle (which will burn for hours), and a solid fuel chemical fire starter enable anyone to make a blaze in any weather.
- If space permits, add bouillon cubes, tea, and sugar. Be aware, however, that food is a low-priority item when you're lost. Your main concern is shelter, warmth, and *getting found.*
- A two-pound coffee can with a fitted plastic lid makes a handy pot, snow shovel, and container for everything.
- Carry a whistle (the pealess designs take up little space) and a small mirror for signaling.
- Two zipper-lock bags. Use them as a cold-weather vapor barrier (wear them against the skin) on your feet or hands and as a container for berries, minnows, tinder, etc.
- Twenty-five feet of strong nylon line suspends your tube tent from trees or becomes a belt to secure your "rain gear." *Warning: Never* seal the ends of a nonporous plastic tube tent. Doing so could cause suffocation!
- Large cotton bandanna. Doubles as a neck warmer, sun and bug hat, cravat, bandage, and spare sock. Use it to strain minnows and crawfish.
- Small, single-bladed knife. A razor blade is no substitute for a sharp knife. If you include a compass in your kit, make it a real one.

Pack everything in the coffee can and seal the lid with several feet of duct tape, which you can use to rig shelters and mend holes in plastic bags.

TABLECLOTH

You are preparing lunch along the edge of a rain-soaked trail. Every depression is a pond, every leaf a pool. You break out the crackers and slice the Swiss and salami. Where can you put them out of the muck?

On a tablecloth, of course! A small (2-foot-square) plastic tablecloth adds dignity to what might otherwise be a dirty free-for-all. My red-checkered tablecloth has painted black ants on top. It always draws a smile, even in rain.

TARPS (RAIN FLIES)

Tarps are essential in a rainy-day camp. Under them you'll comfortably pre-pare meals, make repairs, and otherwise enjoy a day that might be soured by rain. The value of a fly is obvious, whether you're camped on a remote mountain vista or in the gentle confines of a state park. It requires skill and a bit of weather knowledge to pitch a drum-tight fly in a howling storm, yet anyone can learn how in less than an hour. A well-rigged rain fly exempli-fies the experts' edge.

Materials: A 10-by-12-foot (or larger!) nylon tarp for every four people. I ordinarily rig a single fly in modified lean-to configuration, but for severe storms I mate the pair into a giant open tent that everyone can crowd under. No need to purchase expensive tarps (I suggest you get two). Any waterproof nylon—ripstop or taffeta—is fine.

Customize your tarps according to figures T-1 and T-2. Two hours' time and a light-duty sewing machine are all you need.

Tips: Well-sewn nylon loops (get inch-wide nylon webbing at any camp-ing shop) are much more reliable than grommets. If you're a belt-and-suspenders person, you'll replace critically located corner grommets with well-reinforced nylon loops. Allow no more than 18 inches of space between loops or grommets. Be sure to back whatever you sew with heavy material.

Sew an 8-inch-square pole patch of heavy material to the inside center (opposite the center guy line) of your fly, then sew on the two "butterfly pole" loops that are illustrated in figures T-1 and T-2. Thread a 2-foot-long piece of parachute cord through the loops and secure the cords with a heavy-duty cord lock. This will allow you to use—and stabilize—an interior center pole when there are no trees to which you can attach an outside guy line. Nylon stretches and abrades easily, so a reinforcing patch is essential if you plan to use a pole.

To use the butterfly pole loops: Center the pole in the socket and tighten the cord lock. The loops will wrap around the pole and hold it in place when the tarp is buffeted by wind. For extra security, wrap the cords around the pole a few times and tie them with a simple bow. In very high winds, you may need to stake the pole to the ground—simply run a guy line from the butterfly loops to a stake at the base of the pole.

Attach loops of parachute cord to each grommet or loop. Loops should be large enough to allow insertion of a wire stake. Leave at least 6 inches of "tie" hanging, as illustrated. *Tip:* Braided nylon cord holds knots better than the inexpensive sheathed parachute cord sold at hardware stores.

Attach generously sized chute-cord loops to each of the five webbed loops on the face of the fly (figure T-1). Loops should be tied with a sheet bend. One 20-foot-long cord should be permanently secured to the center face loop.

Tip: If you sew matching loops *inside* the tarp opposite those on the outside of the tarp, you'll have a handy place to hang flashlights, candle lanterns, stuff sacks, etc.

Finally, waterproof all seams. I prefer Thompson's Water Seal—an industrial-strength compound used for sealing wood and concrete block. TWS won't crack and peel in winter or get sticky in July. Two applications, spaced an hour apart, provide lifelong protection. Apply the product sparingly with a foam varnish brush. Use TWS on your tent seams, maps, and journals too. Every hardware store has it.

Don't Leave Home without These Items!

When suddenly the sky suddenly turns black and the wind grows deadly still, you generally have only a few moments to pitch tents and get every-

Figure T-1. A customized tarp.

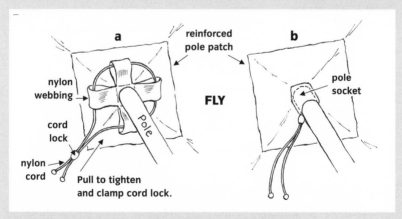

Figure T-2. Close-up of the customized tarp's pole patches.

thing and everybody under a stormproof tarp. There's no time to cut hanks of line; fumble for tent stakes, poles, or ground sheets; or wonder where you put your pocketknife. Suddenly, your worst foul-weather concerns have materialized.

You'll avoid much embarrassment when the weather turns sour if you gather these materials before you take to the woods:

- One hundred feet of ⅛-inch-diameter parachute cord for each tarp you plan to rig. Cut rope into 15- to 20-foot lengths and burn the ends so they won't unravel. Then tightly coil each hank and secure it with the quick-release loop illustrated in figure T-3.

  Tip: Choose brightly colored cord that you won't trip over in failing light.

- Fifty feet of ¼- or ³⁄₁₆-inch-diameter *braided* nylon rope (twisted rope unravels too easily) for each tarp. Singe the ends and coil the ropes by the method illustrated in figures R-1 through R-4.

- A sharp knife. A hand ax and folding saw are useful when you need to cut extension poles from *dead, downed* timber.

Figure T-3. Quick-release loop.

- Inexpensive plastic sheeting can be substituted for nylon tarps (*please* don't leave plastic in the woods) if you have small rubber balls or pebbles. Figure T-4 shows the attachment procedure.

- Waterproof tape for making repairs to nylon and plastic.

Pitching the Fly

When thunderheads loom threateningly overhead and the wind builds to impressive speeds, you generally have only a few minutes to rig a stormproof camp. So keep everything you need to rig your tarp—50 feet of rope, five 20-foot coils of parachute cord, and a dozen stakes—in a nylon stuff sack with cord-lock closure.

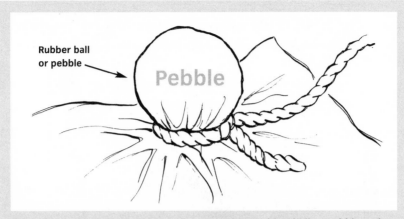

Figure T-4. A simple tarp anchor—all you need is a rubber ball or pebble and cord.

Note: Military-specification kernmantle-style parachute cord that has a lightly textured outer sheath is better than rough-braided civilian cord that has no protective outer sheath. Rough cord holds knots well, but plant matter sticks to it. Get brightly colored cord so you can see it in dim light. You'll find the best cordage at mountaineering shops.

Tip: Stuff your fly, don't roll it. Stuffing is faster and easier on the water-proof coating. Be certain everything is bone dry before you pack it away. Dampness provides a media for microorganisms to attack the fly. Microbes will not attack nylon, but they *will* devour the polyurethane coating on it. Ever see a tent floor whose waterproof coating has peeled? More than likely the tent was put away wet!

Rigs
Single Lean-to
This meat-and-potatoes configuration can be erected alone in about three minutes and will withstand winds of 30 miles an hour. The sloping design spills water effectively and conserves the warmth of a reflector fire.
Procedure:

1. Locate two trees about 15 feet apart and string a drum-tight line between them, about 5 feet off the ground. Use two quick-release half hitches at one end, and a quick-release power cinch at the other.

Quick-
release
knots

Tie edge
of fly to
a tight
line with
a single
"bow"
knot.

Figure T-5. Single lean-to.

2. Take the pair of ties at one corner of the fly and tightly wind one tie of the set clockwise around the rope. Wind the other tie counterclockwise. Take at least four turns around the rope, then secure the ties with an overhand bow.

3. Pull the other corner of the open end of the fly tight along the rope and secure it with the ties, winding them around the rope, as above. The tie wrappings will provide tension to keep the corners of the tarp from slipping inward along the rope when the fly is buffeted by wind.

4. Secure all remaining ties to the rope with a simple overhand bow. Note that by securing the fly at several points along the length of its open end, rather than just at the corners, you distribute the strain across a wide area, thus increasing the strength of the fly. High wind will tear out the corner grommets or loops unless you distribute the load along a main hemline, as illustrated.

5. Pull the back of the fly out tight and stake it.

6. Run the center cord over a tree limb or a horizontal rope strung above and behind the fly. Snug the cord and secure it with a quick-release power cinch. Use an interior center pole if trees are not available. Connect additional lines (use a quick-release sheet bend) to other face loops as needed to produce drum-tight geometry.

    In ultrahigh winds, guy or stake the side hems of the fly to the ground or adjacent trees.

Using Campfire and Single Fly Together

A fire built just under the open edge of the fly will provide substantial heat inside the lean-to. However, since the fly acts as a wind eddy, you must backlog your fire (figure T-6) or it will smoke you out. The bottom of an aluminum canoe works well, as does a large sheet of aluminum foil. You can even use several packs if you keep them well away from the flames. The

Figure T-6. Backlogging a fire.

real purpose of the backing is to draw smoke away from the enclosure, not reflect heat into it. Note that the fire must be completely *outside* the tarp. The backlogs have insufficient area to make up for the size of the wind eddy created by the huge tarp.

When rigging twin tarps, you can foil the smoke with the ingenious procedure illustrated in figure T-7.

For more information: My ninety-minute DVD, *The Forgotten Skills,* shows how to stormproof tents, rig tarps, tie knots, make fires, and more.

Twin Flies with Fire Slit

Here's a secure, airy shelter that will provide luxurious comfort for up to twelve people. Two people can rig it in about ten minutes, even in high winds. You'll need two 10-by-10-foot or larger customized flies and all your rope and cord.

The beauty of this arrangement is that you can build a rain-protected warming fire right underneath the fly. The combination backlog and overhead vent spills smoke through the opening on top. You can "float" the slanted roof, as illustrated, to provide more interior room, or stake it to the ground for protection from blowing wind.

Procedure:

1. Rig the single lean-to configuration shown in figure T-5. In vertical rains, float the back as illustrated in figure T-7. Remember to connect all lines to one another with a quick-release sheet bend.

2. Overlap to the second grommet the hem of the top fly over the hem of the bottom fly. This should provide an approximate 2-foot overlap. Then secure the corner ties of the top fly to the ties on the side hem of the bottom fly.

3. Attach a 20-foot length of chute cord to the center grommet of the top fly (point *a* in figure T-7) and secure this cord to a tree—or line strung between two trees—directly behind the bottom fly. If you won't build a fire under the top fly, you may guy this line to a stake at the base of the bottom fly.

4. Next you'll need a 6-foot-long aluminum or wooden pole. If you don't have a metal pole, cut one from dead, downed wood, or use a shear lashing to extend several short spars to this length. Tie the top of the pole to the center ties on the top fly. Run twin guy lines from the pole

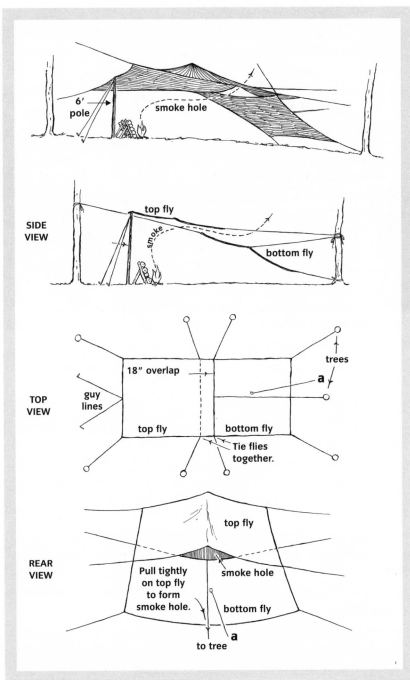

SIDE VIEW
6' pole
smoke hole
top fly
smoke
bottom fly

TOP VIEW
trees
18" overlap
a
guy lines
top fly
bottom fly
Tie flies together.

REAR VIEW
top fly
smoke hole
Pull tightly on top fly to form smoke hole.
bottom fly
a
to tree

Figure T-7. Rigging twin flies with a smoke hole.

Figure T-8. Twin flies with fire slit. Notice the clothes drying on the line and the smoke exiting through the slit in back.

    tip to the stakes below. Secure guy lines with a power cinch. Stake or guy out the corners of the top fly.

5. Go to the back of the bottom fly and tighten the overhead "vent" cord (*a*) until the structure is tight. There should be an approximate 6-inch gap between the overlapped portions of the two flies. The last step is to add additional storm lines on the face and hem of both flies to produce a taut shape that won't pool water. You now have a huge, sturdy shelter that won't pool water or flap in the wind.

Campfire Considerations

Build the fire just inside the hem of the top fly. Backlog it as explained. Smoke will follow the backlogged eddy line to the roof of the top fly and be drawn out through the slit between the two flies. This works slick when there's no wind. You'll have to experiment here, as a good breeze may confuse the eddies and allow the shelter to fill with smoke. You will also discover that if you raise the back of the bottom fly off the ground to provide more headroom, the bottom draft that results will pull smoke away from the vent and into the shelter. Ingenuity and strong backlogging will usually solve most smoke problems.

Special-Purpose Rigs
Cliff and Dan Tundra Tarp

During the summer I guide canoe trips in northern Canada for Piragis Northwoods Company in Ely, Minnesota. I typically travel with a crew of ten, often in very rainy conditions. Rigging twin flies every night is time consuming, so I leave the small tarps at home and instead carry a giant 15-foot-square model that I designed with the help of Cooke Custom Sewing (see appendix B). This *tundra tarp,* as Dan Cooke calls it, has full bug netting sewn to all four sides. The netting rolls and ties out of the way when it's not needed, yet it releases instantly. Surprisingly, there's no need to kill or shoo away insects that are trapped inside the enclosure. The bugs happily entertain themselves by crawling on the inside netting, away from you!

The tundra tarp is ingenious and expensive—and worth every penny when you need a bugproof structure that stays up in high winds. I've used mine on the shores of Hudson Bay in sustained winds of 50 miles an hour! No problems. The outfit weighs about fourteen pounds with three aluminum poles, stakes, lines, and netting. Twelve people can crowd inside. Dan Cooke will build a tundra tarp to your specifications.

Figure T-9. If bugs drive you batty, you'll want a fully netted tundra tarp.

Canoe Prop Method

Prop a canoe on paddles and cover it with your rain tarp, as shown in figure T-10. If you have two canoes, prop them side by side about 6 feet apart, parallel to one another and cover them with a tarp. Stake and guy the tarp and push out the center with a paddle so it won't pool water. *Don't trust this setup in a strong wind!*

If it's *perfectly calm,* you can prop up the back ends of the canoes, as well as the front, to produce a nonsloping shelter with more interior space.

I don't like the canoe prop method. It's hard on paddles and not very secure. But it is useful in light rain and handy when you need protection for a small fire.

Tip: A single canoe prop without fly makes a quick shelter for two in a light, vertical rain. I've used it many times to prepare lunch along a canoe portage on a rainy day.

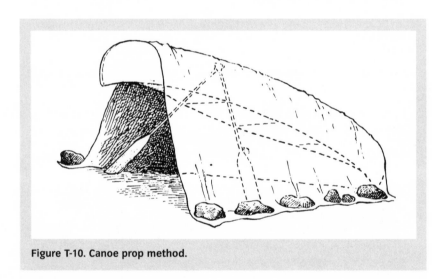

Figure T-10. Canoe prop method.

Quick-Rig Tundra Tarp

You're canoeing in the barren lands where no trees and high winds are the rule. Rig a canoe prop, like that illustrated in figure T-10, and it will go sailing off into the tundra before you can move in. What to do? Why, use your canoes to weight the tarp, of course. And, oh yes, you'll need one 5- to 7-foot aluminum pole.

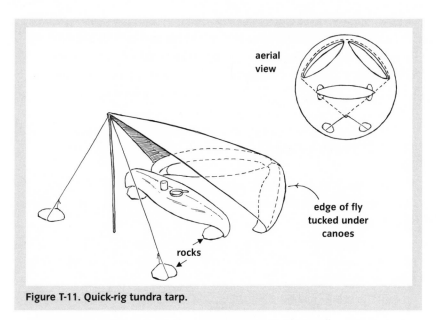

aerial
view

edge of fly
tucked under
canoes

rocks

Figure T-11. Quick-rig tundra tarp.

Procedure:

1. Lay the tarp flat on the ground and weight two adjacent sides with over-turned canoes.
2. Hoist the apex of the shelter on a long pole, then guy the pole and remaining loose fabric in place. Total rigging time? Less than three minutes!

Tips:

• You can construct a more spacious shelter by placing the canoes *inside* the fly, bellies facing the occupants. Drape the tarp partially over the canoes and tie it to them (you'll need several short lengths of cord).

• An overturned canoe blocked up on the sides makes a great table (figure T-11). Remove the side blocks and it becomes a windbreak for your stove.

Single-Walled Sun Tepee

This is similar to the quick-rig tundra tarp illustrated in figure T-11, except stakes, not canoes, are used to secure the back of the tarp. The sun tepee requires one pole and one or two guy lines. For a taut configuration you'll need to guy out the midpoint of the fly—impossible if there are no trees. However, stacking gear against the inside back wall will stiffen the shelter considerably.

As you can see, there are dozens of ways to rig tarps. And that's the problem. Most people are so baffled by all the possible configurations that they never master a single design. My advice? Forget about the cute options suggested in survival texts and become expert at rigging the *single lean-to* (figure T-5) and *twin flies with fire slit* (figure T-7). For desert or barren land camping, the *quick-rig tundra tarp* or its derivative, the *single-walled sun tepee,* is most practical.

TENTS

And the night shall be filled with music
And the cares that infest the day,
Shall fold their tents like Arabs
And as silently steal away.
—Henry Wadsworth Longfellow, *A Psalm of Life*

It's been four hours now and still it continues. The water comes in sheets, cold and unrelenting. Everywhere the ground is drenched with it; every rut holds a pool, every leaf a tiny pond. Contentedly, you peer through the mosquito net of your nylon tent at the vastness of the forest beyond. The sky, deep gray and foreboding, communicates that "more of the same" is on the way.

Overhead, a small aluminum candle lantern provides some warmth and enough light to permit reading a novel. You laze against the loosely rolled sleeping bag and momentarily stare into the dampness of the day. A smug smile flashes briefly: Granted, the 5-by-7-foot A-frame tent is a bit cramped for two. But no matter; it is warm and dry. Be it ever so humble, there is no place like home, even when it is a confining backpack tent pitched on a secluded ridge deep in the Adirondacks.

Five states to the west, a similar scenario is in progress. A man, woman, twelve-year-old girl, and towheaded boy of nine peer wistfully through the netted window of their spacious 9-foot-square umbrella tent. The walls of

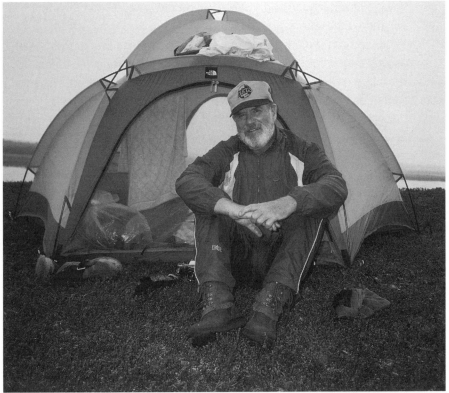

Figure T-12. A happy camper relaxes by his geodesic dome tent. Along the Hood River in Nunavut, Canada.

the ten-ounce canvas Eureka tent rustle contentedly to the rhythm of the wind-whipped rain. Outside, tiny icicles drip from the well-bronzed canvas, but inside, warmed by the glow of a Coleman lantern, it is snug and dry. The 6-foot peak provides plenty of room to stand and dress, and the spacious floor plan encourages games and socializing. This family has been confined for six hours but they are having a very good time. Yet all around, far as the eye can see, the campground is deserted. Where earlier dozens of tents had dotted the treeless field, now, there is only grass and rain. Everyone else has gone—casualties of the persistent precipitation.

At the top of the continent, just above the arctic circle, two canoe campers ride out a polar gale in their low-slung geodesic dome. The state-of-the-art nylon igloo expands and contracts with every gust of the 50-mile-per-hour wind, but it holds firm. Thirty-six hours later, two smiling voyageurs emerge on to the still, sunlit tundra, grateful that their tent had weathered the storm.

As you can see, there is no such thing as a perfect tent or even an all-around one. What's best for car camping is out of place in the tundra or on the hiking trail. Backpacking in the mountains is not like desert hiking or wilderness canoeing. And winter camping imposes new demands. Tents designed to withstand high winds may perform poorly in rain, and vice versa. Those built to withstand snow loads may be too heavy or difficult to pitch. Ones light enough to carry long distances may test your sanity on a rainy day, while larger models may strain the confines of your backpack. And so it goes. When you do find your dream tent, it may simply cost too much.

But don't despair; there is order in the universe. The following principles of tent design and construction will help you separate the wheat from the chaff. Figure T-13 will help you with terminology.

Design and Construction Features

The construction features of most tents are vastly overrated. Thread count, number of stitches per inch, reinforcement of zipper ends and such are proudly touted by tent makers, but in reality these take a back seat to *good design*—a feature not always associated with quality construction or high price. In all my years of canoeing and camping, I've never seen a well-designed tent come apart at the seams or a zipper rip from its stitching.

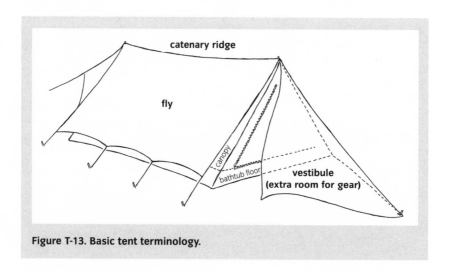

Figure T-13. Basic tent terminology.

But I've experienced enough bent poles, torn flies, and broken zippers to know that fabrics and sloppy sewing are rarely the villains.

If you keep uppermost in your mind that good design, impeccable construction, and high price don't always go hand in hand, you'll be on your way to finding the ideal tent for your purposes and pocketbook.

Design Principles

If you asked a boating expert how to tell a seaworthy canoe from one that's not, he or she might use the following analogy:

Pretend your hands are water and place them on the keel line of the canoe. Now slide your hands up toward the rails. Is there substantial flare here? Good. Water will follow that flare away from the hull rather than into it. But if your hands "tumble home" (follow the inward curve of the canoe above the waterline), water will do the same. It's no mystery why flare-sided dories are more seaworthy than hard-chinned rowboats!

Now try this same test on your tent. Follow the fly to the ground, as if your hands were water. Do your hands fall on unprotected seams? If so, rain will pool here and seep into your tent. And seam sealant (glue) won't keep you dry for very long. The most reliable way to keep seams from leaking is to cover them with waterproof material. A fly that stakes right to the ground will do the trick, but few tents come so equipped. To save weight, many tents have short "cap" flies that don't protect the canopy in wind-driven rain. Some sophisticated tents now feature machine-sealed (heat tape) seams like those applied to the best rainwear. These seams won't leak in any weather.

Exceptions aside, you are best advised to avoid any tent that has perimeter seams that are not fully covered by the fly. The floors of some tents, like the Eureka Timberline, are sewn to the canopy several inches above ground. This bathtub construction puts vulnerable seams under the protection of the fly, where they belong. All the best rain tents have bathtub floors!

Now check the tent corners where the floor seams and door zippers come together. Does the fly drip water onto any stitching? If so, find a way to fix it or keep shopping! Even the well-designed Eureka Timberline scores low in this category.

The entrance and windows are other critical components. Are there generously sized awnings over doors and vents to keep rain out? Are exterior zippers protected by weather flaps? Can you easily turn aside a weather flap with your hand? If so, wind will do the same. Many of the best tents use elastic or Velcro to keep weather flaps in place. Perhaps you can make modifications.

Vestibules are worth their weight in gold on a rainy day. They function as an extra room to store packs and wet gear. More importantly, they protect the entrance (all those exposed seams and zippers we are concerned about) against blowing wind and rain, and they provide a place to cook out of the weather when you're too lazy to rig a rain tarp. Vestibules are generally add-on affairs that attach to the tent canopy with clips or shock cord. If you're serious about camping in rain, you'll *demand* a vestibule!

Geometry

There are A-frames, tepees, tunnels, domes, lean-tos, wall tents, and sophisticated geometric shapes that defy description (figure T-14).

Domes: In terms of space, domes are the most efficient of tent designs. The high, gradually sloping sidewalls of a dome provide a pleasant spacious atmosphere, and the hexagonal or octagonal floor permits occupants to sleep in any direction—a real advantage if the tent is pitched wrong or on a sloping site.

But domes have plenty of faults. Though they shed rain efficiently, they're poorly ventilated (the fly covers the windows and door) and not very stable in wind. *Geodesic* domes, which use a lattice of arrow-shaft aluminum poles, are the exception. However, serious geodesic designs are time consuming to pitch and very expensive. All domes (geodesics included) crush in high winds unless they are well guyed and staked. This means running storm lines through slits in the fly to guy points on the poles. Rigging a dome for gale-force winds is quite a task, though once accomplished, the tent usually holds.

By design, domes cannot utilize bathtub floor construction. The many-faceted floor must be sewn to the canopy at ground level, which leaves plenty of seams for you to glue. Ironically, some of the best domes have short flies that leave perimeter floor seams exposed to the weather. Such construction guarantees a sponge party in prolonged rain.

Geodesic domes were designed as mountaineering tents. Since they're basically freestanding, can be shoved into small crevices, and don't need to be rotated to face into a changing wind, they are ideal for situations where creature comfort, light weight, small packed size, and wind stability are important factors. Good geodesics are at best mediocre rain tents.

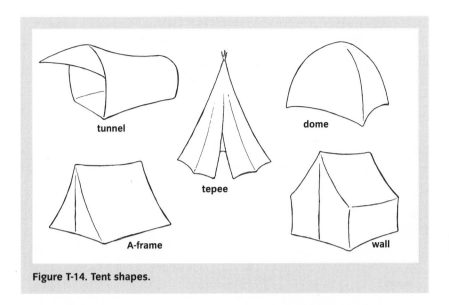

Figure T-14. Tent shapes.

And conventional domes are worse. Inexpensive (cheap!) domes that have fiberglass poles and no awnings over the doors and windows are among the worst tents you can buy. Might as well get a play tent as one of these!

Tepees: The tepee is perhaps the most efficient and ingenious of tent designs. No other tent of comparable size sheds wind and rain as well and is as cool in summer, as warm in winter, and as versatile. The American Indian knew what he was doing when he designed the tepee!

Indian tepees are actually egg shaped, not round as is commonly believed. The long axis of the cone was placed windward to brace the structure against the harsh prairie winds. Ventilation was provided by the doorway and a clever system of flaps at the apex. In winter, fine brush was stacked between the inner tent liner and outer wall to serve as insulation. The original tepee design was ingenious and difficult to improve upon.

The modern nylon tepee is a far cry from its skin-covered ancestor. Aluminum poles provide support and a removable cap fly keeps out the weather. Entry is a zippered door or traditional hole.

Tepees light enough for backpacking share the same wet-weather inadequacies as domes, but they're more rigid, so they remain rock solid in winds that would flatten conventional tents of equal height. However, their flies are slow and awkward to install, they have stakes and guy lines everywhere, and there is no awning over the doorway to keep rain out. Tepees are great for semipermanent camps. Otherwise, forget 'em.

Tunnels are low-to-the-ground affairs that are supported by a network of semirigid aluminum hoops. Designed for severe service, tunnels are among the most wind-stable tents. Their small size makes them light and compact. Inside they are cramped and doghousy, but they're generally more rainproof and better ventilated than domes. For high-altitude work and where weight is critical, tunnels have few peers.

A-frames are by far your best buy. These tents shed rain and wind effectively, allow construction of water-resistant bathtub floors and protective awnings, are well ventilated and pestproof, and are less costly to manufacture than other styles. In its most elementary form (a single I pole at each end), the A-frame is the lightest, most compact, and strongest of all tents. The design is thousands of years old, but it is still a good one.

Umbrella tents are traditional for family camping. And for good reason. They go up easily on any terrain and are almost entirely self-supporting. There's standing room inside and a generous front awning under which to cook and relax. With full-length flies, these tents are rain- and windproof.

The umbrella design is not just for family tents. Some sophisticated backpacking tents are built on this pattern.

Self-supporting tents: Any tent design can be made self-supporting if it's rigged with a tubular exoskeleton and shock-cord suspension system. Note that self-supporting tents remain freestanding only if there is no wind—a fierce storm will send any unanchored tent reeling across the countryside. The real advantage of self-supporting tents is that they require fewer stakes to erect than traditional U-stake-'em models. But these tents do require staking . . . nearly always!

Fabrics

Nylon is the most suitable fabric for lightweight backpacking tents. Cotton tents are too heavy and bulky for most forms of self-propelled travel. Nylon tents need a porous canopy to let body-produced moisture out and a protective waterproof fly to prevent rain from getting in. Check the fit between fly and canopy: The two must not touch at any point (even when stressed by high wind) or condensation and dripping will result.

Poles and Stakes

Poles should be *aluminum,* no ands or ifs! There is no such thing as a good fiberglass or plastic composite pole. *Wands* (nonsupporting members) that are used to hold out awnings and vents are an exception, though even here aluminum is better. It follows that large-diameter aluminum poles of equivalent alloy are less apt to break than smaller poles. I prefer ¾-inch-diameter tempered poles if I can get them. Thin arrow-shaft poles are fine if there are enough of them. All poles should be shock-corded for easy assembly.

Tips:

- Tent poles are less apt to jam together if you polish the joints (a one-time effort) with 400-grit *wet* sandpaper then wipe them with a cloth sprayed with liquid silicone.
- Remedy for stuck pole sections: Heat the joint lightly in the flame of your trail stove. The joint will expand and the poles will part easily.
- Aluminum poles will slide more easily through tight pole sleeves in nylon tents if, before your trip, you squirt talcum powder down the sleeves and lubricate the poles with liquid silicone. One application of silicone and talc lasts several weeks, even in rain. Gun shops sell special dry powdered lubricants that are used for resizing hand-loaded brass cartridge cases. These cartridge-case lubricants work better than talcum powder, but they're much more expensive.

Tent stakes: Twelve-inch-long arrow-shaft aluminum stakes or staples (U-shaped stakes) hold best in sand; sharp aluminum skewers are good for compacted soil; narrow steel-wire stakes are ideal for rocky ground, and so it goes. Ten-inch-long aluminum skewers may be the best all-around tent stake. Carry a variety of tent stakes so you'll always have what works best (see figure T-15).

Tips:

- Eight-inch-long aluminum concrete nails make acceptable low-cost tent stakes. The heavy steel and plastic U-pound-'em stakes sold at discount stores are useful only on big, semipermanent canvas tents.
- Special stakes are unnecessary for camping on snow or sand. Conventional aluminum stakes can be buried or guy lines wound about wooden sticks and then buried. Tin-can lids (with the edges peened in for safety) make good snow stakes. Run the guy lines through holes in the center and bury the lids.

Figure T-15. Types of tent stakes: 6-inch pins (general purpose); 8-inch skewers (better general purpose); 12-inch staples (for soft ground—they have double the holding power); 12-inch arrow-shaft stakes (for sand, mud, and spongy tundra).

Features

Bug netting may be standard mosquito type or no-see-um-proof. I prefer the former as it is stronger, easier to see through, and allows free flow of air. Tightly woven no-see-um-proof netting can be stifling on hot nights. When the tiny gnats begin their act, simply spray your mosquito net with bug dope or close the fabric door panel.

Door panel: A well-designed tent has the door panel *inside* the bug net so you can open the door to peek out without unzipping the screen.

Extras: Some tents have niceties like lantern loops and inside pockets for the storage of small items. These features—which require only a few minutes on a sewing machine to make—add considerable cost to a tent without significantly increasing its utility.

How to Select a Family Tent

My family's first camping tent was a 9-by-9-foot umbrella model with a wet-wax finish, a steel telescoping center pole, and two netted windows with flaps that tied shut. It weighed fifty-two pounds and, when rolled, barely fit into the trunk of the car. In hot weather it smelled like kerosene and paraffin, and in rain it leaked profusely. But it was inexpensive and it enabled us to see a lot of country on not a lot of money.

Family tents, like the times, have changed. They've gotten more expensive, of course, but they're also lighter, stronger, roomier, and more weatherpoof than those of the sixties. And they're easier to pitch too. Guy lines are passé, as are obtrusive center poles and odors. Ties have been replaced by nylon zippers and Velcro, and shock-corded aluminum poles have succeeded steel ones. Even the largest family tents can be erected in less than fifteen minutes.

Your needs: For comfort, you need at least 21 square feet of floor space per person, more if you use cots. Tents with rectangular floors use space more efficiently than those with square or circular floors, which means more room between sleepers.

Weight: Three to four pounds per person is the rule for lightweight backpacking tents; five to six pounds for canoeing and high-altitude expedition tents; and up to ten pounds for drag-'em-out-of-the-car family shelters. Many of the best tents weigh much less than this.

Height: Waiting out a rain in a tent you can't stand in is no fun. However, low-profile tents with sloping sides spill wind better than high-sided umbrella and wall tents, so you may have to make some sacrifices if you camp where there are big winds.

Fabrics: Though nylon is the most popular and best fabric for the construction of small tents, lightweight cotton is still a good choice for family tents where weight is less of a concern. It's impractical to use double-walled (waterproof fly/porous canopy) construction in large tents, so one layer of waterproof nylon is usually used throughout—a design that encourages condensation inside. Big windows and a porous cotton or nylon roof help dispel some moisture, but not enough to prevent these tents from occasionally turning into saunas.

Nonetheless, if you confine your trips to areas where high humidity and rain are infrequent, then you may like an all-nylon tent. In any case, be sure the tent has at least two rain-protected windows. The best nylon family tents have four-way ventilation—three windows and a door.

Speed of pitching: A tent that requires ten minutes to pitch in dry, windless weather may require twice that long to erect in a rainstorm. It's faster to assemble poles than to drive stakes and tie guy lines, so choose a tent that is supported mainly by poles.

Modesty curtains: Family tents are commonly used in areas where there are other campers, so they should be designed to provide privacy without sacrificing ventilation. Some tents have a modesty curtain—a short fabric panel that attaches behind the door—in addition to the regular entry flap. On hot days you can leave the door open for ventilation and close the modesty curtain for privacy.

Clothing loops: Convenience dictates plenty of D rings, loops, or brass hooks at the ridge to hang wet towels, clothing, and your battery-powered lantern. *Warning:* Mantle lanterns put out enough heat to burn through the roof of flame-retardant tents. And they consume lots of precious oxygen as they produce poisonous carbon monoxide. For this reason, you should hang only *flameless* lanterns inside your tent. Heaters, except catalytic ones, are also unsafe in tents.

Winter Tents

Most travelers use their three-season nylon tent for snow camping, which works well enough if they rig a *frost liner* inside. A piece of cotton sheeting, hung from the roof by ties or Velcro, absorbs exhaled moisture that might condense and freeze on the sleeping bags below.

A more gracious style of winter camping, popular a century ago, is again finding favor among those who spend long periods of time in the wilds. A 7-by-9-foot or larger canvas tent is rigged to accept a small sheet-metal stove and pipe. A generously sized canvas fly defies blowing rain, increases interior temperatures, and protects the roof from sparks. The tent *must* be canvas. Hot sparks will melt nylon instantly and cause serious burns! Most winter campers use wall or pyramid-style tents. Authentic period canvas tents—some of which are wonderful for winter camping—are available from Empire Canvas Works, Duluth Pack, Frost River, and Tentsmiths (see appendix B).

In summary, the best tents are largely self-supporting and have full-length flies and bathtub floors that wrap well up the sidewall. Protective awnings over doors and windows are a must, as are heat-treated aluminum poles and one or more vestibules.

Care and Cleaning of Tents

Canvas tents: Sweep 'em out, hose 'em down with water, and let 'em sundry until they are bone dry. Don't use soaps or detergents to clean cotton tents, as these products will remove the waterproof compounds.

Tip: You can restore the water repellency to small sections of cotton tents by rubbing a bar of paraffin across the fibers. Heat from the sun will melt the paraffin and the cotton fibers will absorb it.

Nylon tents should be thoroughly washed at the end of each camping season. Soak the tent for thirty minutes or so in a tub of lukewarm water and mild detergent. Tent manufacturers wisely suggest that you avoid use of detergents and chemical solvents, as these products may dissolve waterproof coatings. However, sparing use of these products remove abrasive dirt, which is your tent's greatest enemy. Sponge troublesome spots with detergent. Tree sap may be removed with a *very small* amount of gasoline or alcohol. Don't overdo it though; gasoline is very hard on waterproof coatings.

Never roll and store a wet tent. Even rot-resistant nylon tents are sewn with cotton/Dacron thread, which can mildew. Damp polyurethane coatings provide food for microorganisms. Generally, it's better to stuff a nylon tent than to fold and roll it. Folding produces harsh creases that can damage waterproof coatings.

Caution: Tents like the Eureka Timberline, with exposed metal hooks and pins that can puncture fabric when the tent is packed, should *always* be rolled, never stuffed!

Sustained exposure to ultraviolet light saps strength from nylon fabrics. A nylon tent may lose half or more of its strength in a single season if it's continually exposed to sunlight. Do sun-dry and air your tent regularly, but don't overdo it!

Nylon tent lines harden and lose strength. They should be replaced occasionally. Tent cords should be brightly colored for high visibility in failing light. I prefer bright yellow or hot pink.

Store tents in a porous cotton or nylon sack. Be sure the bag is large enough. A dry, properly rolled tent that fills its sack when dry won't fit when it's soaked with rain! Never store a tent on a concrete floor or in a damp basement.

Waterproof the seams of a new tent. I prefer to use Thompson's Water Seal rather than glues that crack, peel, and absorb dirt. Apply TWS sparingly with a foam varnish brush. One application per seam side waterproofs seams forever. That said, sealing seams is mostly window dressing. If your tent fly covers every seam and zipper, you can eliminate this step. That's because rain that gets through stitching on the fly will, due to surface tension, slither harmlessly to the ground. There is no particular advantage in sealing floor seams if you use a ground cloth inside your tent.

A whisk broom and small sponge will keep your tent clean and neat. *Tips:*

- Attach a tiny brass hook to the lanyard of your flashlight so you can clip it to a ridge loop or line inside your tent.
- Sew a D ring or nylon loop inside your tent at each end of the ridge. A length of parachute cord strung between the D rings makes a handy clothesline for light items like damp socks. Some campers sew up a miniature hammock of mosquito netting and suspend the hammock from the tent ridge. This "gear loft" will hold all manner of small items.
- It's worthwhile to repeat that a small candle lantern will raise interior tent temperatures by 10 degrees or more and eliminate much dampness.

Stormproofing Your Tent

A sewing machine and sixty minutes are all you need to turn your tent into a bombproof shelter!

You pitch your tent—a four-person Eureka Timberline—on a gentle knoll near a clump of youthful birch trees. There's a better spot 20 feet away—a well-worn area where hundreds of tents have stood before. But there's a slight depression here; a good rain could flood you out. And nearby is a long-dead spruce, its limbs poised menacingly overhead, waiting patiently for a high wind to send it crashing down.

Slowly it begins with the *tap, tap* of intermittent rain. Then it intensifies into unrelenting drizzle. For a while, you stand complacently in the gentle shower and curiously watch the blackening clouds approach. Then you suddenly realize that you have only a few minutes to get things under control before the storm unleashes its fury.

First, you string two parachute-cord guy lines from each peak to stakes below (figure T-16). Next, you weight the corner stakes with rocks then turn your attention to the right sidewall, which is being crushed by the building wind. It would be nice if you could turn the tent into the storm, but the site won't cooperate. Besides, it's too late now; you'll have to make do by shoring up the windward sidewall and poles. You're glad now that you sewed storm-line pull-outs to the fly before you left home. As the wall firms under these tight guy lines, you wonder why they aren't standard equipment on every tent.

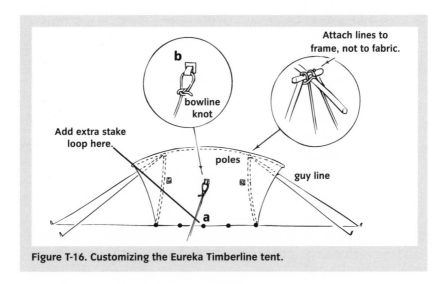

Figure T-16. Customizing the Eureka Timberline tent.

Satisfied now that everything's secure, you retire to the tent, confident you'll stay dry no matter how hard it rains.

Stormproofing Philosophy

Admittedly, staying dry in a deluge requires luck as well as skill. What would you have done if there had been no well-drained spot? Or if rocks or uncooperative ground kept you from placing your tent where you wanted? And don't forget that clump of birch you used for a windscreen.

Nonetheless, even a bad campsite can be made habitable if you correct the shortcomings of your tent and follow these rules.

1. *The right spot:* The section TENT SITE: HOW TO COPE WITH A BAD ONE, beginning on page 220, reviews some things you can do to make a bad site habitable.

2. *Use a ground cloth inside your tent!* Even well-sealed seams will admit water in prolonged rain. And no tent floor will remain watertight forever. The solution is to always use a 4- to 6-mil-thick plastic ground cloth inside your tent. Make the ground cloth large enough so it flows a few inches up the tent walls. If your tent springs a leak, water will be trapped under the groundsheet and you'll stay dry. *Do not* place the ground cloth outside the tent floor (exception—in winter put it outside to prevent the floor from freezing to the ground). Surface water may become trapped between the groundsheet and floor and be pressure

wicked (from body weight) through the floor seams. You'll really have a sponge party if this happens!

Contrary to the claims of tent makers, you don't need a ground cloth under your tent floor to protect it from abrasion. Holes in tent floors usually develop from the inside. If you don't believe this, begin a trip with a new plastic groundsheet inside your tent, then count the holes it accumulates with each day of use. Old beliefs die hard!

3. *Reinforce seams:* If a seam looks weak, it probably is. Reinforce stress points with heavy carpet thread and nylon webbing.

4. *Add extra stakes:* If the hem of your tent looks like it needs additional stake lines, add them!

5. *Double-stake or anchor guy lines in soft ground:* Inserting two stakes per loop—each through a separate hole and at a different angle—doubles the surface area and holding power in soft ground. In sand, use a rock anchor like the one illustrated in figure T-17. *Tip:* Tie 3-foot lengths of parachute cord to each stake loop *before* your camping trip and you

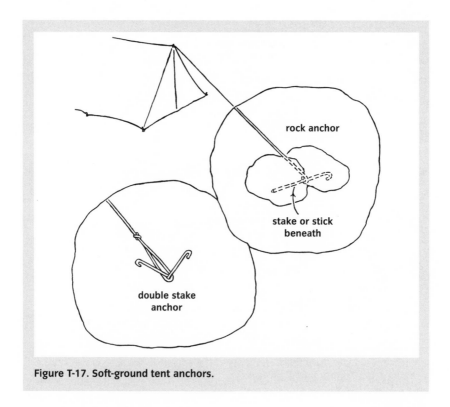

rock anchor

stake or stick beneath

double stake anchor

Figure T-17. Soft-ground tent anchors.

won't have to mess with cutting and tying these anchor lines in a rain-storm.

6. Attach loops of shock cord or bands cut from inner tubes to all stake points and guy lines (figure T-18). Shock cords take up the wind stress normally reserved for seams and fittings. Even a badly sewn, poorly reinforced tent can be used in severe weather if it's rigged with shock cords.

7. Shock-cord your tent poles. Shock-cording kits are available at most camp shops. Color code non-shock-corded pole sections and wands for easy assembly. It's frustrating to look for a center ridge section or spreader bar in failing light. Colored plastic tape sticks to poles better than paint.

Old Tents Reveal New Secrets!
The best turn-of-the-twentieth-century A-frame tents were better foul-weather shelters than modern campers like to admit. Studying one reveals

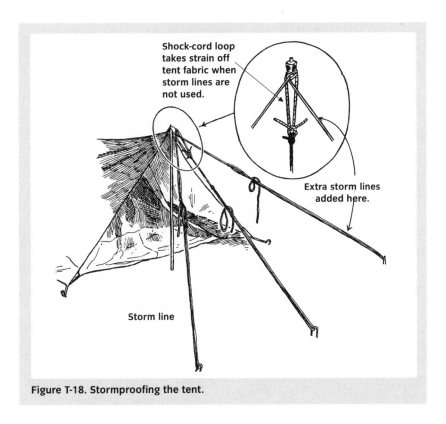

Figure T-18. Stormproofing the tent.

some interesting things about where to place seams, guy lines, and stake points. Let's analyze one of these canvas antiques:

- There's a single vertical pole at each end. The poles are located at the apex of the triangular door and back wall. In essence, they form the "altitude" of each triangle.
- The tent has no floor, so there are no perimeter seams at ground level. A removable rubberized groundsheet, placed inside, protects occupants from flowing ground water and dampness.
- Including the corners, there are *five* stake points per side hem. A center stake halves the length of the sidewall material; the others split the distance between adjacent stakes. There's that apex-of-the-triangle relationship again.
- Guy lines at each end originate on the poles or at heavily reinforced fabric very near the poles. The exoskeleton—not the fabric—absorbs most of the wind stress.

Rigging storm lines is largely a game of triangles. Locate an apex, put in a stake or guy line. This keeps fabric tight by equalizing strain. As any elk hunter will attest, a modern canvas-wall tent will withstand quite a blow. That these tents perform much better than their simple geometry suggests is no mystery to those who use them.

Customizing the Eureka Timberline and Similar Freestanding Tents

Let's use what we've learned to beef up the popular Eureka Timberline tent so it will stand up to a major storm.

First, the hem test. Does the fly cover all exposed perimeter seams? You bet! At least along the sidewalls. The Timberline has a full bathtub floor so fly coverage below the elevated bathtub seams isn't necessary, right?

Wrong! Fabrics wear, and the floor sidewalls are no exception. An extra waterproof layer here is always a plus. Seam coverage on the Timberline is adequate for vertical rain but not for wind-driven weather.

Rule: If your tent has exposed stitching or a fly that can be blown aside by high winds, you may want to extend the fly by sewing on matching material. Make cuts above stake and guy line loops so you won't have to reattach them to the new fabric. Matching (or contrasting) material can be obtained from the tent manufacturer and many outdoor stores (see the section YARD GOODS, page 236). Thrifty Outfitters, a division of Midwest Mountaineering in Minneapolis, is a complete source of tent fabrics, clothing, and equipment repair materials. (See appendix B.)

Move to the corners where the toggle pins plug into the pole ends and note that some corner stitching is exposed to the weather. You'll have to rely on glue (seam sealant) here—a bad idea. Or you can solve the problem instantly by attaching a vestibule to one or both ends of the tent.

Check out the hems along the sidewall. There are just two equidistant stake points, neither of which splits the distance between tent corners. The result is that a strong side wind can compress the center sidewall hem into the porous canopy. Correcting the problem is easy: Just sew a third stake loop to the hem center at point *a* (see figure T-16). Note how this one center stake firms the sidewall.

The Timberline is a comfortable, relatively high tent, with lots of sidewall exposed to the wind. Stiffen each wall by sewing a nylon storm loop to the center of the fly at point *b* of figure T-16. Be sure to back with heavy fabric whatever you sew.

The aluminum A-frame is your final concern. Standard-issue Timberline poles simply aren't designed for winds above 30 miles an hour. (The expedition poles are much sturdier.) Is there a way to stiffen the framework without adding weight or bulk?

You bet! Sew a nylon guy loop to the fly face at the midpoint of each pole that makes up the A-frame. Back the loop on the inside fly with a length of mating Velcro. When the weather gets nasty, secure the Velcro tabs to the poles and guy the outside loops. Since the Velcro tabs secure directly to the poles, there is no stress on the fly fabric—and no danger of tearing it.

Rule: Whenever possible, guy off the framework rather than the tent fabric!

Now, apply this philosophy to each end of the tent. The Timberline is effectively freestanding; there are no forward and aft guy lines to provide stability in oncoming winds. To account for this, the manufacturer has provided a D ring on the ridge at each end. You can attach guy lines directly to these, right?

Wrong! Reread the rule above and you'll see why. The first good blast of air will tear the D rings right off the tent. There's a better way.

1. Sew a Velcro tab to the underside of the fly, opposite the D ring. Secure the tab to the plastic pole junction tube, *then* guy off the D ring.

2. Or disregard the D ring and secure your guy lines directly to the horizontal junction tubes. If possible, attach guy and stake lines to an immovable object like a tree or rock.

For dome tents: Sew Velcro tabs to the inside fly, adjacent to the poles, as illustrated in figure T-19. When high winds develop, Velcro around the poles and run guy lines to stakes or trees. Wind stress will be absorbed by the poles instead of the nylon tent fly.

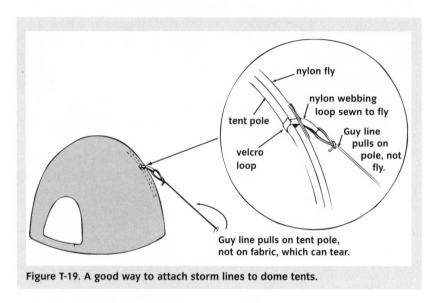

nylon fly

nylon webbing
loop sewn to fly

tent pole

Guy line
pulls on
pole, not
fly.

velcro
loop

Guy line pulls on tent pole,
not on fabric, which can tear.

Figure T-19. A good way to attach storm lines to dome tents.

Stormproofing in Summary
Let's review the rules for stormproofing tents:

- Perimeter floor seams (there should be none!) must be fully covered by the tent fly. Check the tent corners. If there's a problem here, adding a vestibule may solve it. If not, sew on an extension of some sort.
- There should be enough stake points (you can never have too many) along the fly hem to prevent wind-whipped rain from getting under the fly and onto seams. If your tent needs more stake points, add them.
- High-walled tents can be stabilized by attaching a guy line to the center face of the fly. Back your sewing with extra material. Don't run a canopy pull-out cord from the inner fly face to the canopy to increase

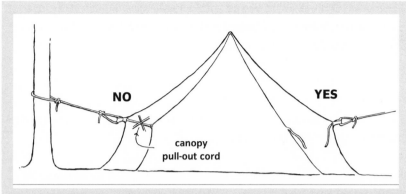

Figure T-20. Disconnect (or cut) canopy cords—they provide a path for rain to enter your tent!

space inside the tent (figure T-20). Rain will wick through the stitching on the fly face and slither down the side-pull cord into the sleeping compartment. If your tent already has a canopy side-pull cord, disconnect it the moment rain begins. If this is impractical, tie a cotton shoelace or handkerchief to the cord somewhere between the fly and canopy. Now any water that wicks through will follow the hanky to the ground (at least for a while!) rather than into your tent.

• Whenever possible, guy directly off the framework of a tent. If you must attach lines to fabric, back what you sew with heavy material.

Now stand back and take a long, proud look at your accomplishments. You have a tent that will keep you dry in any rain. Cost of materials? Under $20. Time involved? About three hours.

TENTS: CLASSICS YOU CAN MAKE

In the 1950s, when I was a Boy Scout, I owned a Spartan 5-by-7-foot canvas "wedge" tent (figure T-21). There were no zippers, bug nets, or windows and no floor. A rubberized poncho doubled as a ground cloth, and in buggy weather I wore a head net. With two wooden poles and ten stakes, the little pup tent weighed exactly seven pounds—a respectable weight for a hiking tent, even by today's standards.

I used the wedgie in all types of weather—backpacked all over upper Michigan with it—and can recall only one time when I was wet and cold. It was my "go light" philosophy and a cold, two-day rain that did me in. I got just what I deserved when I placed my dry sleeping bag on top of my wet poncho. From then on, I carried a special ground cloth for use inside my tent.

In the 1960s I bought my first nylon backpacking tent—a three-person Gerry Fireside. More commodious and half the weight of the wedge, it featured true double-walled (waterproof fly over porous canopy) construction. The Gerry had a window in back and an integral floor and bug net. Man, was I living! For more than a decade, the little tent was a constant companion on canoe camping trips in Minnesota and Canada. It never failed me in any weather.

Though I now own more sophisticated tents, I continue to use the Gerry for solo canoeing. Admittedly, my other tents are geometrically better, but none are lighter, more compact, and faster to pitch. With its built-in (sewn to the ridge) rain fly and shock-corded I poles, the Fireside goes up in less than a minute. Few modern tents can do as well.

Admittedly, for high-altitude and severe-weather use, state-of-the-art tents outshine the old-timers by a wide margin. But for general camping in forested areas, many turn-of-the-century tents are better. At any rate, the best of the nostalgic designs were lighter, better ventilated, and roomier than most people think.

Many of the old tent designs—like the wall, wedge, baker, and forester—are still in production. Attempts to modernize these designs by substituting nylon for canvas has generally been unsuccessful. That's because breathable canvas still is the best material (and certainly the most durable) for large, airy tents. Though I spent considerable time under canvas when I was a kid, I now prefer nylon tents by a wide margin. Nonetheless, the traditional tents of the past have much to recommend them. Reproduced in figures T-22, T-24, and T-25 are three of the most popular models from the 1912 Abercrombie Company camp catalog for your interest and amusement. Study the specifications and you'll discover how light and versatile these shelters were. You may even want to build one yourself. Plans for the simplest models are included for your convenience.

Wedge Tent

Simplest of all designs, the wedge is versatile and cozy (figure T-21). When constructed with a doorway at each end, the structure can be opened to

Closed wedge tent   Open wedge tent

Figure T-21. The wedge tent.

face a fire. Snap or Velcro a mosquito bar to the roof and you have a tent that is similar to the convertible A-tent recommended by the legendary outdoorsman Calvin Rutstrum in his book *The New Way of the Wilderness* (see appendix A). The design is so simple you can easily draw your own plans from the specifications.

Note: A twin-door version of this classic tent is manufactured in mildew-resistant army duck by Tentsmiths (see appendix B).

Forester Tent

This ultralight tent (figure T-22) was designed around 1910 by *Field & Stream*'s editor, Warren Miller. Nothing more than a tapered tarp, the forester tent goes up fast on any terrain and is very wind resistant. The 1912 Abercrombie catalog lists a weight of just two and three-fourth pounds for the 8-by-8-foot version—this, in cotton canvas. Try finding a two-person *nylon* tent that light today!

Build a campfire out front and you'll discover how well the cone-shaped entrance funnels heat to the occupants inside. The forester was a standard offering in Boy Scout catalogs for nearly fifty years. David Abercrombie wrote about the material used in this and other Abercrombie manufactured tents in the company's 1912 *Camp Outfits* catalog:

> The cloth is treated by a copper process which makes it waterproof, rot proof
> and vermin proof, and leaves it perfectly pliable and soft. Even the white ant
> will not attack it; neither does it burn as readily as unprocessed material and

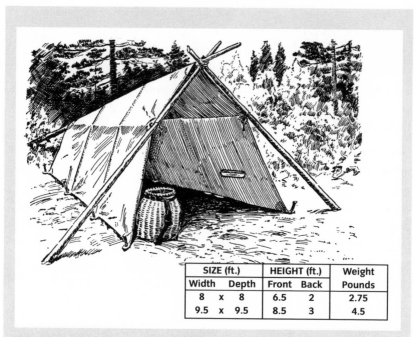

| SIZE (ft.) | | HEIGHT (ft.) | | Weight |
Width	Depth	Front	Back	Pounds
8 x 8		6.5	2	2.75
9.5 x 9.5		8.5	3	4.5

Figure T-22. Forester tent, from 1912 Abercrombie catalog.

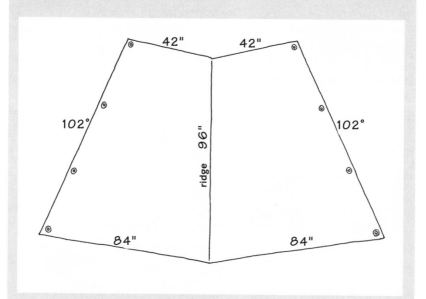

Figure T-23. Forester tent pattern.

it is not affected by either tropic heat or Arctic cold, changes in temperature making little differences in its feeling.

It is a non-conductor of heat, which makes it a cool summer and a warm winter tent. The color is a great advantage, the green being a shade that is easy for the eyes, and flies and gnats are not so troublesome in a green tent.

Baker Tent

Everyone who has camped out for long eventually comes to know and love the baker tent (figure T-24). Guy out the fly and build a cheery fire beneath; gather the crew and deal the cards. There's room enough for all, even when heavy rain blows up. Add a sod cloth, bug net, side wings, and a privacy screen out front, and you have a snug four-season shelter that's as much at home in Patagonia as at a friendly KOA campground. Baker tents once were the backbone of every nineteenth-century hunting camp, and in parts of the American West, they remain so today. Note that the 1912 *Camp Outfits* catalog listed the 8-by-6½-foot model at just nine pounds—lighter even than today's popular nylon Eureka Timberline.

You can buy a modern baker tent from Tentsmiths and many western outfitters.

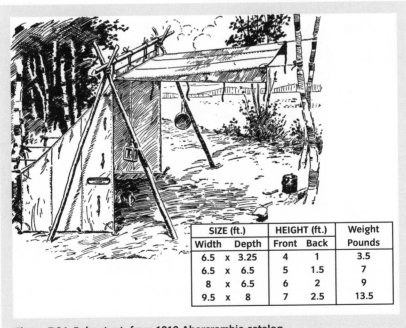

SIZE (ft.)		HEIGHT (ft.)		Weight
Width	Depth	Front	Back	Pounds
6.5 x 3.25		4	1	3.5
6.5 x 6.5		5	1.5	7
8 x 6.5		6	2	9
9.5 x 8		7	2.5	13.5

Figure T-24. Baker tent, from 1912 Abercrombie catalog.

Miners' Tent

When it comes to efficient utilization of space, the miners' tent is hard to beat. Four pegs and a tie at the top (or interior pole) stabilize this tent in winds that would flatten most conventional designs. Spread the door flaps and feel the heat of your campfire. Button up tight and listen to the patter of rain while you stay dry inside. The miner is great for winter camping too: Just run the pipe of your sheet-metal stove through a thimble in the roof and watch things heat up fast inside.

Pyramid tents like these were popular in the cowboy days and well into the twentieth century. Journals of the early arctic explorers praised the miner tent for its light weight, wind stability, and ease of pitching. Look around and you'll discover that this ancient design is still going strong. If you can draw a triangle, you can build this tent.

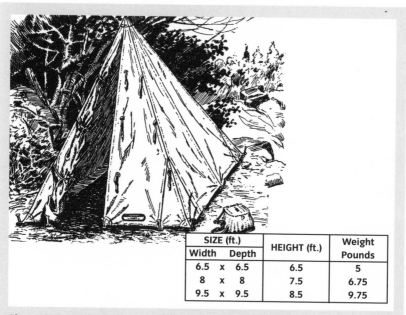

SIZE (ft.)		HEIGHT (ft.)	Weight
Width	Depth		Pounds
6.5 x 6.5		6.5	5
8 x 8		7.5	6.75
9.5 x 9.5		8.5	9.75

Figure T-25. Miners' tent, from 1912 Abercrombie catalog.

Whelen Lean-to

The Whelen lean-to was designed by the famous outdoorsman Col. Townsend Whelen. A retired army officer, Colonel Whelen wrote prolifically about guns, hunting, and camping. Even when it was no longer fashionable, he preferred to base his hunts out of tents rather than RVs or motels.

Whelen disliked the popular campfire tents of the day because their sloping back walls reflected campfire heat onto the floor rather than the occupants. And everyone had to sleep with their head or feet toward the fire, which cooked one end and froze the other. "Much smarter to sleep sideways, so all parts get done at once," snipped the colonel.

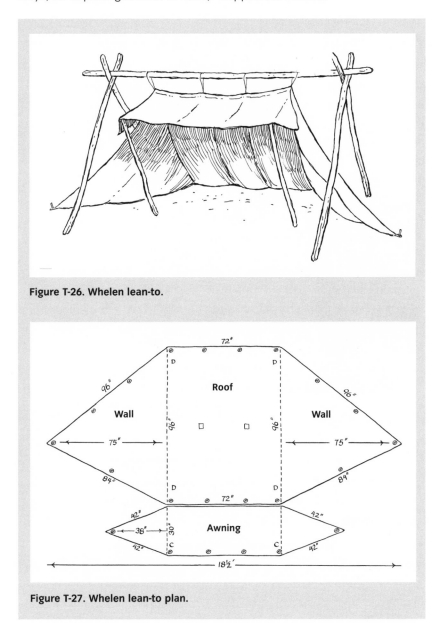

Figure T-26. Whelen lean-to.

Figure T-27. Whelen lean-to plan.

Whelen added a short vertical wall to the back of a conventional lean-to, then he sewed on a generous awning and side flaps. Voilà! The Whelen lean-to was born. It's interesting to note that Eureka and Cooke Custom Sewing offer a facsimile of this still-popular 1926 design—in waterproof nylon, of course!

TENT SITE: HOW TO COPE WITH A BAD ONE

The camping literature is rich with advice on how to choose a good campsite. Requirements generally include high, flat ground with good drainage; a south-facing slope (so you can enjoy the morning sun); and an open vista so a welcome breeze will blow away bothersome insects. In reality, a rank novice can tell a good tent spot when she sees one. Everyone knows enough not to pitch a tent on bumpy ground, on a rock face, or in a depression. However, most camping today is carefully regulated, and some programmed sites are downright awful. In most cases you'll have to accept the inadequacies of the place and make the best of it. Here are some suggestions to do just that:

1. Always use a ground cloth *inside* your tent. The exception is in winter when you are camping on snow (with no chance of rain). Then the ground cloth should be placed under the tent to prevent the floor from freezing to the ground. Stormproof your tent as suggested in the TENTS section.

2. Know the shortcomings of your tent and correct them. For example, the most weather-vulnerable portion of any tent is the door end, where zippers and seams come together. A vestibule will solve this problem instantly; however, not all tents come so equipped. If the ground slopes, pitch the tent with the weather-vulnerable end downhill, so groundwater will run away from the seams rather than onto them.

3. If the site drainage is bad and there are a number of tents in your party, pitch each tent far enough away from its neighbor so that tent roofs won't funnel water onto nearby tents. Closely spaced tents act as gutters in a heavy rain!

4. Please do not "improve" the lay of the ground by attacking it with a hatchet and Rambo knife. Instead, use foam pads or air mattresses. Level your sleeping system by placing additional clothing beneath your trail bed.

5. There will not always be trees available from which to rig cooking flies. An extra set of collapsible tent poles will provide anchor points for tarps.

6. If, despite all your precautions, a heavy rain threatens to wipe you out, create water-diversion bars by placing logs alongside your tent's perimeter. The logs will function much like the erosion-control bars used for trail maintenance. After the rain, return logs to the forest so you'll leave no trace of your presence.

7. An antirain dance or thoughtful plea to the Great Spirit will sometimes cause the brunt of a storm to bypass a bad tent spot.

TOOLS

For predictable outings close to home, a Swiss Army knife and duct tape are all you need. For an ultracompact tool kit, I like the original Leatherman multitool.

Figure T-28. Expeditions demand specialized tools. Here's what I bring on my Canadian canoe trips: file; sanding board; C clamps; awl; twist drills; heavy-duty scissors; dental tool; pliers; 4-inch crescent wrench; Leatherman original multitool; instant epoxy; duct tape; sewing needles and copper wire in tube; nylon strapping tape; assortment of bolts, nuts, rivets, snaps, washers, and gaskets; diaper pins; hot glue sticks; eyeglass repair kit; Therm-a-Rest repair kit; machine oil.

For backcountry trips, add to your kit an assortment of bolts, nuts, and washers; a small coil of light copper wire; five-minute epoxy; a file; and some diaper pins and you're set for most emergencies.

Expeditions demand specialized tools. Figure T-28 shows some of the things I bring on my Canadian canoe trips.

TOWELS

Cloth dish towels have no place on a wilderness trip. They trap and spread bacteria and absorb soot and dirt. Once soaked, they usually stay that way for days. Try these as towels on your next campout:

- A synthetic (cloth) chamois will absorb about ten times its weight in water. You'll find this product at kitchen supply and auto shops and at state and county fairs. Outdoor stores sell the highly absorbent Pack-Towl, which comes in three sizes. A cloth chamois is my first line of defense against heavy spills. It works nearly as well as a sponge but it dries much faster.
- Absorbent paper toweling: Two sheets of paper toweling per meal will dry dishes for four, if you first "chamois dry" your cookware.
- The Boy Scouts consider toilet tissue so useful they call it "AP" (all-purpose) paper. Use it to blow your nose, nurse a cut, clean a stove, etc. Uses are endless. *Tip:* To save weight and bulk, remove the card-board tube and place the roll inside a zipper-lock bag. Pull the paper from the *center* of the roll (tube removed) and you'll have a steady stream of tissue that you won't have to unroll.
- A cotton bandanna, lightweight cotton dish towel, or cloth baby diaper is the only wash towel you'll need on a wilderness camping trip.

ULTRAVIOLET PROTECTION

If you want to make your plastic canoe, polyethylene dry box, car dashboard and rubber moldings, carpeted cartop carriers, and other sun-sensitive materials last almost forever, treat them regularly with 303 Protectant. Many vinyl makers and vinyl accessory companies recommend 303 by name. Bell Canoeworks, in Zimmerman, Minnesota, says that 303 is the best UV protectant you can buy for use on their exquisite Kevlar/carbon-fiber composite canoes.

A 303 customer treated one panel of a nylon life vest with 303 Protectant and placed it on an aluminum roof in Portland, Oregon. He checked the vest four years later and discovered that the 303-treated panel looked fine, while the rest of the vest had completely disintegrated!

303 Protectant contains no petrochemicals, silicone oils, or petroleum distillates. It's not greasy or oily and it repels dust, dirt, and stains. I store my canoe trailer outside year-round and regularly use 303 to preserve the tires. It works!

V

VAPOR-BARRIER LINERS (VBLS)

A vapor barrier is a waterproof fabric (urethane-coated nylon or plastic) that you wear next to your skin. Warm clothes are layered over that. Perspiration can't get through the waterproof fabric to dampen your clothes and reduce their insulating properties, so you stay warm even when you're inactive. It's like wearing a wet suit—you're warm but not very comfortable. Some people don't mind the damp feeling; others can't tolerate it.

VBLs were popular in the 1970s, especially for use as sleeping-bag liners. But the choir has quieted. In 2003 I attended an arctic survival school in Spitsbergen, Norway. It never warmed above twenty-four degrees below zero. Our instructor was a top winter-survival expert in the Norwegian army. He did not recommend vapor barriers.

WANIGANS

Wanigans are rigid boxes commonly used in the fur trade to carry hard goods like knives, guns, and axes that would be uncomfortable in a standard soft pack. Modern campers can use wanigans for the same purpose. For auto camping, nothing beats a well-organized wanigan camp kitchen, which has compartments for tin cans, utensils, and soft goods. Most commercial models have a plywood lid that doubles as work area and cutting board. You can get detailed plans for making a camp kitchen from many scout and YMCA camps.

Smaller hard packs are handy for canoe camping, picnicking, berry picking, and any activity requiring a strong, rigid container. The traditional hard pack for canoeing is the Maine pack basket, which is available from L.L. Bean, Inc. and Duluth Pack (see appendix B). If you place a woven ash basket into a waterproof sack (the army-surplus waterproof clothes bag is

Figure W-1. Wanigans, from left to right: pickle barrel with Ostrom Outdoors harness, Cooke Custom Sewing foam-lined food pack, Stormy Bay wanigan (no longer manufactured).

Figure W-2. The York Pack.

just the right size), then set this unit into a tailored backpack, you'll have a strong, watertight container that's comfortable to carry.

Tip: Make a number of narrow fabric pockets and attach these to the inside rim of your pack basket. Store sunglasses, a fillet knife, and other small items in these handy organizers.

A less-expensive solution is to nest a cheap rectangular plastic trash container inside a soft pack. This outfit will protect all your breakables.

A medium-size plastic ice chest (cooler) can also be pressed into service as a wanigan. It will be easier to carry if you strap it to a tubular aluminum pack frame.

Aluminum and plastic wanigans (usually called "dry boxes") are available from western raft companies. The York Pack (figure W-2) is a popular model.

Round Wanigans: Many years ago a resourceful Canadian canoeist, who was on the prowl for a low-cost wanigan, tried an experiment: He packed some hard items that would gouge his back in a giant plastic pickle barrel. His canoe capsized and everything in the barrel came through dry. The word that there was a new round wanigan in town spread like an Ontario bush fire, and soon everyone copied the plan. Then capitalism reared its ugly head, and the smelly plastic jars that were once free for the asking began to sell for big bucks. (Any relationship to the true story of how this all began is purely coincidental!)

Pickle barrels are more watertight than any wanigan, but they are a pain to pack and portage. A few pack makers, notably Ostrom Outdoors and Headstrong Packs (www.ostrom packs.com; www.headstrong packs.com; see appendix B). offer clever foam-padded har-nesses, which help (figure W-3). Barrels were unpopular in the States until recently; now most every canoe shop has them.

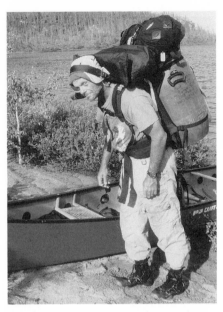

Figure W-3. Pickle barrel packs are water-proof but *not* bearproof! This Ostrom-designed pack harness makes the barrel very comfortable to carry. PHOTO: OSTROM OUTDOORS

WATERPROOF BAGS AND BOXES

To make a plastic bag water-proof, tightly twist the neck of the bag and fold it over. Secure the gooseneck with a rubber band (figure W-4). This procedure is recommended by the Boy Scouts.

Aloksak waterproof and waterproof/odorproof plastic bags (www.watchfuleyedesigns.com or www.aloksak.com; see appendix B): These inexpensive plastic bags look like ordinary zipper-lock bags, but they are much stronger and are waterproof to depths exceeding 190 feet, even when placed under mild compression. They have a patented triple seal and come in sizes to fit everything from passports and cell phones to topographic maps and bulky clothes. Odorproof (they block *all* odors!) ver-sions, originally developed for the safe disposal of hazardous biological wastes, are also available.

Waterproof boxes: A waterproof box is only as good as its seal. Quality control is never 100 percent, so carefully eyeball the seal, inch by inch, before you buy. A magnifying glass will show imperfections. The slightest dent or cut will let water in.

After each use in the field: It takes just one tiny plant seed, blade of grass, or dirt particle to corrupt the seal of a waterproof box. You'll get a perfect seal every time if, just before you close the box, you wipe the full

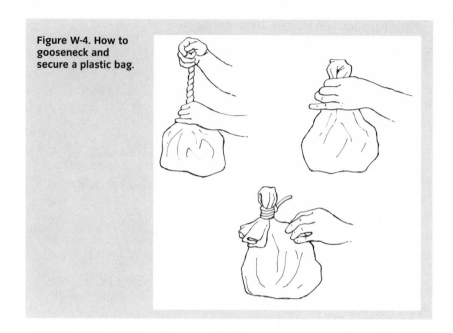

Figure W-4. How to gooseneck and secure a plastic bag.

length of the seal with a cotton bandanna, preferably one moistened with water. I've religiously followed this procedure for years and I've never had a problem, even when my canoe capsized and the box was submerged in a pounding current for many minutes.

A few times each season: Use a Q-tip to clean the seal with water. Rubbing alcohol will remove tree sap and insect fragments. Apply silicone spray and you're done.

Tip: Plastic deteriorates and becomes brittle after long exposure to sunlight. Occasionally (once a year is enough) spray the outside of your waterproof plastic boxes with a nonoily ultraviolet protectant (I prefer 303 Protectant).

WATER TREATMENT

There are few places in North America where you can safely drink water from a lake or stream. And conditions don't seem to be improving. Water quality—and just plain availability of water—remains a major environmental concern. Unless you always camp where the quality of drinking water is guaranteed, you should carry your water or treat it by one of these methods.

Field Methods of Water Treatment

1. *Boiling* is the most reliable way to kill almost everything. Even cryptosporidium, which can survive exposure to iodine, chlorine, and bleach, is killed by boiling. If you are uncertain about the quality of your drinking water, boiling is the best way to make it safe. Simply bring your water to a rolling boil then shut off your stove. There's no need to adjust boiling times for altitude.

2. *Filtration:* Mechanical filters have improved steadily since the first edition of *Camping's Top Secrets.* There are a lot more options than two decades ago. If you opt for mechanical filtration, choose a large-capacity unit whose pores will remove the smallest infectious agents you are likely to encounter. By comparison, a filter with a 4-micron absolute pore size will stop giardia; a 1-micron filter will halt cryptosporidium. "Absolute" pore size means that no hole in the filter is smaller than the diameter indicated. Generally, large pores mean fast delivery, while small pores slow the flow. The industry standard for removing bacteria is 0.45 microns (absolute). Be sure you can easily replace or clean the filter. Naturally, it's wise to carry a spare.

   Note: Some filters use iodine to "purify" the water after it has been filtered. The drawback is that the iodine imparts a bitter aftertaste that some people find objectionable. An optional carbon cartridge removes some of the bad taste.

3. *Chemical treatment:* Halazone tablets are an old standby that have been available from corner drugstores for years. If you use Halazone, take an unopened bottle on each trip. The product loses considerable strength when exposed to air and heat.

   Aqua Mira (called Pristine in Canada) is the latest high-tech water purification pill. It comes in two bottles. You mix drops of each together, and the chlorine dioxide that is formed kills microorganisms in about thirty minutes. It's easy to use and it has very little chlorine aftertaste.

   MSR (www.msrcorp.com; see appendix B) recently released an impressive Magic Marker–size purifier called the MIOX, which uses electricity and salt to produce a powerful disinfectant that kills everything. Simple and fast, it's ideal for purifying large volumes of water. The water has minimal aftertaste.

   Important: Any chlorine-based system will leave an aftertaste if you don't allow the chlorine gas to evaporate. No problem if you purify your water in an open container (pot or bucket). If you don't, you should aerate the mix before you drink it—simply pour the water back and forth from one poly bottle to another several times.

Chlorine: Liquid chlorine bleach with 4 to 6 percent available chlorine may be used to purify water. Use two drops of bleach per quart of clear water and four drops per quart of cold or cloudy water. Let treated water stand for thirty minutes before using. You should be able to smell the chlorine gas. If not, repeat the dosage and let it stand another fifteen minutes before using. If the water is very cold or cloudy, let it stand overnight before using.

Note: None of the chemicals work very well in cold, cloudy water. Under these conditions, your best bet is to boil your water!

My preference? I like the MSR MIOX and the archaic Katadyn Pocket Filter, which is beautifully machined from aluminum. The Katadyn is terribly slow and frightfully expensive, but it's easy to maintain and reliable. And its ceramic filter leaves no bitter aftertaste. For an ultralight kit, Aqua Mira is the way to go.

Tip: You can sterilize your camp dishes by simply adding a splash of chlorine bleach to the final rinse water. Or add a convenient EfferSan tablet (www.activon.com; see appendix B). EfferSan tablets have 30 percent available chlorine in a handy dry form.

Iodine: Place six grams of iodine (your pharmacist will weigh it out for you) in a one-ounce amber bottle. Fill the bottle with water. The iodine crystals will dissolve until a saturated solution results, then no more crystals will dissolve.

Sterilize a quarter canteen of water by pouring about half (the amount isn't critical) the iodine solution into the canteen. Let the canteen stand at least thirty minutes before drinking. Allow additional time for cold or cloudy water.

Recharge the iodine bottle with fresh water after each use. Only a small amount of iodine will dissolve from the crystals each time, so you may continue to use the "iodine decant bottle" dozens of times until no more crystals are visible.

Caution: Do not allow any iodine crystals to enter your canteen. Large doses of iodine can be fatal! (Iodine is a rather heavy metal and is visible in solution, so you'll have no trouble seeing the crystals or containing them in your bottle.)

You may also treat your water with a commercial tablet that releases iodine. Potable Aqua (sold nearly everywhere) is highly recommended.

A 2 percent tincture of iodine solution may also be used to purify water. Use six to eight drops of iodine per quart of drinking water. Let the chemical work for at least thirty minutes before you drink the water. Double the dosage and working time if the water is cold or cloudy.

Note: Products that release chlorine will not destroy giardia cysts under all conditions, and they won't destroy cryptosporidium cysts under any conditions! If you suspect contamination by these parasites, boil your water or use a water filter with an absolute pore size of 1 to 2 microns or smaller. Authorities generally agree that compounds that release iodine are more reliable than those that emit chlorine.

4. *Ultraviolet light treatment:* The Hydro-Photon company (www.hydro-photon.com) recently introduced a penlike device that uses ultraviolet light to purify water. Called the SteriPEN, the device weighs seven ounces and runs off four AA batteries. It's safe to use, reasonably fast, and treated water has no aftertaste. It's designed to purify one liter of water or less at a time—it won't purify a big bucket. The concern is its high cost (about $150 at this writing) and its fragile (very pricey) ultraviolet bulb.

Where Not to Get Your Drinking Water

1. Go well away from the shoreline to get drinking water. If you're camping at a spot frequented by man or animals, go upstream of the source to get water. On lakes, go a minimum of 150 feet from shore, and the farther (and deeper) the better.

    Tip: Place a rock in your largest cooking pot and lower it deep into the lake with a long rope. Work the bucket up and down like a yo-yo to guarantee good exchange of water. Water taken 20 feet or more below the lake surface is apt to be most trustworthy.

2. Avoid water that has a greenish color. The green tinge indicates the presence of algae, which attracts microorganisms. Tan-colored water, however, is usually safe. Invariably, this color suggests natural runoff of tannic acid from adjacent conifer stands (quite common throughout the upper Midwest).

3. Take your drinking water from fast-moving areas; avoid backwaters,

stagnant areas, and eddies, which are breeding places for microorganisms.

4. Never drink any water that has been contaminated by wastes from a paper mill. Instead, secure your water from incoming streams or springs.

5. Don't take water near beaver dams or lodges. Beaver are the favored hosts of *Giardia lamblia,* a small protozoan that may cause severe discomfort. Giardia enters a water supply through the feces of the host. Its cyst can survive up to two months in 46-degree Fahrenheit water, and up to one month in 70-degree water!

   The infection carried by the organism is called giardiasis, characterized by severe diarrhea, cramps, nausea, and vomiting. Incubation time is one to two weeks, though some people have gone as long as two months without getting sick. If untreated, the disease may go on for years!

   Giardiasis is usually diagnosed by stool examination, which is not always reliable. Most physicians just haven't had enough experience with the disease to correctly diagnose it. As a result, many victims suffer for months before they get the help they need. Not everyone who is exposed to the giardia parasite comes down with the disease. Indeed, most people are simply carriers.

6. Contrary to popular belief, clear water tumbling over sunny rocks *may not* be safe to drink. While ultraviolet light does kill microorganisms, flowing water mixes them and increases the chance they'll get in your drinking water. Better to take your drinking water from the deep sunlit pool nearby.

7. Take water from small tributaries that flow into a stream. The closer to the source of the tributary, the better.

8. Water from a still, deep pool should be taken near the surface and as far from shore as possible. Harmful microbes tend to lurk just below the surface of calm water, out of reach of sunlight.

Treatment for giardiasis and cryptosporodiosis: Metronidazole (Flagyl) and furazolidone (Furoxone) are the recommended prescription drugs for treating giardiasis. It's a good idea to carry a supply on long trips. There is no treatment for cryptosporodiosis, whose symptoms are similar to giardiasis. Cryptosporodiosis usually runs its course in one to two weeks.

WEATHER FORECASTING

Every outdoors person should have a basic understanding of weather phe-nomena and be able to make reasonably accurate short-term weather pre-dictions. Some campers take forecasting quite seriously; they arm themselves with min/max thermometers, barometers, cloud charts, and weather tables. Whether or not this paraphernalia will improve your short-range forecasts is debatable. After all, primitive man is right on target more than 80 percent of the time simply by looking at the sky, sensing the wind, and "feeling" the weather. You can approximate this enviable suc-cess rate by applying these time-proven principles:

1. "Red sky at night, sailor's delight; red sky in the morning, sailor take warning." Translation: A red morning sky indicates possible rain that day; a red evening sky suggests the next day will be clear. The color dif-ference relates to the reflective value of the low-lying cloud cover.

2. Check the grass, tent, canoe bottom, or whatever for the presence of dew in late evening or early morning. A heavy dew at either of these times usually suggests eight to twelve hours of good weather.

3. Watch the smoke from your campfire. If it hangs low (a function of low pressure) to the ground, rain is on the way. If it rises high into a nice ver-tical column (high pressure), count on good weather.

4. Check out the air bubbles in your coffee cup. They'll ring the edges of the cup when a low pressure (rain) system sets in.

5. You can sometimes smell a coming storm, as the low pressure allows methane (swamp gas) to rise and drift with the current. In boggy areas the odor is quite pronounced.

6. "When the peacock loudly bawls, there'll be both rain and squalls." Translation: Birds sing loudly just before a storm.

7. Geese and seagulls usually won't fly just before a storm. Low-pressure air is thin and it's hard for them to get airborne.

8. The ears of many animals are sensitive to low pressure. Wolves will howl before a storm. Dogs will become nervous and emit howls or howl-like sounds.

9. To determine the distance of a lightning strike, count the seconds between the flash and the thunder boom. Divide by five and you'll have your answer in miles.

10. Noises all become louder and more vibrant just before a rain, because the sound is reflected and magnified by the low clouds. The croaking of frogs, yodel of loons, etc., will echo loudly if rain is imminent.

11. Be alert for changes in wind direction. Storms are whirlpools of wind that rotate counterclockwise in the Northern Hemisphere (remember high school science?). The adage "Wind from the south brings rain in its mouth" is the keystone here, as the wind that precedes a storm usually blows from the south. Counterclockwise wind shifts therefore usually bring rain, while clockwise movements indicate fair weather. You can keep these directional changes straight by remembering the rhymes . . .

    "Wind from the east brings weather that's a beast." (Suggests a counterclockwise wind shift from south to east, east to north, and so on.)

    "Wind from the west brings weather that's best." (Suggests a clockwise wind shift from south to west, north to east, etc.)

12. Most everyone knows that frogs emerge from the water just before a storm and croak their fool heads off. Frogs breathe partly through their skin (which must be kept moist), so when the humidity rises just before a storm, they climb ashore and sing happily.

13. If you're a canoeist, you know that about eight to twelve hours before a storm, mosquitoes and blackflies begin to swarm and bite more than usual. Up to two hours before the storm they quit biting altogether.

14. Check out the rainbow: A heavy red may mean more rain; vibrant rich blue suggests clear skies ahead.

15. Here's an old Down East proverb: "Filly tails make lofty ships wear low sails." Translation: Thin, hairlike clouds forecast rain within the day. These "filly tails" are really streaks of ice thrown skyward by the rising air of a coming storm.

16. "A mackerel sky [tiny scalelike clouds that resemble a mackerel's back], just twenty-four hours dry." Translation: Expect rain within the next day!

17. Any fireflies around? When rain approaches, these little insects light up the woods, according to this rhyme: "When the little glow bug lights his lamp, the air around is surely damp."

18. Listen for the rustle of leaves as the wind precedes the storm.

19. If you can't see the sharp points on a half moon, rain may be on its way. Translation: Low clouds and haze distort sharp images.

20. Bright, twinkling stars usually indicate high altitude winds, which may be bringing in a storm.

21. There's a good chance that foul weather (rain or snow) will fall within three days of a new moon phase.

22. "The weather out west had best be best, for tomorrow will bring it to you to test!" This means that in all likelihood, the weather system to your west will be at your location tomorrow.

23. In summer a sun dog, or halo around the sun, generally predicts the coming of rain. Sun dogs are caused by sunlight streaming through the ice particles of high cirrostratus clouds. A halo around the moon may also indicate rain.

24. "Evening fog will not burn soon, but morning fog will burn before high noon." Invariably, a fog-borne day will become perfectly clear (an ideal day) by noon. Fog forms when water vapor reaches the dew point and condenses on dust particles near the ground. When the day heats up, the fog evaporates and turns to invisible water vapor.

25. "Short notice, soon it will pass. Long notice, expect it to last." Watch the clouds. If they take several days to build, a warm front—and prolonged rain—is usually in the offing. If the storm system builds suddenly, it will probably pass quickly.

26. And of course everyone knows: "Rain before seven, dry by eleven."

Y

YARD GOODS AND REPAIR MATERIALS

Tools You'll Need to Make Repairs

Sewing machine: From time to time you'll have to mend tears in tents, sleeping bags, tarps, and clothing. Of course you can send things out for repair, but it's less expensive—and frankly more fun—to do it yourself. By and large you'll be sewing lightweight fabrics, so any light-duty sewing machine will do. Many years ago I purchased a coal black, 1958 Singer. It sews forward and backward, that's all. I've used the old Singer to patch countless packs and tarps and to build more than twenty nylon splash covers for canoes. I paid $75 for the Singer, complete with maple cabinet. Good buys on old machines are still available.

Sailmaker's needles and waxed thread: Sailmaker's needles are available from Tandy Leather Company and others who sell leather supply products. Half a dozen heavy-duty needles and a bobbin of waxed thread should last for years. Use *two* needles when you sew. Figure Y-1 shows how to make a strong machinelike stitch that will never let go. *Tip:* This "double-needle machine stitch" is the one to use when sewing a knife or ax sheath. At home, use an electric drill to make the needle holes in thick leather. In the field, a thin awl will do.

Sewing awl: The awls that come on Swiss Army knives and multipurpose tools are too coarse for fine work. Get a small, sharp awl at your local fabric store.

Speedy Stitcher sewing awl: The Speedy Stitcher has been around for decades. It has a self-contained bobbin and a strong, replaceable needle. A heavy wooden handle allows you bore through thick material. In all, the Speedy Stitcher is a solid and practical little machine, though it's a bit cumbersome for go-light trips. Two sailmaker's needles and a sharp awl are slower to use but produce results as good as the Speeder Stitcher.

Don't forget to include in your repair kit: swatches of material to match your equipment; buckles; 1-inch-wide nylon webbing; two-piece, solid brass snaps (a Tandy Leather Company item); instant epoxy; nylon filament tape; gray duct tape; tweezers; needle-nose pliers; scissors; safety pins.

Thrifty Outfitters (see appendix B) in Minneapolis is an excellent source of fabrics, hardware, and repair materials. As mentioned earlier, Thrifty is the Midwest's only authorized repair center for Gore-Tex products.

Here's the lowdown on all the modern "yard goods."

Cotton

Cotton is a marvelous material for large, semipermanent tents and for any application that requires breathability and durability. Military tents are still constructed from cotton canvas duck, as are most of the high-grade wall tents you see in western hunting camps.

Canvas breathes as it sheds water, which means that tents made of this fabric are wonderfully comfortable (no condensation) in wet weather. Worn canvas is easily restored to waterproof condition by painting on chemicals that can be purchased in most hardware stores. Mending the damaged polyurethane coatings on nylon fabrics is at best difficult.

Cotton has a nonskid surface, has a nice soft "hand," and feels good against the skin. It's ideal as a covering for foam sleeping pads and seat

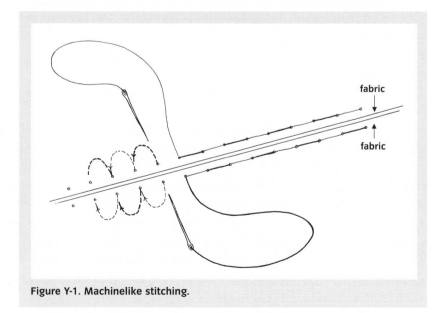

fabric

fabric

Figure Y-1. Machinelike stitching.

and boat cushions, for tent and tool bags, and for hats. A cotton-poplin parka is luxurious and will ward off quite a shower if treated with water-repellent chemicals. Cotton fabrics retain water repellents much more willingly than do nylon materials. Note that nylon *stretches* when it gets wet, whereas canvas *shrinks.*

Being a natural fiber, cotton also has considerable flex. Haul a heavy nylon pack across sharp granite and the nylon fibers won't give much. Do the same with a canvas pack and the cotton fibers will stretch and return to shape. The result is that canvas packs often outlive nylon ones, even though they are technically less strong. Some of my canvas Duluth packs are thirty years old and are still serviceable.

Army duck is the strongest and heaviest (and most expensive!) of the cotton fabrics. It is woven so that each warp yarn passes over (or under) a single filling yarn (similar to those loop pot holders you made as a child). "Duck" is available in weights from 7 to 15 ounces per square yard. The army prefers 12- to 15-ounce fabrics for their heavy truck tarps and bivouac tents, but 7- to 8-ounce weights are better for family campers. Army duck is the king of cotton tent fabrics.

Twill is woven so that each warp yarn passes over two or more filling yarns. It's less strong than duck and is used mostly to make military uniforms. It's tough stuff and it weighs about 8 ounces per square yard.

Drill is a three-leaf twill made from fairly coarse yarns. It's more loosely woven than duck and less expensive. The cheapest canvas tents are often made from drill.

Cotton-poplin is a tightly woven fabric that's produced by using yarns that are heavier and more coarse than the warp yarns. Poplin comes in weights of 4 to 11 ounces per square yard. Some family-size wall tents are woven from 5½-ounce fabric.

Egyptian, pima, and Supima cotton: Egyptian cotton has the longest fibers of all cottons, and it makes into the strongest and silkiest yarn. It is by far the most luxurious fabric for the interior shells of sleeping bags; no other material feels better against the skin. Pima cotton was developed by U.S. growers to compete with the Egyptian product, and it is nearly as good. Supima is the top of the pima crop. Tightly woven high-grade cotton isn't used much in its pure form anymore (it's very expensive). However, it is a marvelous material for sleeping bags, windshells, and summer shirts.

Ventile cotton was originally developed by the British to keep downed RAF fliers from freezing in the North Sea. It is so tightly woven that it will repel a shower for twenty minutes or more without the aid of chemical water repellents. Until the advent of Gore-Tex, all the best parkas in the world were made from Ventile. Unfortunately, this fabric is heavy when dry, heavier when wet, very expensive, and difficult to find. It is a wonderfully luxurious and long-lived material.

Waxed cotton: Wax or oil is applied to densely woven cotton duck—a method of waterproofing that dates from the days of iron men and wooden ships. Now scores of fashionable parkas—notably Australian Outback riding garments—are waterproofed by this method. Pluses include a soft, draping hand and luxurious texture, good breathability and durability, an attractive natural odor, and a techy but traditional look. Waxed-cotton garments must be periodically maintained by rubbing in more oil. These garments work well in moderate rains but not in bad storms. They are no match for today's best rain gear. Waxed-cotton parkas have become a cult thing among outdoor enthusiasts: They are quite expensive.

Microfibers

Microfibers (nylon, polyester, and acrylic) are extremely fine—about one hundred times thinner than human hair! Their small diameter gives them unique properties that thicker, conventional fibers can't match. For example, they can bend more easily than thicker fibers, so they feel soft and luxurious against the skin. They resist pilling, keep their shape through many washings, and dry almost instantly.

Microfiber liners are widely used in wind- and raincoats because they're wonderful at wicking moisture away from the skin. A microfiber lining will make any garment feel less clammy in damp weather. A drawback is their sensitivity to heat—campfires (especially, sparks!) and hot clothes driers are deadly.

Nylon Fabrics

Nylon is used for everything from tents to boots. Nylon is strong, light, and relatively inexpensive. On the negative side, it degrades rapidly in ultraviolet light and stretches considerably when wet. It also shrinks over the years.

Taffeta is a flat-woven fabric that weighs between 2.5 and 3.5 ounces per square yard. Taffeta is more prone to tear than ripstop, but it has greater resistance to abrasion, the reason why most tent flies and floors are made of this material.

Polyurethane-coated nylon taffeta is the fabric of choice for lightweight rain gear, stuff sacks, and backpack tarps. Uncoated (porous) taffeta is a popular fabric for garments. Uncoated taffeta has no water repellency. Waterproof coatings last for years, not decades. It's best to toss your rain gear at the first sign of a leak than to attempt repairs with the expensive paint-on chemicals sold at camping stores.

Ripstop has a gridwork of heavy threads woven in at quarter-inch intervals to increase fabric strength. It weighs 1.5 to 2.0 ounces per square yard. Ripstop is widely used for lightweight tent canopies, sleeping-bag shells, and wind garments. Coated ripstop makes a nice lightweight rain tarp.

Vinyl-coated nylon is a heavy-weight plastic-coated nylon used largely for heavy-duty tent floors and tarps. It's much stronger and more resistant to abrasion than coated taffeta, but its vinyl coating may soften or peel if it is exposed to heavy doses of harsh solvents, such as those used in some insecticides.

Cordura is the toughest nylon of all. It resists abrasion and puncture far better than any other fabric of equal weight. Many of the best backpacks are made from it, and it's widely used in the manufacturing of lightweight hiking boots. However, heavy-weight Cordura does not accept waterproofing compounds very well. Invariably tiny pinholes (which you can see when the fabric is held up to a strong light) of untreated material remain, which will admit some water.

Packcloth is a medium-weight nylon weave with a heavy polyurethane coating. Packcloth is lighter, less abrasion resistant, and more waterproof than Cordura. It also costs less than Cordura.

Coated oxford cloth (which weighs about six ounces per square yard) is a strong, absolutely watertight fabric used in the manufacture of lightweight backpacks. This is the same stuff that Eureka uses for flooring in their outfitter Timberline tents. It is the best material I've found for making fabric splash covers for canoes.

Taslan nylon: Nylon yarn is textured with jets of air to make it feel soft and cottony. Taslan nylon fabrics are lightweight, durable, and very resistant to abrasion. Taslan nylon is much less "slippery" than regular nylon.

Ballistics cloth is a 1050+ denier nylon. The yarn was originally developed as a tire cord then later refined into cloth for military flak vests. Ballistics cloth is exceptionally strong and abrasion resistant. It is less flexible than Cordura or cotton canvas. Like all synthetic fibers, ballistics cloth must be coated with polyurethane to make it waterproof.

Note: All these nylon fabrics can be had with or without waterproof coatings. Weight and cost of the fabrics will vary depending upon the type and amount of coating applied.

Polyethylene and Polypropylene

Polyethylene-coated polyethylene is a tough polyethylene fabric with a polyethylene plastic coating on both sides. The material is mildewproof and is commonly used for heavy-duty tent floors and tarps. Both vinyl-coated nylon and polyethylene-coated polyethylene are much more dimensionally stable (less wet stretch/dry shrinkage) than polyurethane-coated nylon.

Propex (Condessa) is a woven polypropylene that is designed for use in luggage. It resists solvents, stains, molds, abrasion and tears. The (coated) material weighs about twelve ounces per square yard and looks and feels almost exactly like eighteen-ounce canvas. Tough stuff . . . and very beautiful.

Blends

Sixty/forty cloth (60 percent cotton/40 percent nylon) is woven with nylon threads in one direction and cotton in the other. The nylon supplies strength, the cotton provides water repellency and a luxurious feel. A lot of great mountain parkas are built from 60/40 cloth.

Sixty-five/thirty-five cloth: Cotton and polyester yarns are blended together then woven into the garment. Threads of each yarn run in both directions. This fabric is supposed to be more water repellent and have greater strength than 60/40 cloth.

There are also a number of exotic blends that feature cotton, polyester, and nylon in varying weaves and amounts. Generally, the higher the nylon content, the stronger, lighter and less water repellent the garment. More cotton and polyester mean a softer hand, higher water repellency, and heavier weight. In practice, the differences between these similar fabrics are relatively insignificant.

Here are some other common fabric terms you may encounter:

Acrylic: The generic name for fibers made from polyacrylonitrile. Acrylics are soft, washable, nonallergenic, and quick drying. In the days before fleece, acrylics were *the* substitute for wool. They are still a good choice for growing kids and those on a budget.

Olefin (polypropylene): A paraffin-based fiber that doesn't absorb water. See the discussion of polypropylene long underwear in the CLOTHING section.

Spandex (Dupont calls it Lycra) is very stretchy but has a good memory for shape. It's always used in combination with other fibers like cotton or nylon.

Triblend: Three different fibers woven together—like cotton/nylon/polyester. Each fiber contributes something special to the blend.

Tricot: A strong double-thread weave that doesn't easily tear or fray.

Appendix A: Recommended Reading

Basic Essentials: Knots for the Outdoors, second edition. Cliff Jacobson. Globe Pequot Press, 1999. All the knots and hitches you need to know for camping. Includes left-handed illustrations of every knot and hitch.

Basic Essentials: Map and Compass, third edition. Cliff Jacobson. Falcon, 2006. All you need to know to navigate by map and compass and GPS. Widely used by schools, scouts, and summer camps.

Bear Attacks: The Deadly Truth. James Gary Shelton. Pallister Publishing, 1998. This book examines the lives of people who have survived bear attacks. Emphasis is on what went wrong.

Bear Attacks: Their Causes and Avoidance, revised edition. Stephen Herrero. Lyons Press, 2002. The most authoritative guide available. All the research is here!

Bear Attacks II: Myth and Reality. James Gary Shelton. Pallister Publishing, 2001. Firsthand accounts of bear attacks are analyzed to determine cause.

Bear Aware, third edition. Bill Schneider. Falcon, 2004. Solid advice for those who camp in western national parks like Yellowstone.

Bear Encounter Survival Guide. James Gary Shelton. Pallister Publishing, 1997. A refreshing look at bearhavior from a British Columbia woodsman who has spent the better part of his life around bears.

Camping and Woodcraft. Horace Kephart. Facsimile edition: University of Tennessee Press, 1988. First published in 1917, this classic started the camping revolution. There's still much to learn from this old camping book.

Canoeing and Camping: Beyond the Basics, third edition. Cliff Jacobson. Falcon, 2006. Skills, equipment, and sage advice for canoeing wilderness waters—beginners through experts.

Expedition Canoeing: A Guide to Canoeing Wild Rivers in North America, fourth edition. Cliff Jacobson. Falcon, 2005. Experts consider this the premier guide to canoeing and exploring North America's waterways. Includes advice from the world's top paddlers. Now in its twentieth anniversary edition.

GPS Land Navigation. Michael Ferguson. Glassford Publishing, 1997. The most complete and intuitive text for learning about global positioning and coordinate systems.

The New Way of the Wilderness: The Classic Guide to Survival in the Wild, reprint. Cal Rutstrum. University of Minnesota Press, 2000. A must read for every serious camper, written by a master who spent long periods in the wilderness. I am proud to admit that Rutstrum was my mentor.

Wilderness Medicine: Beyond First Aid, fifth edition. William W. Forgey, M.D. Globe Pequot Press, 1999. The most practical and useful first-aid text for those who don't have much medical knowledge. Offers prescription and nonprescription advice and describes innovative first-aid kits you can assemble.

Woodcraft and Camping. George W. Sears Nessmuk. Dover, 1963. This camping classic was first published in 1920. "Nessmuk" canoed the Adirondacks alone in the early part of the twentieth century. His wisdom and sage advice continues today. If you love camping, you'll love this book!

Appendix B: Sources of Recommended Products

Aloksak waterproof plastic bags by Watchful Eye Designs: (800) 355–1126; www.aloksak.com, www.watchfuleyedesigns.com. Waterproof and odorproof zipper-lock bags. Used by government agencies and the military.

The Backpacker's Pantry Outback Oven: (303) 581–0518; www.backpackers pantry.com. Perfect bakestuff every time. Built-in oven thermometer.

Badger Healing Balm: (800) 603–6100; www.badgerbalm.com. Heals cracked skin fast. Its alcohol-free formula won't irritate cuts.

Chosen Valley Canoe Accessories: (507) 867–3961; www.gear4portaging.com. The universal pot handle system I inspired, plus high-tech canoeing accessories.

Chota: (877) 462–4682; www.chotaoutdoorgear.com. My favorite boots for canoeing and wet-weather camping.

Cooke Custom Sewing: (651) 784–8777; www.cookecustomsewing.com. Superior tarps, packs, winter mukluks, and specialized canoeing gear.

Counter Assault: (800) 695–3394, (406) 257–4740; www.counterassault.com. Pepper spray that will discourage bears.

DMT (Diamond Machining Technology): (800) 666–4DMT; www.dmtsharp.com. Diamond sharpening hones.

Duluth Pack: (800) 777–4439; www.duluthpack.com. Traditional canvas canoe packs and camping accessories.

EfferSan Sanitizer by Activon Products: (800) 841–0410; www.activon.com. Dry chlorine tablets that you add to rinse water to purify camp dishes.

Empire Canvas Works: (715) 378–4216; www.empirecanvasworks.com. Canvas summer and winter tents, mushing clothes, canoeing accessories, and more.

Fast Bucksaw: (651) 437–2566; www.fastbucksaw.com. Best folding camp saw I've found. Made by hand in small batches. Expect to wait weeks for delivery.

FoodSaver by Tilia: (877) 777–5670; http://foodsaver.jardindirect.com. Vacuum-sealing machine with enough power to crush a tin can.

Frost River: (800) 375–9394; www.frostriver.com. McAllister waxed canvas packs (the tiny Nessmuk is my favorite), tents, garment bags, briefcases, and more.

Granite Gear: (218) 834–6157; www.granitegear.com. Impeccable packs and paddling accessories that will stand up to the hardest use.

Gransfors Bruk axes: (843) 875–0240 (USA), (905) 681–3993 (Canada); www.gransfors.us. Best axes on the planet!

Grohmann Knives: (888) 7–KNIVES; www.grohmannknives.com. The #1 Original, the flat-ground carbon camper, is my favorite factory knife.

Headstrong Packs: (604) 628–2436 (USA), (416) 693–6083 (Canada); www.headstrongpacks.com. Sturdy and very comfortable barrel harness.

Icebreaker pure merino wool underwear and outerwear: www.icebreaker.com. Supersoft, itch-free, 100 percent merino wool layered garments.

Idaho Knife Works: (509) 994–9394; www.idahoknifeworks.com. Source of the Cliff knife I designed and other terrific knives with carbon-steel blades.

Klar Ullfrotté merino wool-polyamide underwear and outerwear: (800) 433–2863; www.ullfrotte.com. Merino wool layered garments. Extremely soft and warm. Widely worn by police, military personnel, and rescue teams.

MIOX water purifier from MSR: (800) 531–9531; www.msrcorp.com. A fast and simple purifier in a compact size.

Nalgene bottles by United States Plastics Corporation: (800) 809–4217; www.usplastic.com. Is there anyone who hasn't heard of Nalgene plastic bottles?

N/R Laboratories No-Rinse shampoo and body bath: (800) 223–9348. Ideal products for trips where clean water is hard to find.

The Original Bug Shirt: (800) 998–9096, (705) 729–5620 (Canada); www.bugshirt.com. Highly recommended if bugs drive you batty.

Ostrom Outdoors: (877) 678–7661, (807) 473–4499 (Canada); www.ostrompacks.com. Superbly designed high-tech packs and paddling accessories for those who demand the very best. Their barrel harness is awesome!

Razor Edge Systems, Inc.: (800) 541–1458, (218) 365–6419; www.razoredgesystems.com. Unique, effective sharpening system for knives.

Sawyer repellents: (800) 940–4464, (727) 725–1177; www.sawyerproducts.com. Insect repellents, insecticides, and tick pliers.

Smartwool: (888) 879–9665; www.smartwool.com. Super-soft, pure merino wool socks and underwear.

Steger mukluks: (800) 685–5857; www.mukluks.com. The most comfortable and beautiful mukluks on the planet.

SteriPEN: (888) 826–6234; www.hydro-photon.com. Water purification "pen" that uses ultraviolet light to purify water.

Surefire: (800) 828–8809 (USA), (714) 545–9444 (Canada); www.surefire.com. Ultra-high-powered tactical flashlights (bulb and LED)—many times more powerful than traditional lights. They are widely used by law enforcement personnel and are so bright they can disable an attacker—or a determined wild animal.

Tentsmiths: (603) 447–2344; www.tentsmiths.com. Old-time tents made from traditional canvas.

Thermax and Thermistat long underwear from Cabela's, Inc.: (800) 237–4444; www.cabelas.com. A comfortable and odor-free alternative to wool.

Thrifty Outfitters: (800) 866–3162, (612) 339–6290; www.thriftyoutfitters.com. If Thrifty can't fix it, forget it! Certified Gore-Tex repair facility.

Tingley rubber boots: (800) 631–5498; www.tingleyrubber.com. Inexpensive knee-high rubber boots that fit over running shoes.

TrailBlazer Outdoor Quality Products: (800) 565–6564; www.trailblazer products.com. Sawvivor and Trailblazer aluminum saws.

Uncle Keith's Northern Canadian Bug-Free Insect Repellent Jacket, available from the Arctic Trading Company: (800) 665–0431, (204) 675–8804; www .arctictradingcompany.com. Very effective DEET-impregnated open-mesh bug jacket—a favorite of arctic adventurers.

Glossary of Common Camping Terms

agonic line: A line of zero compass declination along which the compass needle points to both true and magnetic north.

A-frame tent: An inverted V-shaped tent with one or two poles at each end.

anorak: A shell parka that goes on over the head. Anoraks have a chest-length zipper or snaps. They conserve heat better than full-zip parkas.

Arkansas stone: A medium-hard mineral stone used for putting a fine edge on knives.

azimuth: Commonly used to indicate a directional bearing in degrees or mils. Technically, *azimuth* relates direction to one (or a fraction of one) of the 360 degrees of the compass rose. A *bearing* (often used synonymously with azimuth) relates direction to the north or south cardinal point. Example: An azimuth of 330 degrees equals a bearing of north 30° west. An azimuth of 160 degrees equals a bearing of south 20° east, etc.

baffle: Fabric panels sewn to the inner and outer shell of a sleeping bag. Baffles keep the insulation in place. Down bags must be baffled. Most synthetic bags feature quilted insulation.

bannock: The traditional trail bread. Usually made in a skillet by a combination of frying and reflective baking.

bathtub floor: A tent floor that wraps 6 inches or more up sidewalls of the tent before it is sewn in. This construction eliminates ground-level perimeter seams, which can leak.

Bean boots: Slang for *Maine Hunting Shoe,* the leather-top/rubber-bottom boots invented by Leon Bean.

bearing: A compass direction (see *azimuth*).

billy can: A straight-sided cooking pot with a wire bail.

*bivouac: T*echnically, a temporary encampment. Modern usage connotes an emergency or bush camp made where no other camp has stood.

blousing bands: Elastic bands used by the military to secure pant-leg bottoms around boots. Blousing bands are useful for sealing trouser legs against mosquitoes and blackflies.

breathable: Refers to the porosity of fabrics. Breathable materials are not waterproof.

bug jacket: A fabric mesh jacket impregnated with insect repellent.

cagoule: A waterproof, ankle-length, over-the-head parka used by mountaineers for bivouacking. Cagoules have tailored hoods and drawstring hems. The wearer pulls his legs inside, draws the hem tight, and "outlasts" the elements.

canopy: The (usually porous) roof of a tent. Not to be confused with the waterproof tent fly.

cap fly: Three-quarter-length tent fly. Tents with cap flies are not as weatherproof as those with full-length flies.

catenary cut: The natural curve formed by a rope tightly strung between two trees. A tent that has a catenary cut rigs tighter (has less sidewall sag) than one without catenary cut. Catenary cut is a feature of the best tents.

chute cord: Slang for parachute cord.

contour lines: Thin brown lines on maps connecting points of equal elevation.

cord lock: Spring-loaded nylon clamp used to secure the drawstring closures of stuff sacks.

crash out: To bushwhack out of a forested area to a trail, road, or meadow.

cruiser compass: A needle compass that has the numbers on the dial reversed (running counterclockwise rather than clockwise) to permit reading bearings in the same plane as the observer's eye. Cruiser compasses are still used by some professionals, but there are better choices for campers. The design of these instruments originated in the nineteenth century, and they are now outdated.

cryptosporidium: A protozoan you won't want in your drinking water! Causes symptoms similar to giardiasis. Cryptosporidium cysts may be killed by boiling or removed by filtering. They resist most chemicals.

declination: The difference between true or geographic north and magnetic north. Declination (also called *variation* by mariners) is expressed in degrees east or west of the agonic line.

DEET: Slang for N,N-diethyl-meta-toluamide, the active ingredient in most insect repellents.

diamond stone: A type of man-made sharpening stone that contains powdered diamonds. Diamond stones are lubricated with water (not cutting oil). They remove metal much faster than traditional oil stones.

differential cut: When the inner shell of a sleeping bag is cut smaller than the outer shell to produce a Thermos-bottle effect. The merits of this construction are still being argued by equipment freaks.

dining fly: An overhead tarp (fly) used for protection from rain. Usually erected just before meals, hence the descriptive name.

double-wall tent: A tent with a double-layered wall. All modern nylon tents are built this way, featuring a breathable taffeta canopy (inner wall) and a watertight ripstop fly (outer wall). Double-wall canvas tents are sometimes used in winter (with a sheepherder stove) to conserve heat.

draft tube: A down-filled tube that runs the length of a sleeping bag zipper to prevent cold air from filtering through the zipper teeth.

dropped-point knife: The favored style for hunting knives. The point is centered (similar to a spear point) on the blade. Dropped-point knives are ideal for skinning game animals but are not the most suitable style for camp knives.

Duluth pack: A voluminous envelope-style pack (usually canvas) popular with canoeists.

Dutch oven: A unique oven consisting of a heavy-walled pot and cover with a large retaining rim. Coals from the fire are placed on top of the pot lid and the affair is set into the hot ashes. Heat from the top does most of the baking.

EVA (ethyl vinyl acetate): Strongest, most resilient, and most expensive of the closed-cell foams. EVA makes an excellent trail mattress.

fanny pack: Small, zippered nylon pack that's attached to a waist belt.

ferrule: The metal sleeve attached to fiberglass tent poles. Ferrules form a joint between pole sections.

filling power (of down): Same as *loft*. It's the thickness of a sleeping bag lying flat and fluffed. Generally speaking, the greater the loft of a sleeping bag, the warmer it will be.

fisherman's shirt: Same as a *cagoule,* only calf length and without a drawstring hem.

flat-fell seam: Overlapping construction. The seam goes through four layers of material.

fleece: See *pile.*

floating dial compass: A compass in which the needle is part of the numbered compass dial, which rotates as a unit. This allows the instrument to be read in the same plane as the eye of the user. Some styles are very accurate.

foam pad: A sleeping mattress made of either open- or closed-cell foam.

frame pack: A pack with an exterior aluminum or fiber framework.

frost liner: A detachable inner roof for a tent. Absorbs moisture that could otherwise condense, freeze, and drop on sleeping occupants. Frost liners are made from cotton or cotton-polyester fabric and are needed only in below-freezing conditions.

fuel bottle: Traditionally refers to Sigg aluminum bottles, which are used for the storage of gasoline and kerosene.

gators: Nylon anklets (usually with side zippers) used by skiers and mountaineers. Gators prevent snow from getting in your boot tops, and they add extra warmth.

gelatin-mold oven: An oven made from a large-ring aluminum gelatin mold.

geodesic dome: A dome-shaped tent with a strong faceted framework of tubular aluminum. Geodesic domes are the Cadillac of domes!

giardia: The causative pathogen of giardiasis.

giardiasis: A waterborne disease carried by the protozoan giardia. Giardia is commonly carried by beavers. Incubation time is one to two weeks.

GPS (Global Positioning System) unit: An electronic unit that receives positioning information from twenty-four orbiting satellites. With a civilian-model GPS, you can locate your position anywhere on Earth in a matter of minutes. Accuracy is 3 meters or less! Most units run on small batteries.

hip belt: A padded waist belt that secures to a backpack—makes carrying the pack much more comfortable.

hollow-ground knife: A knife with an edge ground to a concave bevel, which produces a thin, razor-sharp edge and a stiff spine.

hood closure: The tie cord and fastener that secure the hood of a sleeping bag around the sleeper's face.

hypothermia: A potentially lethal physical state caused by lowering of the body's core temperature due to exposure to cold, wet weather. Also called exposure sickness.

internal frame pack: A hiking pack with internal stays. The stays give the pack shape and make it more comfortable to carry than a traditional soft pack.

I-pole tent: A tent with a single vertical pole at each end.

kindling: Pencil-thin pieces of wood used to nurture a fire to a reliable blaze.

layering: Wearing several thin layers of clothes, one over the other. Layering is the most efficient clothing system for cold weather.

lensatic compass: A compass that features a built-in magnifying lens for ease of reading directions. The old army lensatic compass (no longer used) is the best example of this type of instrument. Lensatic compasses are impractical for camping (they don't have built-in protractors), slow to use, and no more accurate than modern orienteering instruments.

lock-back knife: A folding knife with an integral lock that secures the blade when open. Some modern lock backs are really side locks or front locks. Lock-back knives do not have pressure springs like ordinary jackknives, so they can be opened easily with one hand while wearing mittens.

loft: Thickness of a sleeping bag while laying flat and fluffed. Generally speaking, the higher the loft, the warmer the bag.

map index: A specially gridded small-scale map that lists maps in print, how and where to get them, and their cost.

millar mitts: Fingerless gloves used by mountaineers for technical climbing. Millar mitts are great for fishing, canoeing, and general hiking.

mocha: A popular camp drink of hot chocolate and coffee.

moleskin: Soft-surfaced bandaging material used to protect blisters. The sticky side of moleskin is placed over the unbroken blister; the cushioned surface absorbs the friction from socks and boots.

mountain parka: A generic name for full-zipper, thigh-length parkas. Mountain parkas usually have lots of pockets. They're traditionally constructed from 60/40 (60 percent nylon, 40 percent cotton) cloth, which is doubled for added warmth. The U.S. Army field jacket is a true mountain parka.

orienteering: An international sport that combines the skills of map and compass reading with cross-country running.

orienteering compass: A compass with a built-in protractor that allows you to determine directions from a map without orienting the map to north. This is the most practical compass style for outdoor use.

overlapping V-tube construction (sleeping bags): A type of baffle construction in which down is secured into V-shaped tubes that overlap one another. Some very warm winter sleeping bags are built this way.

pack basket: A basket pack traditionally woven from splints of black ash. This original American Indian–made item is still going strong in the New England area and is available from L.L. Bean. Pack baskets are ideal for berry picking, picnicking, canoe trips, and auto camping. They will protect your breakables. Compared to fabric packs, they are quite inexpensive.

parka: A thigh-length shell garment with integral hood. Parkas may be lined or filled with down, polyester, or other insulation for use in cold weather.

pelican case: Hard plastic, absolutely waterproof case that comes in many shapes and sizes—the Cadillac of waterproof cases.

pile: A luxuriously soft fabric made from polyester. Pile absorbs little water and it dries quickly. Pile has almost replaced wool as the material for cold-weather camping.

Polarguard: A synthetic polyester material widely used in sleeping bags and parkas. Polarguard is considered one of the best synthetic insulators.

poly bottle: Short for polyethylene bottle.

poncho: A rectangular, hooded rain garment. Ponchos provide good ventilation and can be worn over a hiking pack. They do not supply reliable protection from rain.

prime (as in *priming* a gasoline or kerosene stove): Stoves are usually primed by filling an integral spirit cup with gasoline or alcohol, then setting the fuel aflame. Stoves can be overprimed. If too much gasoline is forced into the spirit cup, the unit may ignite into a ball of uncontrollable flames.

prismatic compass: A compass with a built-in sighting prism. Prismatic compasses are a step up from lensatic types. They're expensive but not very versatile.

Quallofil: A synthetic material developed for use in sleeping bags and parkas. Each filament has four longitudinal holes that trap air and add warmth. Quallofil is one of the best synthetic insulators.

quick-release knot: A knot that can be removed by a simple pull of the tail. The most common quick-release knot is the bow used for tying your shoes.

quilt construction: A type of sleeping-bag construction in which the insulation is sewn (quiltlike) in place. This is an inexpensive way to make a summer-weight sleeping bag. This construction is suitable for winter use if the bag is double-quilted.

reflector oven: An aluminum sheet-metal oven that bakes by means of reflected heat. Reflector ovens are hard to keep clean and are cumbersome. They require an open flame for baking and cannot be used on stoves or over charcoal. They are very efficient if you have a nice bright fire.

ridge vent: The triangular window at the ridge of A-frame tents.

ripstop nylon: A lightweight nylon fabric that has heavier threads sewn in at approximate ¼-inch intervals. Ripstop is less likely to tear than taffeta but it has less resistance to abrasion.

seam sealer: A special glue, available at all camping shops, used to waterproof the stitching on tents and rain gear.

self-supporting tent: Theoretically, a tent that needs no staking. However, all self-supporting tents must be staked or they'll blow away in the wind.

semimummy bag: A sleeping bag with a barrel shape and no hood. A good choice for those who feel confined by the mummy shape but want lighter weight and more warmth than that supplied by standard rectangular sleeping bags.

sewn-through construction: Same as *quilt construction.*

shell (garments): Refers to unlined garments, or the interior or exterior wall of a sleeping bag.

sidewall baffle: A baffle that is opposite the zipper on a sleeping bag; it keeps the down from shifting along the length of the bag.

sixty/forty parka: A parka made from fabric that consists of 60 percent nylon and 40 percent cotton. The term 60/40 is now generic; it defines any mountain-style parka, regardless of the fabric composition. See *mountain parka.*

snow flaps: Earlike flaps sewn to the perimeter of a tent floor. Snow flaps are folded outward then piled with snow, eliminating the need for staking the tent. Snow flaps are an extra-cost feature of special-purpose winter tents.

sou'wester: The traditional rain hat of sailors and commercial fishermen. The sou'wester was developed centuries ago and is still the best of all foul-weather hats. The best sou'westers have ear flaps, a chin strap, and a flannel lining.

space-filler cut: Where the inner and outer shells of a sleeping bag are cut the same size. This construction allows the inner liner and fill to better conform to the curves of your body than the Thermos-bottle shape of the *differential cut.* The merits/demerits of space-filler versus differential cut are still being argued by sleeping-bag manufacturers.

space blanket: A mylar-coated blanket used in survival kits. Space blankets are waterproof and are very warm for their size and weight. Every camping shop has them.

spreader bar: Same as a *wand.* Used for spreading out a portion of a tent.

sternum strap: A short nylon strap that connects the shoulder straps of a hiking pack. A properly adjusted sternum strap transfers some of the pack load to the chest.

storm flap: A panel of material that backs the zipper of a parka and prevents the storm from getting in.

stuff sack: Traditionally a nylon sack in which a sleeping bag is stored. The term now defines any nylon bag with drawstring closure.

Svea: Brand name of the venerable Svea stove.

Swiss Army knife: Originally the issue knife of the Swiss Army. Now generic for any scout-style multitool pocket knife.

tinder: Ultrafine dry material used for starting a fire.

Tingleys: Tingley brand rubber boots slip over street shoes. They grip like iron, even on wet rocks, wear like steel, weigh almost nothing, and are inexpensive. Most construction supply stores have them.

topo map: A topographic map that shows the lay of the land by means of contour lines.

trenching (also called "ditching"): Digging a trench around a tent to carry away groundwater that accumulates during a heavy rain. This form of guttering is illegal in all wilderness areas. Ground cloths and tent floors have eliminated the need to trench tents.

tumpline: A head strap used to carry heavy loads. Voyageurs carried hundreds of pounds of furs with only a tumpline. Today this feature is found only on traditional canvas Duluth packs, which are used for wilderness canoeing.

UTM (Universal Transverse Mercator): A metric coordinate map grid that is universally used by the U.S. and Canadian military. UTM grid lines are always 1 km (0.62 mile) apart. UTM coordinates are easier to use than latitude/longitude grids because their "easting" and "northing" values are decimal based.

vapor-barrier liner (VBL): A waterproof fabric that's worn next to the skin. Warm clothes are layered on top. You stay warm because perspiration can't get through the waterproof fabric to dampen your clothes and reduce their insulation value.

vestibule: An alcove or extension that secures to one or both ends of a tent. Vestibules provide a place to store gear out of the weather.

Wachita stone: A medium-hard mineral oil stone used for sharpening knives.

Wellies: Short for "Wellingtons"—the traditional knee-high (green) British rubber boot used by gardeners, hunters, and just about everyone else—a cult boot.

white-print map: A provisional map that's similar to a blueprint. White prints are up-to-date maps that show the location of logging and mining roads and man-made structures. These maps are designed for professional use; they are not listed in standard map indexes.

Index